Sartre and the Artist

Jean-Paul Sartre, by Alberto Giacometti
1949, pencil, 11½ x 8⅞ in.
Collection Ruth and Herman Vollmer, New York
(Museum of Modern Art, New York)

SARTRE

AND THE

Artist

GEORGE HOWARD BAUER

THE UNIVERSITY OF CHICAGO PRESS
Chicago and London

Standard Book Number: 226–03930–7
Library of Congress Catalog Card Number: 76–88232

The University of Chicago Press, Chicago 60637
The University of Chicago Press, Ltd., London W.C. 1

JE NE PEINTS PAS L'ESTRE.
JE PEINTS LE PASSAGE.

MONTAIGNE

Contents

Illustrations

Acknowledgments

THIS BOOK GREW out of a conflict between a passionate interest in art history and a firm commitment to literature. As a graduate student at Indiana University, I was torn between a career in French literature and a career in art history. My greatest debt is to Professor Albert Elsen who brings to his teaching and his writings an excitement and vitality that is absorbed by his students. He originally suggested the topic of this work and inspired its completion. It is the means by which I have sought to reconcile what at first appeared to be an impossible choice between art and literature. I am also indebted to Professor Robert Champigny for his encouragement and advice at all stages of this study, in its original form a dissertation written at Indiana University. My warmest thanks go to all those who read this work at one stage or another: Professors Joel Hunt, John Jacobi, James Edie, Charlotte Gerrard, Edward Seeber, Francis Very, Roger Kempf, Charles Newman, and Andrew McKenna. I must express my appreciation to the museums, photographic services, and private collectors who provided photographs and granted permissions to reproduce them in this book. In my search for information, I have been generously aided by Professor Meyer Schapiro of Columbia University; Madame Henri-Georges Adam; Lotte Drew-Bear of Feigen Galleries; Alice Adam and Alan Frumkin of Frumkin Galleries; Richard Olson, Antonia Fodor, and Inge Burnham of Deering Library; and Professors James Breckenridge and Jack Burnham of the Art Department of Northwestern University. Special thanks go to Jerre Nugent and Sherry Davidson for their time and interest in the typing of this manuscript. The translations from the French are my own.

G. H. B.

1

Introduction

THROUGHOUT HIS CAREER, Jean-Paul Sartre has been concerned with the artist, his activity, and the aesthetic objects created by him. In his philosophical works, he frequently uses painting, sculpture, and poetry as illustrative examples in the presentation of his ideas. The characters of his novels and plays come into contact with art in their daily lives and are frequently themselves writers, painters, or poets. Sartre has also published a number of essays on poets, painters, and sculptors. The purpose of this study is to examine Sartre's preoccupation, in his novels, plays, and critical essays, with art objects and with the existence of the artist and his creative activity.

Sartre has not published a fully elaborated system of his aesthetics, but his fiction, drama, and criticism complement the ideas he has put forward in his studies of the imagination and the image [1] and in his theory of literature as expressed in *Qu'est-ce que la littérature?* (*What Is Literature?*).[2] These works have served as a basis for a number of studies which examine Sartre's aesthetics from a purely philosophical or theoretical point of view.[3] The most complete of these considerations of Sartre's ideas

1. *L'Imagination;* "Transcendance de l'ego"; "Structure intentionnelle de l'image"; "Idée fondamentale de la 'Phénoménologie' de Husserl"; *Esquisse d'une théorie des émotions; L'Imaginaire.*
2. In *Les Temps modernes* (Feb.–July 1947). Subsequently published in *Situations,* vol. 2.
3. Isère, "Ambiguïté de l'esthétique de Sartre"; Ames, "Existentialism and the Arts"; Vendôme, "Jean-Paul Sartre et la littérature"; Rau, "Aesthetic Views of Jean-Paul Sartre"; Morpurgo-Tagliabue, "L'Existentialisme et l'esthétique," pp. 509–91, in his *L'Esthétique contemporaine;* Champigny, "Writers and Readers," in his *Stages on Sartre's Way;* Kaelin, *Existential Aesthetic;* Kohut, *"Was ist Literatur?";* Cumming, "Literature of Extreme Situations," in *Aesthetics Today,* ed. Philipson, pp. 377–412.

relating to art is that of Eugene F. Kaelin, who compares and contrasts Sartre with Merleau-Ponty and interprets his ideas in the light of British and American aesthetics. Kaelin eliminates Sartre's literary work by arguing for a separation of his creative efforts from his philosophical writing:

> It is not unreasonable to separate the literary efforts of Sartre from his already dense body of purely philosophic work. Our ground here is not that literature cannot be philosophy, but that historically considered, the literary interpretations of his philosophy are secondary; they were intended, in the main, merely to reach that larger section of his audience which is composed of readers for whom philosophy is too forbidding a fare.[4]

However, Kaelin, Karl Kohut, and Guido Morpurgo-Tagliabue all draw upon Sartre's *Saint Genet, comédien et martyr* and his *Baudelaire* to discuss the major aesthetic ideas. Only Champigny, in his "Writers and Readers," and Cumming discuss the theories in relation to Sartre's literary production. These critics put forward their objections to Sartre's major ideas—the separation of prose and poetry, the work of art as imaginary object, and committed literature. For the purposes of this study a discussion of the criticisms of these elements is not relevant, but a consideration of Sartre's expression of these ideas in *L'Imagination, L'Imaginaire*, and *Qu'est-ce que la littérature?* will provide a working definition of art. To the concept of art as an imaginary object and the distinction between prose and poetry, the opposition between *existence* and *being* must be added to provide a framework for a discussion of Sartre's novels, plays, and essays which deal with art and the artist.

Sartre's definition of the work of art as imaginary object is found in his conclusion to *L'Imaginaire*. He states categorically that "the work of art is an unreality."[5] His discussion initially focuses on a painting of Charles VIII in the Uffizi of Florence.[6] In the aesthetic experience the attention of the viewer is at first fixed on the real object before him. By "real" Sartre means the

---

4. *Existential Aesthetic*, p. 20.
5. "L'œuvre d'art est un irréel." *L'Imaginaire*, p. 239.
6. This painting is a curious choice on which to base a discussion of the work of art. The artist of this profile portrait is unknown and the painting is of minor importance. However, it is an example of the official portrait which fascinated Sartre at this time. It is reproduced in the article on Charles VIII in the *Larousse du XXe siècle*, 2: 151.

frame, the pigment, and the canvas which confront the viewer, and he demonstrates that as long as the viewer dwells on these real elements he will see only the physical object. The aesthetic object appears only when the viewer's awareness of the physical properties of the painting as a part of his own experiential world gives way to an awareness of the man in the painting. The figure seen is not the same object as the rectangular canvas covered with pigment. He is an object, but unreal: "We understood from the very first that this Charles VIII was an object. But obviously it is not the same object as the painting, the canvas, the real layers of paint. As long as we focus our gaze on the canvas and the frame themselves, the aesthetic object will not appear."[7] For Sartre, this aesthetic object does not belong to the real world but appears when the real world is negated by "the intentional act of an imagining consciousness."[8] The aesthetic object is not part of the world of experience but is grasped through the act of the viewer.

Sartre contends that the work of art has traditionally created a confusion between the real and the imaginary. He insists on a separation between the real world and the aesthetic object: "What is *beautiful* is a being which cannot be experienced as a perception and which, by its very nature, is outside of the world."[9] This *being*—characterized as imaginary—stands apart from the world in which the spectator exists. The opposition between *existence* and *being*—between the real and the imaginary—is emphasized in *La Nausée* (*Nausea*) when the protagonist, Roquentin, explains that the jazz melody does not *exist* but *is*. It is described as being beyond the real world. Like the *Charles VIII*, the melody is not the voice and the notes any more than the painting is the pigment and the canvas: "It doesn't exist because it has nothing 'de trop': it is all the rest which in relation to it is 'de trop.' It is."[10] The spectator *exists* in the real world,

7. "Nous avons compris d'abord que ce Charles VIII était un objet. Mais ce n'est pas bien entendu le même objet que le tableau, la toile, les couches réelles de peinture. Tant que nous considérons la toile et le cadre pour eux-mêmes, l'objet esthétique n'apparaîtra pas." *L'Imaginaire*, p. 239.
8. "L'acte intentionnel d'une conscience imageante." *Ibid.*
9. "Ce qui est 'beau,' au contraire, c'est un être qui ne saurait se donner à la perception et qui, dans sa nature même, est isolé de l'univers." *Ibid.*, p. 240.
10. "Elle [the melody] n'existe pas, puisqu'elle n'a rien de trop: c'est tout le reste qui est de trop par rapport à elle. Elle 'est.'" *La Nausée*, p. 218.

but, as will be seen in the novel, he is tempted to be like the work of art. As Roquentin says, "I, too, wanted to *be*."[11] The clear distinction between *being* and *existence* in the literary works and critical essays discussed in this study becomes considerably more complex in Sartre's *L'Etre et le néant* (*Being and Nothingness*).[12] In treating the novels and theater, a second use of *being* needs to be added to these two categories—to indicate the crude material *being* of objects in opposition to the imaginary *being* of the work of art. This brute *being* of things in the world of man's experience is frequently represented by stone as a symbol. For Sartre all *being* is outside of man who *exists*. The body is an object which *is* in the world, but man is not his body. On the contrary in his *existence*, his consciousness is a hole to be filled. This emptiness which seeks fullness is tempted to imitate the being of objects which are themselves and nothing else. In them there is nothing "de trop." It is precisely this consciousness which is in excess because "any positional consciousness of an object is at the same time a non-positional consciousness of itself."[13] *Existence* cannot assimilate *being*. The real world contains objects which contrast sharply with the individual who *exists* but cannot *be* like a stone which coincides with itself. Sartre's definition of the work of art as imaginary places it in opposition to the world in which man exists. Because man cannot achieve *being* in life, Sartre will frequently show his characters confronted by the temptation of *being* as it is found in the work of art. In his creative works, the art object—particularly those that are anthropomorphic in character—represents a continual attraction for those who confuse the real and the imaginary. The definition of the work of art as imaginary distinctly separates man in the world from his tendency to assume an aesthetic attitude toward life. For Sartre, "Beauty is a value which is only applicable to the imaginary and which requires the negation of the world in its essential structure. That is why it is stupid to confuse the moral with the aesthetic."[14]

11. "Et moi aussi j'ai voulu 'être.'" *Ibid.*
12. The several meanings of *being* as it is used in this philosophical work are fully treated by Champigny's "Le Mot 'être' dans *L'Etre et le néant*."
13. "Toute conscience positionelle d'objet est en même temps conscience non-positionelle d'elle-même." *L'Etre et le néant*, p. 19.
14. "La beauté est une valeur qui ne saurait jamais s'appliquer qu'à l'imaginaire et qui comporte la néantisation du monde dans sa structure essentielle. C'est pourquoi il est stupide de confondre la morale et l'esthétique." *L'Imaginaire*, p. 245.

To a consideration of Sartre's definition of *being* and *existence* which depends upon his characterizations of the work of art as imaginary, it is necessary to add his separation of prose from poetry. This distinction is the result of Sartre's concept of committed literature [15] which he puts forward in "Présentation des *Temps modernes*." [16] From this new concern with commitment, literature must receive new life and fulfill its purpose to an even greater degree than previously: "The concern must be to serve literature by giving it new blood, and at the same time to serve the collective whole by attempting to provide a literature which befits it." [17] But because prose and poetry are traditionally linked, the question arises as to whether it is possible to include the latter in the commitment he proposes: "And poetry? And painting? And music? Do you want to commit them too?" [18] Sartre's answer is negative but qualified: "No, we do not want to 'commit' painting, sculpture, and music 'too,' or at least not in the same way." [19] The question is the result of confusion in the minds of those who would like to believe that "at bottom there was only one art which expresses itself indifferently in one or another of these languages." [20] For Sartre, each of the arts must be considered on its own terms. Literary and artistic theory are separate.

Each of the arts is distinct not only in its created form, but also in the elements with which it is constructed: "It is one thing to work with colors and sounds, and another to express oneself with words. Notes, colors, and forms are not signs; they refer to nothing exterior to themselves." [21] The artist, unlike the prose

15. An excellent discussion of committed literature appears in Kohut's *"Was ist Literatur?"* He treats the commitment of the artist in particular in his chapter, "Ansätze aus einer allgemeinen Theorie der engagierten Kunst," pp. 177–97.

16. *Situations,* 2: 9–30.

17. "La préoccupation doit être de servir la littérature en lui infusant un sang nouveau, tout autant que de servir la collectivité en essayant de lui donner la littérature qui lui convient." *Situations,* 2: 30.

18. "Et la poésie? Et la peinture? Et la musique? Est-ce que vous voulez aussi les engager?" *Ibid.,* p. 57.

19. "Non, nous ne voulons pas 'engager aussi' peinture, sculpture, et musique, ou du moins, pas de la même manière." *Ibid.,* p. 59.

20. "Il n'y avait, au fond, qu'un seul art qui s'exprimât indifféremment dans l'un ou l'autre de ces langages." *Ibid.*

21. "C'est une chose que de travailler sur des couleurs et des sons, c'en est une autre de s'exprimer par des mots. Les notes, les couleurs, les formes ne sont pas des signes, elles ne renvoient à rien qui leur soit extérieur." *Ibid.,* p. 60.

writer, deals with the qualities of things and transforms these qualities of objects into the work of art—an imaginary object. In stating this Sartre returns to the ideas he expressed in his discussion of painting in *L'Imaginaire*. The materials of creation used by the sculptor or musician are defined by Sartre as things in opposition to the raw materials available to the writer. This distinction between the writer and the artist is not made in the discussion of the art object in *L'Imaginaire* in which he placed them in the same categories: "What we have just shown regarding painting could easily be applied to the art of fiction, poetry, and drama." [22] But the desire to commit the writer requires the separation of literature from music, painting, and sculpture, because these arts do not have communication as their aim. For Sartre, art is not a language either in the component creative elements or in the resultant imaginary object. The result of the creative act is not required to have a meaning—at least not a meaning capable of being expressed in words or in relation to the real world, whether it be a landscape or a face. Sartre insists on the object quality which is in itself sufficient:

> The painter does not want to trace signs on a canvas, he wants to create an object; if he puts together red, yellow, and green, there is no reason for the created whole to have a definable signification, that is, to refer by name to another object. [23]

The painting or symphony corresponds to the personal tendencies of the artist through his selection of the materials of creation, but does not express the emotion of the artist by any means other than the combination of the qualities of the objects with which he creates. The emotions of the artist are absorbed and lost in his creative materials never to be recognized again as such, in the imaginary work of art. For Sartre, the artist does not use subject and material either to mean or to provoke an emotion in the viewer because it is removed from the real world in the creative process. In discussing a painting of Tintoretto, Sartre explains

22. "Ce que nous venons de montrer à propos de la peinture, il serait trop facile de le montrer aussi à propos de l'art du roman, de la poésie et de l'art dramatique." *L'Imaginaire*, p. 242.
23. "Le peintre ne veut pas tracer des signes sur sa toile, il veut créer une chose; et s'il met ensemble du rouge, du jaune et du vert, il n'y a aucune raison pour que leur assemblage possède une signification définissable, c'est-à-dire renvoie nommément à un autre objet." *Situations*, 2: 61.

that "Tintoretto did not choose that yellow rent in the sky above
Golgotha in order to 'signify' anguish or to 'provoke' it, it 'is'
anguish and yellow sky at the same time." [24] The act of painting
has transformed the emotion into an object,[25] but like the pigment employed it relates to beauty and not to morality. It is, as
Sartre says, "anguish become thing." [26] The colors of painting
and the sounds of music, in Sartre's opinion, are not used as a
language. The error of Greuze (Pl. 8) is to have chosen to speak
in his painting and to have considered his work as a symbol,
whereas for Sartre the work of art should remain an object which
does not have communication as its aim. The artist who chooses
to represent an event or a landscape rather than to create the
imaginary art object functions as a writer, not as an artist. The
writer communicates through words and meaning. The artist,
that is, the painter, the musician, the sculptor, does not—or
should not. Klee, in Sartre's eyes, makes the mistake of wishing
his paintings to be both objects and symbols. The artist must not
use his art as a language to convince or communicate.[27]

The distinction made between literature and art creates certain
difficulties with respect to the poet because the prose writer and
the poet both use words as the raw materials for their works.

24. "Cette déchirure jaune du ciel au-dessus du Golgotha, le Tintoret ne l'a pas choisie pour 'signifier' l'angoisse, ni non plus pour la
'provoquer,' elle est angoisse, et ciel jaune en même temps." Ibid.
25. Another example of the transubstantiation of the artist's emotion
is Picasso's creation of the art object: "Picasso's long harlequins, ambiguous and eternal, haunted with inexplicable meaning, inseparable
from their stooping thinness and their faded diamond-patterned tights,
are an emotion become flesh, an emotion which the flesh has absorbed
as a blotter absorbs ink, an emotion which is unrecognizable, lost,
stranger to itself, flung to the four corners of space and yet present."
"Les longs Arlequins de Picasso, ambigus et éternels, hantés par un sens
indéchiffrable, inséparable de leur maigreur voûtée et des losanges
délavés de leurs maillots, ils sont une émotion qui s'est faite chair et
que la chair a bue comme le buvard boit l'encre, une émotion mécon-
naissable, perdue, étrangère à elle-même, écartelée aux quatre coins de
l'espace et pourtant présente." Ibid., p. 63.
26. "Une angoisse faite chose." Ibid., p. 61.
27. Compare Sartre's comment on Picasso's Guernica (Pl. 24):
"And that masterpiece, The Massacre of Guernica, does anyone believe
that it won over a single heart to the Spanish cause? And yet something
is said that can never quite be heard and that would take an infinity of
words to express." "Et le Massacre de Guernica, ce chef-d'œuvre, croit-
on qu'il ait gagné un seul cœur à la cause espagnole? Et pourtant quelque chose est dit qu'on ne peut jamais tout à fait entendre et qu'il
faudrait une infinité de mots pour exprimer." Ibid., p. 63.

Sartre is quick to point out that language is not used in the same way in creating works of prose. The poet, the painter, or sculptor makes an object. Unlike the prose writer, "poets are men who refuse to utilize language." [28] The poet conceives of words as things—as materials comparable to stone, pigment, and notes— with which to create his own poetic reality. The language of the prose writer is that of speech in which words are used as a means of communication, but the poet sees them as "natural things which grow naturally on the earth like grass and trees." [29]

Separated from the writer who uses words, the poet belongs with the painter, the musician, the sculptor: "A distinction must be made: the realm of signs is prose; poetry is on the side of painting, sculpture, and music." [30] The poet in his use of words is unable to forgo meaning because this alone gives words their verbal unity. He cannot treat them just as sounds because these are inseparably joined in the words' meaning. The poet conceives of language as "a structure of the external world." [31] Words reflect the material quality of the world. Words are no longer either utensils which contain meaning or barriers to communication, but magic devices which permit the poet to encounter them as things and as meaning. Thus, through his attitude the poet encounters the metaphors dreamed of by Picasso when "he wished to make a matchbox which was entirely a bat without ceasing to be a matchbox." [32] The poet accomplishes this, not through using a word which literally means a certain aspect of the world, but by creating images which will poetically bring into being the very aspect he would indicate: "Thus, a double reciprocal relation of magical resemblance and signification is established between the word and the thing signified." [33]

This dual aspect of the poetic word is characterized by Sartre

28. "Les poètes sont des hommes qui refusent d'*utiliser le langage*." *Ibid.*
29. "Des choses naturelles qui croissent naturellement sur la terre comme l'herbe et les arbres." *Ibid.*, p. 64.
30. "Encore faut-il distinguer: l'empire des signes, c'est la prose; la poésie est du côté de la peinture, de la sculpture, de la musique." *Ibid.*, p. 63.
31. "Une structure du monde extérieur." *Ibid.*, p. 65.
32. "Il souhaitait faire une boîte d'allumettes qui fût tout entière chauve-souris sans cesser d'être boîte d'allumettes." *Ibid.*, p. 69.
33. "Ainsi s'établit entre le mot et la chose signifiée un double rapport réciproque de ressemblance magique et de signification." *Ibid.*, p. 66.

as a microcosm which like a mirror exists in itself but reflects as well the world of things. Poetic words, as has been said, become things and are joined in the created work in much the same manner as the painter brings together his pigments. The poet creates by bringing these microcosms together to create the poem, an object: "And when the poet joins together several of these microcosms, the act is like that of painters when they put their colors together on the canvas: it might be thought that he is composing a sentence, but it only seems like that; he is creating an object." [34] The magic fusing of these microcosms governed by repelling and attracting qualities serves as the basis for poetic unity. Sartre views the poet and the painter at work as having a preconceived idea of the object to be created. This is not the final created work but an intuited form on which the work is based. Like Valéry,[35] Sartre's poet begins with rhythm or structure of the sentence and the words follow. This process involves not the ordinary syntactic structures of language based on meaning; "Rather it is related to the creative project by which Picasso, even before touching his brush, prefigures in space the thing that will become a juggler or a harlequin." [36]

In this way Sartre answers the question of the commitment of the poet by placing him with the painter. Together with the sculptor and musician they make up the definition of Sartre's artist. Tintoretto's anguish becomes the painting. Political hatred, social indignation, rage become the poem. These feelings and emotions are at the source of the work of art but are not experienced in the created work as such. The prose writer retains these emotions and explains them. For the poet it is an entirely different matter: "If the poet lets his feelings flow into his poem, he ceases to recognize them; the words take hold of them,

---

34. "Et quand le poète joint ensemble plusieurs de ces microcosmes, il en est de lui comme des peintres quand ils assemblent leurs couleurs sur la toile: on croirait qu'il compose une phrase, mais c'est une apparence; il crée un objet." *Ibid.*, p. 67.

35. In his essay on the composition of the *Cimetière marin*, in *Variété* 3: 68, Valéry says of his poem that "this intention was at first only an empty rhythm, or one filled with useless syllables, which appeared to obsess me for a period of time." "Cette intention ne fut d'abord qu'une figure rythmique vide, ou remplie de syllabes vaines, qui me vint obséder quelque temps."

36. "Il se rapprocherait plutôt du projet créateur par quoi Picasso préfigure dans l'espace avant même de toucher à son pinceau, cette chose qui deviendra un saltimbanque ou un Arlequin." *Situations*, 2: 68.

penetrate them, and metamorphose them; they do not signify them, even in his eyes." [37] The emotion becomes in the poem, in the painting, a thing with the attendant opaqueness of things: "The word, the sentence-object, inexhaustible as things, everywhere overflow the feeling which has produced them." [38] For Sartre, the poet and the prose writer are separated for good. Their respective worlds are at opposite poles: "What do they have in common? The prose writer writes, true, and the poet writes too. But these two acts of writing have nothing in common except the movement of the hand that traces the letters." [39]

In this study, Sartre's definition of the artist as the creator of an imaginary object of sculpture, painting, poetry, or music will serve as a basis for a discussion of art and the artist in his creative works and critical essays. Previous studies of Sartre's work have touched upon his preoccupation with the art object and its creator only briefly. Only La Nausée has provoked significant critical commentary on Sartre's use of painting and music in relation to the protagonist, Roquentin. The following chapter will develop more fully the use of the fine arts in this novel. Sartre's continuing interest in sculpture in anthropomorphic form as evidenced in his drama will reveal his attitudes towards the sculptor's art in the context of his ideas of *being* and *existence*. His *Les Chemins de la liberté* (*Roads to Freedom*) will provide additional examples of his obsession with projects of *being* [40] portrayed in terms of the sculptor's art as well as his criticisms of painting and poetry. Finally, his essays on sculp-

---

37. "S'il coule ses passions dans son poème, il cesse de les reconnaître: les mots les prennent, s'en pénètrent et les métamorphosent: ils ne les signifient pas, même à ses yeux." *Ibid.,* p. 69.

38. "Le mot, la phrase-chose, inépuisables comme des choses débordent de partout le sentiment qui les a suscités." *Ibid.*

39. "Qu'y a-t-il de commun entre eux? Le prosateur écrit, c'est vrai, et le poète écrit aussi. Mais entre ces deux actes d'écrire il n'y a de commun que le mouvement de la main qui trace les lettres." *Ibid.,* p. 70.

40. In his *Critique de la raison dialectique* (Paris: Gallimard, 1960), Sartre explains that "man defines himself by his project. This material being continually transcends the condition made for him; he reveals and determines his situation by transcending it in order to objectify himself, through his work, his action, or his gesture." "Donc l'homme se définit par son projet. Cet être matériel dépasse perpétuellement la condition qui lui est faite; il dévoile et détermine sa situation en la transcendant pour s'objectiver; par le travail, l'action ou le geste." P. 95.

ture,[41] painting,[42] poetry,[43] and music [44] will be discussed in order to discover those stylistic attributes which Sartre chooses to praise, to answer the question of whether Sartre was consistent in applying his stylistic predilections to specific artists and their works. The aesthetic ideas are rooted in Sartre's own representations of art, in his fiction and drama and in his consideration of the lives and works of individual artists. In his preoccupation with art, he preferred an artistic style reminiscent of certain qualities of the baroque by which man is represented in the process of becoming.[45] This will be seen to arise from Sartre's rejection of art that is used to create the myth of *being*.

41. Alexander Calder in "Mobiles de Calder," *Alexander Calder*, pp. 9–19; David Hare in "Sculptures à 'n' dimensions," pp. 1–4; Alberto Giacometti in "Recherche de l'absolu."
42. Alberto Giacometti in "Les Peintures de Giacometti"; Tintoretto in "Le Séquestré de Venise," Robert Lapoujade in "Le Peintre sans privilèges"; "André Masson," in *Vingt-deux Dessins;* Wols in "Doigts et non-doigts."
43. Francis Ponge in "A Propos du *Parti pris des choses"*; Baudelaire in his introduction to Baudelaire's *Ecrits intimes;* French African poets in "Orphée noir," *Anthologie de la nouvelle poésie,* ed. Sédar-Senghor pp. lx–xliv; Jean Genet in *Saint Genet;* "Mallarmé," in *Les Ecrivains célèbres,* ed. Queneau, 3:148–51.
44. In his preface to Leibowitz, *L'Artiste et sa conscience,* pp. 9–40. Reprinted in *Situations,* vol. 4 (Paris: Gallimard, 1964), pp. 17–37.
45. In comparing the classical to the baroque, Heinrich Wölfflin observes that "the baroque uses the same system of forms, but in place of the perfect, the completed, gives the restless, the becoming, in place of the limited, the conceivable, gives the limitless, the colossal. The ideal of beautiful proportions vanishes, interest concentrates not on being, but on happening." *Principles of Art History,* p. 10.

2

La Nausée:
Melancholy of the Artist

CRITICS OF *La Nausée* have usually seen in it Sartre's philosophical preoccupations and rarely his interest in the artist and the work of art.[1] The protagonist, Antoine Roquentin, has been seen as an individual who concerns himself with his existence as a man rather than as an artist. This emphasis has been fruitful in revealing the philosophical meaning of Roquentin's encounter with nausea. But the critics have not treated the aesthetic and creative aspects of the hero's life as fully as possible. They do touch on Roquentin's concern with the work of art in two major themes of the novel, the jazz melody and the portraits in the museum at Bouville. But these two elements should be reconsidered and related to Roquentin's problematical involvement in the creation of a work of art. The rich detail relevant to Roquentin's aesthetic and creative experience, for example the Khmer statuette, the statue of Impétraz, the church of Sainte-Cécile, *Eugénie Grandet* of Balzac, *La Chartreuse de Parme* of Stendhal, and the illustrated edition of Michelet among others, requires consideration. These works are related to one another and to the experience of Roquentin. One can even say that Sartre uses the artist's existence and the existence and creation of individual works of art as a basic element in the construction of the novel.

A work of art that does not appear in the novel itself will pro-

1. A summary of articles and books on Sartre's work was published by Douglas in *Critical Bibliography of Existentialism*. This should be supplemented by the "Sartre Bibliography" which appeared in *Yale French Studies* no. 30 (1963): 108–19. Among the most perceptive and rewarding of these critical studies, for the treatment of his work as a whole, are those of Campbell, *Jean-Paul Sartre*; Albérès, *Jean-Paul Sartre*; Murdoch, *Sartre: Romantic Rationalist*; Champigny, *Stages on Sartre's Way*; and Jameson, *Sartre: The Origins of a Style.*

vide a basis for a reading of *La Nausée* and for a consideration of the meaning and importance of art and the artist for Sartre in this work. The literary tradition of boredom, *ennui,* spleen, or melancholy is suggested to the reader from his first contact with the bachelor protagonist, but until the publication of the second volume of Simone de Beauvoir's memoirs, *La Force de l'âge* (*Prime of Life*), it was not generally known that the original title of Sartre's novel was *Melancholia.*[2] The tradition is rich in French literature, particularly in the art and literature of the nineteenth century. Melancholy as a feeling or attitude is frequently embodied for these writers and artists in an engraving of Albrecht Dürer, *Melencolia I* (Pl. 1). The haunting quality of this brooding, seated figure caught the imagination of such writers as Gérard de Nerval in his *Aurélia*[3] and *Voyage en Orient,*[4] Jules Michelet in his *Histoire de France,*[5] and Théophile Gautier in his long poem "Melancholia."[6] Gautier sees the artist Dürer as having painted his own portrait in which he contemplates the human condition and thinks,

> To run so brief a span, how bitter is life,
> How vain is science, and how chimerical is art.[7]

In a setting appropriate for Faust, the figure is described by the poet, as full of bitterness and doubt, reflecting on man's knowledge. Gautier's interpretation of the engraving suggests the hero of Sartre's *La Nausée,* and it is not surprising to learn from Simone de Beauvoir that it was this work of Dürer, so admired by Sartre,[8] that provided him the original title for his novel. She relates that it was Gallimard who suggested the present title. Sartre accepted the new title even though Simone de Beauvoir had reservations about the change. She feared that the public

2. *Force de l'âge,* p. 292. Since coming upon the original title in *Force de l'âge,* I have found no reference to it except as a parenthetical remark by Mona Tobin Houston in her article, "The Sartre of Madame de Beauvoir," p. 26, and a brief reference by A. James Arnold in his "*La Nausée* Revisited," p. 204.

3. *Œuvres,* ed. Lemaître 1: 757–58.

4. *Ibid.,* 2: 51–52.

5. *Œuvres complètes,* 8: 81–85.

6. *Œuvres complètes* 1: 215–22.

7. "Que pour durer si peu la vie est bien amère, Que la science est vaine et que l'art est chimère." *Ibid.,* p. 219.

8. Was *Melencolia I* illustrated in one of the art books Sartre remembers in his grandfather's library? The gifts of former students included works on Rubens, Van Dyck, Rembrandt, and Dürer. *Les Mots,* p. 38.

would expect a "roman naturaliste."[9] The change was made but the richness of the relation between the Dürer *Melencolia I* and the novel remains so striking that it cannot be disregarded. The enigmatic title *Melencolia I* calls for an explanation. Erwin Panofsky suggests that a modern definition of melancholy cannot adequately explain the work.[10] The theory of the four humors and the characterization of the fourth, melancholy humor, by Panofsky, is the basis for his interpretation of the central figure as that of the artist. The mysterious number "I" on the wings of the bat hovering over the body of water by which the figure sits is explained by Panofsky on the basis of Dürer's major literary source for this work: *De Occulta Philosophia* by Cornelius Agrippa of Nettesheim.[11] This work divides geniuses under the spell of melancholy into three categories of which the Dürer title represents the first category or the "Artist's Melancholy." Panofsky's long and closely reasoned analysis shows the figure to be that of the artist, and he concludes that the work is

the objective statement of a general philosophy and the subjective confession of an individual man. It fuses, and transforms, two great representational and literary traditions, that of Melancholy as one of the four humors and that of Geometry as one of the Seven Liberal Arts. It typifies the artist of the Renaissance who respects practical skill, but longs all the more fervently for mathematical theory— who feels "inspired" by celestial influences and eternal ideas, but suffers all the more deeply from his human frailty and intellectual finiteness. It epitomizes the Neo-Platonic theory of Saturnian genius as revised by Agrippa of Nettesheim. But in doing all this it is in a sense a spiritual self-portrait of Albrecht Dürer.[12]

Panofsky's evidence explains the title and demonstrates the figure to be the artist in deep concentration who has rejected practical, active existence in order to reflect on "eternal ideas," "human frailty," and on art in their relation to his life.

9. Her account of the circumstances of the acceptance and publication of *La Nausée* is found in *Force de l'âge*, pp. 292–309. Claude-Edmonde Magny also expresses reservations concerning the present title in *Sandales d'Empédocle*, p. 162.
    10. *Albrecht Dürer.*
    11. Panofsky's discussion of *Melencolia I* is found in his chapter on the "Reorientation in the Graphic Arts," 1: 156–71.
    12. *Ibid.*, p. 171.

This scholarly iconological study of the meaning of Dürer's engraving helps to show the work's rich implications for a reading of *La Nausée.* The same meaning has been intuited by other writers who use *Melencolia I* in their work. Gautier, in the previously cited lines, suggests the angel as a representation of the artist reflecting upon the philosophical and artistic problems which confront him. He describes the artist's search for the meaning of the secrets of nature.

> In disarray around him a thousand objects are spread,
> These are the attributes of the sciences and the arts;
> Rule and hammer, emblematic circle,
> Hour-glass, bell, and magic square,
> A Faustian collection, full of nameless things;
> Yet, he is an angel, not a demon.
> That great ring of keys which hangs at his waist
> Is used by him to open the secrets of nature.
> He has plumbed the depths of all human knowledge.[13]

The despair and disillusion of the figure who has cast these "thousand objects" aside in an effort to reach some unattainable idea directly through creation is caught by Michelet in the answer he imagines the figure giving, "Don't you see that badly chiseled block, irregular in form, which divine Geometry will never restore to the prism of crystals? Prismatic, it was regular, symmetrical. What have I done? Without attaining art, I have shattered nature." [14] Each writer gives to the engraving a new interpretation in the context of his own work, but the frequency

13. "Sans ordre autour de lui mille objets sont épars,
Ce sont des attributs de sciences et d'arts;
La règle et le marteau, le cercle emblématique,
Le sablier, la cloche et la table mystique,
Un mobilier de Faust, plein de choses sans nom;
Cependant c'est un ange et non pas un démon.
Ce gros trousseau de clefs qui pend à sa ceinture
Lui sert à crocheter les secrets de nature.
Il a touché le fond de tout savoir humain." Gautier,
Œuvres complètes, 1: 219.
14. "Tu ne vois pas ce bloc mal équarri, de forme irrégulière, et que la divine géométrie ne ramènera pas au prisme des cristaux? Prismatique il était régulier, harmonique. Qu'ai-je fait! Sans arriver à l'art, j'ai brisé la nature." *Histoire de France,* 8: 83. Baudelaire suggests the importance of carefully interpreting the detail of such "œuvres d'art philosophiques" but chastises Michelet by saying that "his interpretation is suspect, particularly in reference to the syringe." *Œuvres complètes,* ed. le Dantec, p. 1101.

of the use of *Melencolia I* to represent the artist in the act of philosophical contemplation reveals the powerful attraction of the work itself. Calvin S. Brown suggests in his study, "James Thomson and d'Annunzio on Dürer's *Melencolia*,"[15] that the reasons for the frequent use of the engraving are its "familiarity," its style as "strictly representational," its elements as a "collection of separable objects," and that these objects have a "standard symbolic significance."[16] These qualities certainly were among those for which Sartre would have chosen the title; and we can see Dürer's engraving in Roquentin, seated by the ocean, contemplating his existence, seeking to justify his life by his creative activity, and yearning for the purity of the *being* of a work of art or a geometrical form.

Let us consider, in *La Nausée*, the incident which gave rise to Roquentin's withdrawal from his previous activity into this melancholy. The crisis in his life seems to antedate the incident of the pebble, which is generally considered to be the source of his problem.[17] His decision to return to Bouville stems from his experiencing an art object which has in itself a two-fold *being:* it is a thing of stone and a work of art. In the presence of a colleague who is urging him to accept an offer to join him on an archeological expedition, Roquentin seems paralyzed and fixes his gaze on a small Khmer statuette (Pl. 2). For the first time he experiences his existence as flesh in its disagreeable warm viscosity. From this encounter with *being* in the form of the work of art and in the *being* of an object he is forced to consider his life. Roquentin recounts that on seeing the statuette he had the feeling of being filled with lymph or lukewarm milk. His irritation is centered on the Khmer figure: "The statue seemed to me disagreeable and stupid."[18] Here is the source of his first realization of boredom, his first questioning of his existence. He expresses it as a feeling of emptiness. Fredric Jameson in his study of Sartre's style describes this important moment as "a moment in which freedom suddenly stirs convulsively, shatters the crust of habits that had seemed to be forming around it, emerges

15. Pp. 31–35.
16. Brown, "James Thomson and d'Annunzio," p. 34.
17. Champigny, *Stages on Sartre's Way,* p. 85. Roquentin himself returns to the pebble as the origin of his story, but at the moment of confrontation with the root he is also faced with the statue of Velléda. This is but another example of the twofold aspect of the problem begun by the Khmer figure. Crude *being* is here embodied in the root, the work of art in the statue at the center of the garden.
18. "La statue me parut désagréable et stupide." *La Nausée,* p. 17.

without any connections at all, without any obligations, into a world which had gradually forgotten it was there."[19] But in his treatment of the essentially negative quality of the experience and the passivity of Roquentin, Jameson does not consider the cause of the event, the statue. Accompanying this experience of vacuity there appears before Roquentin "a voluminous and insipid idea." He does not at that time understand its meaning. Later he comes to understand it by remembering his distressing silence before the Khmer statuette. Jameson correctly interprets the meaning of the "idée" as Roquentin's realization that there are no "aventures,"[20] but again does not relate this revelation to Roquentin's experience of the statuette. Sartre frequently links stone and statue in his writings. For him stone is the material employed by the artist to make the human form eternal.[21] "The stone is Sartre's favorite symbol of being. The stone coincides with itself."[22] This stone is a work of art as well, and for Sartre the work of art represents *being,* but it is different from the stone because the work of art is imaginary.[23] Thus, in this moment, in this problem imperfectly understood by Roquentin, the events and subsequent understanding of them are prepared by this object. Stone and statuette, crude material *being* and ideal imaginary *being,* are joined in the small Khmer statue. Roquentin will think on the duality of the statuette's *being* and the meaning of this duality for his own existence throughout his wrestling with the angel of melancholy.

Just as in the Dürer engraving, also in the poetry and sculpture of the nineteenth century the theme of melancholy is associated with the artist. The artist's problems of creation, particularly his moments of inactivity and frustrated boredom when he is confronted with his incapacity to create, invite him to consider the meaning and significance of his creative activity. The artist's melancholy is experienced in isolation and frustration. Rodin's *Thinker,* as Albert Elsen suggests,[24] invites comparison with the Dürer *Melencolia I* "both in spirit and in form."[25] The *Thinker* was originally conceived by Rodin as a portrait of the artist, in

19. Jameson, *Sartre: The Origins of a Style,* p. 50.
20. *Ibid.,* p. 143.
21. In his "Sculptures à 'n' dimensions," p. 1.
22. Champigny, *Stages on Sartre's Way,* p. 85.
23. The work of art as an imaginary object has been discussed in the first chapter.
24. *Rodin's Gates of Hell.*
25. *Ibid.,* p. 129.

this case Dante, contemplating the plan of his work. Elsen sees the sculpture as a "personal projection of the artist, his deep thought indicative of the effort demanded by creation." [26] For Dante and for Sartre, the relation of the artist to society is as crucial as the artist's own relationship to the work of art. Roquentin's first crisis, as I have indicated above, is the contemplation of the Khmer figure. His withdrawal from active participation in life stems from that moment. Roquentin, as will be seen, would be a sculpture, if this were possible, but his initial reaction is withdrawal from what he thought was a life of adventure and a return to a project which would be his creative life. The problem posed for him by the statue precipitates his return to work on a biography of M. de Rollebon.

From the active experience of adventures in the world of archeology and travel, he turns to a concern with the past, but his major project is that of writing a book, *his* book. Formerly, he reveals to us, he had been caught up with the idea of the man, M. de Rollebon, but gradually the problem of justifying his own life through a creative endeavor replaces his intellectual preoccupation with the man. Roquentin's *raison d'être* becomes the writing of a book, *his* book, in order to give form, shape, and meaning to the flaccid object he found himself to be when confronted with the statuette and the pebble. He reaches out for substance in the book he is writing and speaks of "a greater and greater need to write it." [27] In writing his book, not the biography of the historical Rollebon, he will attempt to transform his life into the eternal hardness of the work of art embodied in the Khmer statuette. His attempt will be futile because he has chosen the wrong means of achieving this hardness. Biography will not work. He learns this only after successive encounters with works of art. The statue of Impétraz, architecture in the form of the church of Sainte-Cécile, the portraits of the museum of Bouville, the novel *Eugénie Grandet,* and his own diary will each confront him before he abandons his book.

Bouville, the provincial city perched precariously on the mud of the seashore, is an appropriate choice not only for Roquentin but for the melancholy figure of Dürer. The Saturn-dominated mood, as Panofsky notes, "was supposed to be coessential with earth." [28] Bouville, "Mud City," becomes the place for the measured ordering of Roquentin's life, and like the seated angel he

26. *Rodin,* p. 53.
27. "Un besoin de plus en plus fort de l'écrire." *La Nausée,* p. 26.
28. *Albrecht Dürer,* 1: 157.

surrounds himself with the precise tools of the geometer in his attempt to measure and record the life of M. de Rollebon. Roquentin will place not only the life of his subject but his own life in the scales of the Dürer engraving; with the magic square, the compass, the hourglass—even the Sartrean stone in the form of a truncated rhomboid—he will attempt to apply to this endeavor "the rules of mathematics, that is, in the language of Plato and the *Book of Wisdom*, of 'measure, number and weight.' " [29] His neat, well-planned schedule of study and writing, from nine to one in the Bouville library, is an attempt to order his existence just as he weighs, considers, measures the life of the Marquis and ties it neatly into logical bundles of episodes and events, of chapters and volumes.

In the course of his work the material quality of objects intrudes upon his existence and the rock quality of the statue of stone penetrates his newly ordered world and assumes an extraordinary place in his life. Dürer provides the hard, cold stone as a major object for the contemplation of his brooding, winged figure who flies no more, but it is a stone carved and changed into geometric configuration. Fixed and permanent, this rock will take on meaning for Roquentin in its parallel—the jazz melody. From the Khmer statue to the pebble and other objects he encounters in his daily activities, things move in upon him. They touch him. The experience he has had with the Marquis's life provides the *modus operandi*. He seeks significant events and tries to place them in time sequence and proper perspective. Roquentin even attempts to apply the geometrical approach to overcoming his growing uneasiness. He describes the box containing the ink with which he is writing, "Well, it's a parallelopiped rectangle, it opens . . ." [30] He breaks off in mid-sentence because he has become aware that in writing there is a danger: "You exaggerate everything. You're always ready to pounce on something. You continually force the truth." [31] In applying his technique Roquentin draws upon the contrast he sees between his life and the life of those around him. Perhaps the most striking thing for him is the discovery that in rejecting his life of adventure he is left alone. He has separated himself from men in society and in so doing he has lost the company of men. In

29. *Ibid.*
30. "Eh bien! c'est un parallélépipède rectangle, il se détache sur . . ." *La Nausée*, p. 11.
31. "On s'exagère tout, on est aux aguets, on force continuellement la vérité." *Ibid.*

coming together men bring only the events of their lives, but they make dramatic happenings of these unimportant, colorless events in their lives by recounting them to one another. The impossibility of Roquentin's doing so is intensified by his solitary life. During this time Roquentin observes other aspects of art—sculpture, architecture, and painting. Frequently in discussing *La Nausée,* critics allude to some of the plastic arts in the novel, but they do not see that Roquentin's experience of these art objects is gradually destroying any possibility of completing the biography he has undertaken. An event such as the smoking of a pipe in the courtyard before the statue of Impétraz is mentioned by Victor Brombert for its "comic vision," and simply as an illustration of the hostility of Roquentin toward the "smug bourgeois." [32] Certainly it is both of these, but beyond social satire it is the characterization of one use of the work of art. The handsome setting of the pink brick courtyard, once a place of gaiety, has now become, because of the complicity of the artist, a place of instruction. A place of beauty and delight now embodies inherited, sacred bourgeois values. The artist has been an accessory to the eternalizing of the writer and scholar, Impétraz, through the casting of his once fleshly existence in the *being* of the bronze work of art. Roquentin writes of the lie of the work of art that changes the small man into the bronze giant in his social costume of dress hat armed with the mass of papers he has written. The writer and scholar, Impétraz, takes on new weight and importance in this form lent him by the artist for eternity, just as the ideas of the bourgeoisie found support in the activities of Impétraz's life. "At the service of their narrow and weighty small ideas he has placed his authority and the immense erudition drawn from the volumes he clutches in his hand." [33] Sartre underlines the sufficiency of the presence of the statue in this role. The work need never be looked upon, because it serves its purpose by the power embodied in the ideas it fixes for eternity. "The women in black feel relieved, they can tranquilly go about their

---

32. *Intellectual Hero,* p. 183. Albérès in his *Jean-Paul Sartre* sees him as representing the provincial life of Bouville: "symbole de tout ce qu'a de conventionnel l'existence médiocre de la petite ville." "symbol of all that is conventional in the mediocre existence of the small city." P. 32.
33. "Au service de leurs petites idées étroites et solides il a mis son autorité et l'immense érudition puisée dans les in-folio que sa lourde main écrase." *La Nausée,* p. 44.

business, running their households, walking their dogs." [34] The statue stands watch over the ideas which justify their existence. But these ideas were weighed and found wanting by Roquentin. He is not unaware of the function and purpose of this work of art for he sees that there is a "mute power" in its *being,* but Roquentin will not be forced from his contemplation of the statue by its powerful presence. He will defy it just as he defies the values which it represents. The green spotting of time attacks the work in its very eternal presence and spreads the epidemic from statue to statue. He is alone in his awareness of this leprosy when he sees the bronze as a horrible sorcerer, an enchanter of the bourgeoisie, created by the sculptor.

The contrast between the insect-like existence of the human being and the substantial *being* of eternalized human form in the statue of Impétraz is reinforced in the carefully documented birth of a church for the wealthy families of the city. The ruling class calls for the artistic transformations of "a dark, stinking bowel, with a great gutter between the paving stones in which fish heads and guts rushed along" into "the gathering place of the elegant and the distinguished." [35] The consecration of the street as a place of social ritual must carry the blessing of the Almighty. Inspired by the example of the nation's wise decision to have a church built on Montmartre in order to demonstrate concretely the presence and support of the existing hierarchy by God, the wife of the mayor of Bouville is visited by a saint with a similar project for this provincial mudhole. To answer the question implicit in her vision, "Was it bearable for the élite to sully themselves every Sunday going to Saint-René or Saint-Claudien to hear mass with shopkeepers?" [36] and the unworthy condition it revealed, Sainte-Cécile-de-la-Mer came into being. Divinely inspired to reinforce the power of the worthy few, this creation required a million francs annually during fourteen long years before its weight was added to that of the statue of Impétraz. The bronze replacing the scholar's fleshly existence is joined by the stone of Sainte-Cécile resting solidly on the former Place de la

34. "Les dames en noir se sentent soulagées, elles peuvent vaquer tranquillement aux soins du ménage, promener leur chien." *Ibid.*
35. "Un boyau noir et puant, avec une rigole qui charriait, entre les pavés, des têtes et des entrailles de poissons" into "le rendez-vous des élégants et des notables." *Ibid.,* pp. 60–61.
36. "Etait-il supportable que l'élite se crottât tous les dimanches pour aller à Saint-René ou à Saint-Claudien entendre la messe avec les boutiquiers?" *Ibid.,* p. 60.

Halle-aux-Morues. Sacred architecture and Sunday require one another. Both intensify the barrier that divides Roquentin from the great families of Bouville on their Sunday stroll following their offer of thanks to God and Sainte-Cécile for the rights and privileges bestowed upon them. And the magnificent new boulevard required by the church becomes the scene for the frequently praised satire of the Bouvillois. But above the comic scene recorded by Roquentin in his diary, "the Eglise Sainte-Cécile raises its monstrous white mass." [37] The hidden magic behind the white façade of the church, like the artistic sorcery of the sculpture, is felt by Roquentin in his privileged position of spectator.

In the creation of this statue and this church the artist has served the cause of the bourgeoisie. The involvement of the artist is implied but never discussed as in the museum scene to follow. The point of interest here is the function of the work of art. The sanctification of reassuring ideas occurs in the casting of the bronze figure and in the building of the church. These ideas require a physical manifestation in order to help secure their place in a fixed world. If Roquentin penetrates the hollow shell which contains the ideas of order, privileges, and rights, it is because of his noninvolvement. The detached position provided by his separation from society makes possible his freedom from the spell of the sorcerer, Impétraz. Sartre uses this technique of detachment from the sacred world of architecture, as he has done with sculpture, to show how the work of art reinforces the power of the ruling class of Bouville. From the statue in the courtyard Roquentin directs his detached observation to the setting in which the Bouvillois play out their lives and from which they derive a feeling of order and well-being. The leaders of the city realized the necessity of physically representing the power of the Deity in architectural form to solidify their position. They called upon a sister art. The architect joins the sculptor in forging the myth of the bourgeoisie—its power, its prestige, its rights.

One of the finest passages of the novel links Impétraz and the church of Sainte-Cécile to a whole generation of the elite of the city enshrined for the future "in little painted sanctuaries." [38] In his visit to the museum of Bouville, Roquentin, like Aeneas, visits the world of the dead. Here his existence is placed in opposition to the public life of the saintly leaders of the city. His avoidance of responsibility, the very life he leads, is a threat to

37. "L'église Sainte-Cécile dresse sa monstrueuse masse blanche." *Ibid.*, p. 64.
38. "Dans des petits sanctuaires peints." *Ibid.*, p. 122.

the established order of society. He is a threat to these people in their role of deputy, of grandfather, of ambassador, or mayor— all those official roles of a public existence. The museum provides a setting for their continued participation in the life of the community. As if to anticipate the visit of Roquentin, the entrance to the Renaudas-Bordurin wing has recently been graced with a handsome canvas by Richard Séverand. This gift of the state, *La Mort du célibataire* (*Death of the Bachelor*), is a last word of warning to those who, like Roquentin, live only for themselves. None of the pictures he will see portrays a bachelor. The agony of the lonely death which awaits him and all those who do not participate in society is revealed by the artist in all its horror. Indifference and betrayal characterize the end of the celibate. No immortality for the irresponsible. Roquentin is not deterred by this attempt to bring shame on his existence. He is armed with the growing awareness of the use to which art is put by society. His purpose is to reexamine a portrait of Olivier Blévigne which had disturbed him on a previous visit.

But once across the threshold he finds himself caught by the spell of the presence of these distinguished hundred and fifty bourgeois. The power of the artist has captured their right to exist and in doing so the work of art calls into question Roquentin's existence. Standing before these works, he expresses to himself something he has gradually come to think: "I [haven't] the right to exist. I appeared by chance, I [exist] like a stone, a plant, a microbe." [39] In their painted niches these leaders have the right to exist. They *are*. Roquentin finds in these official portraits the solidity he lacks. Seeing the heroes and heroines pass before him like those that Anchises showed to Aeneas, he asks, "[Am] I not a mere apparition?" [40] As he closely observes several of the portraits, Roquentin comments upon the admirable technique of the painter. Each of the two great painters, Bordurin and Renaudas, has a specialty, and Roquentin in his sensitivity comments on their technical facility: "In these portraits, which were above all painted for moral edification and to which accuracy of detail was scrupulously applied, artistic considerations were not excluded." [41] Renaudas's favorite subjects, the distin-

39. "Je n'avais pas le droit d'exister. J'étais apparu par hasard, j'existais comme une pierre, une plante, un microbe." *Ibid.*, p. 111.
40. "N'étais-je pas une simple apparence?" *Ibid.*, p. 113.
41. "De ces portraits, peints surtout aux fins de l'édification morale et dont l'exactitude était poussée jusqu'au scrupule, le souci d'art n'était pas exclu." *Ibid.*, p. 112.

guished old men of the group, permitted the artist to demonstrate his genius for painting hair gone white in venerable old age and the capable hands of the worthy writer, artist, professor, or lawyer. The shrewdly chosen accessories for the portraits inevitably include a reference to the creative strength of the individual. Quill pen, finely bound books, handsome libraries allude to the worth of the person portrayed. The presence of these men in the gilt frames previously gave Roquentin a headache, but on this occasion he is suddenly able to free himself from their domination.

The aspect of art that Sartre presents up to this point in the visit to the museum is the role of the painter in the service of the ruling classes. The architect and sculptor of Sainte-Cécile and Impétraz both fall into this category. In another work, *Visages, précédé de Portraits officiels* (*Faces, preceded by Official Portraits*),[42] Sartre develops ideas from this incident in the Bouville museum. He insists that artists of this type are used by the rulers or ruling classes as a means of oppression. In the service of the church or the monarchy—in this case the ruling elite of Bouville —the artist's role becomes that of creating the official portrait which will effectively convince the viewer, be he subject of the king or believer in God, of his own inferiority. The artist accepts as justification of his existence the embodying in his work— whether music, painting, or sculpture—of the superior qualities of power, merit, divine right, and terrestrial or celestial glory. The function is the same in praising the creation of the world by God or the creation of the Empire by Napoleon. At such moments in history, when his role is defined by the society and not by himself, "the artist is at ease."[43]

The artist accomplishes his task by creating an object that constantly asserts the importance and rights of the ruling class. In "Portraits officiels," the court painter is satirized by Sartre for his self-imposed servility. The painter is aware of the essential weakness of the monarch as man and, while knowing this, still goes about producing the paintings which aid the privileged being in his official capacity. "They free the prince from the

---

42. These works originally published in *Verve,* Nos. 5–6 (July–Oct. 1939): 9–12 and pp. 43–44, show the relation between his famous satire of the portraits of the Bouville museum and his less well-known essay, "Portraits officiels." This essay on official portraits was unsigned when published in *Verve* in 1939.

43. "L'artiste est à l'aise." Sartre in his preface to *L'Artiste et sa conscience* of Leibowitz, p. 11.

worry of thinking his divine right." [44] In order to accomplish this, the artist must forgo portraiture and accept, instead, the portrayal of privilege and worth. He must concern himself first with Charles VIII or Louis XIV and the external signs of power. Conscious of the human follies and foibles of Charles and Louis, he proceeds to accomplish the official portrait. "It is enough to see how the symbols of power are heaped around Francis I and Louis XIV." [45] The painter piles stuff on stuff in order to hide the naked body of the monarch: "Not so naked: the face of a king is always clothed. The truth is that the aim of the official portrait is to justify." [46] The artist provides an image which is unlike the man who shoulders the weight and responsibility of power. The body in its nakedness, the face in its exposed vulnerability, the flesh in its essential human weakness disappear with every brush stroke of the skillful court painter. What remains is the royal personage created by the artist. "Do They have bodies? At the ends of those trappings appear hands, handsome and insignificant hands, symbols, too, like the gilt hand of the scepter." [47] The creation of the official presence is completed in an instant simply by adding the details of likeness, but a handsome idealized face must replace the overlarge Roman nose or discreetly mask the pimples or warts: "Authentic expressions, such as guile, cowardly anxiety, and baseness, have no place in these portraits" (Pl. 3, 4). [48]

The creative act Sartre criticizes in the artist as court painter, musician, or sculptor is that of conscious participation by the artist in tyranny and oppression. The painter creates the august personage with his pigment and brush. "Even before encountering his model, the painter knows already the look which he is required to fix on the canvas—strength, calm, serenity, and justice." [49] There is no naïve encounter with the sitter as man.

44. "Ils déchargent le prince du soin de penser son droit divin." *Visages*, p. 14.
45. "Il suffit de voir comme on accumule autour de François Ier et de Louis XIV les signes de leur puissance." *Ibid.*
46. "Pas si nue: un visage de roi est toujours habillé. C'est que le portrait officiel vise à justifier." *Ibid.*, p. 15.
47. "Ont-Ils des corps? Au bout de ces étoffes paraissent des mains, belles et quelconques, symboles aussi comme la main dorée du sceptre." *Ibid.*, p. 16.
48. "C'est que les expressions véritables, la ruse, l'inquiétude traquée, la bassesse, n'ont pas de place sur ces portraits." *Ibid.*, p. 17.
49. "Avant même d'avoir rencontré son modèle, le peintre connaît déjà l'air qu'il faut fixer sur la toile: force, calme, sérénité, justice." *Ibid.*

The artist proceeds to his canvas from a conscious knowledge of the projected creation and consults the world of the human only for the details essential to recognition. From this object created by the artist, the product of his moment of creativity, the monarch, the prince of the church, and the privileged class derive power and demand obeisance: "Thus the purpose of the official portrait is to effect the union of the prince with his subjects. The official portrait, which protects man from himself, is understood to be a religious object." [50] The painter has created a talisman and knows full well the power which resides in this creative act, but once it is created, only the magic presence is essential; "it is perhaps not necessary to look at them at all." [51]

Now, here in the Bouville museum, it is this talismanic aspect which has fixed Roquentin. He stares again at the work of art as he had stared at the Khmer statue before. What he sensed of the sorcery involved in the statue of Impétraz is finally revealed to him in the portraits in the Bouville museum. His headache does not come upon him this time. The hero has learned about this function of the art object. Roquentin's previous confrontation of a portrait of Philip II in the library of the Escorial (Pl. 5) [52] reveals to him now "that when you stare hard into a face aglow with right, it is only an instant before this light dies out, and nothing but an ashy residue remains." [53] This residue, seen for itself when he examines the paint substance, frees him. [54] Just as Sartre has understood Rigaud and Clouet in "Portraits officiels," Roquentin understands the work of the painters Renaudas and Bordurin. The leaders of the community "had placed themselves in the hands of a renowned painter in order that he should

50. "Aussi la fonction du portrait officiel est-elle de réaliser l'union du prince et de ses sujets. On a compris que le portrait officiel, qui défend l'homme contre lui-même, est un objet religieux." *Ibid.*

51. "Il n'est peut-être pas très nécessaire de les regarder." *Ibid.*, p. 18.

52. Sartre's choice of El Escorial underlines his interpretation of the role of official portraiture in supporting the monarchy. Under Philip II, as Professor David Robb comments in *Harper History of Painting,* "Painting in Spain meant painting for the Church and the crown; . . . from Spaniards they asked only what was needed for official or ecclesiastic purposes." P. 561.

53. "Que, lorsqu'on regarde en face un visage de droit, au bout d'un moment, cet éclat s'éteint, qu'un résidu cendreux demeure." *La Nausée,* p. 116.

54. Jameson discusses this allusion to the Philip II portrait, but he sees it only as Roquentin's ability to stare people down. It should be interpreted as well in the light of the aesthetic preoccupations of the protagonist. "Laughter of *Nausea,*" p. 28.

discreetly perform on their faces the dredgings, drillings, and irrigations by which, all around Bouville, they had transformed the sea and the land." [55] The meaning of this experience is clear. The Bouvillois have not been saved. They will not exist for posterity. The ability of the painter to transform the flesh [56] and change it into hard, permanent *being* did not work for them. If we, like Roquentin, can discover behind the pigment the weakness of the flesh, the animal existence felt before these works, then we are freed from their power. From his reading of a satirical newspaper, *Le Satirique Bouvillois*, Roquentin discovers the lie of the painter. Blévigne was a tiny, insignificant man. Bordurin disguised his weakness by placing him in a theatrical setting suitable for his dwarfish proportions. "Admirable power of art. Of this little man with the high-pitched voice, nothing would be handed down to posterity except a threatening face, a superb gesture, and the blood-red eyes of a bull." [57] The lie of the artist, the painting, is immortal, not the man he has painted. Roquentin's life cannot be saved by a similar operation. His work on Rollebon will not be sufficient to save him from the gratuitousness he feels before the Khmer statue. Another solution must be found.

But just as Roquentin is to abandon the heroes of Bouville, Sartre brings his experience to a rich end by reminding the reader that this is indeed the world of the dead visited by Aeneas. As Roquentin stands before this residue that interests him so greatly, two visitors to the museum, caught under the spell of the official presence, discover a painting of the tragic youth of Bouville. Octave, the son of Olivier Blévigne, died in the bloom of youth. He contained in his person all the dreams of this powerful Bouville family for generations to come. The attitude of Roquentin as contrasted to that of this couple is used to emphasize the meaning of Roquentin's experience. The portrait causes the woman to exclaim: "How painful it must have been for his dear

---

55. "S'étaient confiés à un peintre en renom pour qu'il opérât discrètement sur leurs visages ces dragages, ces forages, ces irrigations par lesquels tout autour de Bouville, ils avaient transformé la mer et les champs." *La Nausée,* p. 117.
    56. Champigny, *Stages on Sartre's Way,* p. 26, notes that "Artistically, it takes a Rubens, or a Baudelaire, to redeem flesh, or perhaps, mask it with the very colors or words which suggest it."
    57. "Admirable puissance de l'art. De ce petit homme à la voix suraiguë, rien ne passerait à la postérité, qu'une face menaçante, qu'un geste superbe et des yeux sanglants de taureau." *La Nausée,* p. 121.

mother!" [58] The comment recalls to the reader the emotion of
Octavia, mother of Marcellus, on reading Virgil's description of
her son. The young Marcellus, chosen as heir to Augustus, died at
an early age. The power of the art of Virgil caused Octavia to
faint,[59] but the Marcellus of flesh and bone was dead. Nothing
will pass to posterity but the poem of Virgil. Sartre's use of the
incident dramatically reinforces the idea of the experience in the
museum of Bouville. His quotation from the *Aeneid*, "Tu Marcellus eris!" [60] from the passage eulogizing the boy who embodied the disappointed hopes of Augustus and of all Rome, is
addressed by Roquentin not to the young Marcellus-Octave of
Bouville but to the Bouvillois themselves. The unfulfilled promise of the artist to make them immortal is thrown back at them.
The flesh is dead. They have been unable to overcome death
through art. Only the residue remains to decorate their tombs.
But Roquentin's quotation continues, "Manibus date lilia plenis.
. . ." [61] The reference is an allusion to the useless act of official
portraiture heaped upon these shades. "Adieu, lovely lilies, so
delicate in your little painted sanctuaries, adieu, lovely lilies, our
pride and reason for existing, adieu you Bastards." [62] The painted
lilies which fill the Bouville museum, the *raison d'être* of the
community in their presence but also the justification of Roquentin's life in his painter-biographer role, are forever left behind
when he leaves the museum. Like Aeneas he leaves the world of
the shades through the gates of ivory. Behind him are the false
dreams of art. The experience is over. He records in his diary:
"I'm no longer writing my book on Rollebon; it's finished, I
can't write it any more. What am I going to do with my life?" [63]

It has been noted that Roquentin added a personal diary to his
project of writing the life of the Marquis. In this attempt to
describe objectively his own life in order to overcome his uneasy
awareness that something had gone wrong, he finds himself
comparing his experience to that of those around him. Observing
the socially acquired habit of these individuals of recounting

58. "Ce que sa maman a dû avoir de la peine!" *Ibid.*
59. Knight, *Roman Vergil*, p. 299.
60. Virgil, *Works*, trans. Fairclough, 2: 883.
61. *Ibid.*
62. "Adieu beaux lys tout en finesse dans vos petits sanctuaires
peints, adieu beaux lys, notre orgueil et notre raison d'être, adieu
Salauds." *La Nausée*, pp. 122–23.
63. "Je n'écris plus mon livre sur Rollebon; c'est fini, je ne peux
plus l'écrire. Qu'est-ce que je vais faire de ma vie?" *Ibid.*, p. 123.

their meaningless activities to one another, Roquentin comprehends that he has lost this ability to relate things that happen because of his self-imposed separation from people. He does not play the game: "I am not in the habit of telling myself what happens in my life, so I cannot quite recapture the succession of events, I cannot distinguish what is important." [64] He finds it difficult to see himself through the eyes of another. Choosing among the events of his own daily schedule inevitably falsifies existence as it is lived. This leads him to compare his own life with that of the Marquis. But both his diary and the book he is writing on M. de Rollebon are distortions. The biography is no longer characterized as inevitable truth growing from a study of the abundant documents available to him. In his acute distress he has the impression of creating "a work of pure imagination." [65] The writing of a novel logically comes to mind, and he struggles with the idea that "the characters of a novel would seem more real, or in any case would be more agreeable." [66] He becomes furious with his work, which has lost its consoling, justifying aspect. He comes to feel contempt for the Marquis and comments bitterly: "I don't consider historical research to be important enough to waste my time over a dead man whose hand, if he were alive, I would not deign to touch." [67] In spite of this outburst he throws himself into his work in reaction to his worst moments of nausea. His book becomes the only thing to which he can turn. He realizes the new importance of this endeavor when he says: "M. de Rollebon now represents the only justification for my existence." [68]

In the course of his work he returns frequently to the concept of the hero of a novel, and the clarity and logic of this imaginary existence intrigue him. On Friday afternoon when he enters the library after having defied the power of Impétraz, Roquentin does not feel like writing. He picks up a copy of *Eugénie Grandet* and begins reading on page twenty-seven. He cannot

64. "Je n'ai pas l'habitude de me raconter ce qui m'arrive, alors je ne retrouve pas bien la succession des événements, je ne distingue pas ce qui est important." *Ibid.,* p. 22.
65. "Un travail de pure imagination." *Ibid.,* p. 27.
66. "Des personnages de roman auraient l'air plus vrais, seraient, en tout cas plus plaisants." *Ibid.*
67. "Je n'estime pas assez les recherches historiques pour perdre mon temps avec un mort dont, s'il était en vie, je ne daignerais pas toucher la main." *Ibid.,* p. 79.
68. "M. de Rollebon, à l'heure qu'il est, représente la seule justification de mon existence." *Ibid.,* p. 94.

find "the courage to begin with the beginning." [69] Until late that afternoon he follows the activities of the heroine, and he takes up his own research only with difficulty. The following day when he returns to the library his thoughts go back to the idea of events and adventures. In a man's life the most banal event can become an adventure when it is remembered and recounted. Through the telling of events one is able to invent what has been happening. Roquentin reflects that one attempts to live one's life as if it were being recounted. A choice must be made. Life must be lived or made into a tale or story. There is no beginning or end in life itself. "Nothing happens while you live. The scenery changes, people come and go, that's all. There are never any beginnings." [70]

The senseless, formless experience of life is given meaning only in the novel. The author of *Eugénie Grandet* fixes the life of the heroine into ordered, meaningful patterns. The novelist begins with the end, for it is the end of the novel that transforms the experience of the heroine's life: "Her moroseness, her money troubles are much more precious than ours, they are gilded by the light of future passions." [71] In comparing the man who recounts his life with the author who tells the life of the heroine, Roquentin finds that the man is incapable of beginning from the end. He takes the novel and leaves the library with the awareness that "adventures are in books." [72]

The next day he carries the novel with him on his Sunday walk. The book becomes something solid and fixed to which he can cling. Philip Thody sees the event which occurs in the café as a satire of "the attempt of 'realist' literature to express life as it is." [73] The incident is built on a contrast between the long quotation from *Eugénie Grandet* and the conversation of the people in the café. Roquentin is interrupted in his reading of the novel by their meaningless dialogue. An interpretation of this simply as a criticism of realist literature and its failure to give form and meaning to life [74] does not take into account the

69. "Le courage de commencer par le début." *Ibid.*, p. 45.
70. "Quand on vit, il n'arrive rien. Les décors changent, les gens entrent et sortent, voilà tout. Il n'y a jamais de commencements." *Ibid.*, p. 57.
71. "Sa morosité, ses ennuis d'argent sont bien plus précieux que les nôtres, ils sont tout dorés par la lumière des passions futures." *Ibid.*, p. 58.
72. "Les aventures sont dans les livres." *Ibid.*, p. 55.
73. *Sartre*, p. 10.
74. *Ibid.*

continuing efforts of Roquentin to find in his reading the inevitable succession of the mode of existence of the heroine: "Adventures are in books. Naturally, everything recounted in books can really happen, but not in the same way. It is to this way of happening that I clung so tightly." [75] Through his reading of the novel he decides that this feeling of adventure is based on the irreversibility of time. The sustaining power of this fixed succession of events is underlined by Sartre in his portrayal of Roquentin's subsequent search for a refuge in the world of Stendhal's *La Chartreuse de Parme*. The following day his experience in the museum reveals the failure of the inhabitants of Bouville to justify their lives through the commissioning of a work of art. Balzac and Stendhal do not fail because the imaginary existence of their hero and heroine is characterized by ordered time, but the painters, Renaudas and Bordurin, cannot justify the existence of Blévigne. Just as the elite of this provincial city had seized upon the painter in an effort to give a meaning to their lives, M. de Rollebon, as Roquentin says, "stood before me and seized my life in order to present his own. I was no longer aware that I existed, I no longer existed in myself, but in him." [76] At the end of his visit to the museum Roquentin frees himself from the community leaders, the *raison d'être* of the community embodied in their portraits, and this experience helps release him from his own *raison d'être,* the Marquis de Rollebon. He must ask himself once again, "What am I going to do now?" [77]

In connection with this irreversibility of time, Roquentin thinks of his mistress who tries to give to her life a quality of similar import. Just as he has sought reassurance in novels, Roquentin hopes to find help in Anny's attempt to achieve the fixed *being* of the work of art. Anny wants to *be.* She tries to remain unchanging, eternal. His pleasure on receiving her letter is that of finding once again this characteristic, "this unwavering devotion to the most insignificant detail of her appearance." [78] Her life has been an attempt to become a work of art through

75. "Les aventures sont dans les livres. Et naturellement, tout ce qu'on raconte dans les livres peut arriver pour de vrai, mais pas de la même manière. C'est à cette manière d'arriver que je tenais si fort." *La Nausée,* p. 56.

76. "Se tenait en face de moi et s'était emparé de ma vie pour me représenter la sienne. Je ne m'apercevais plus que j'existais, je n'existais plus en moi, mais en lui." *Ibid.,* p. 127.

77. "Qu'est-ce que je vais faire à présent?" *Ibid.*

78. "Cette fidélité puissante et sévère au moindre trait de son image." *Ibid.,* p. 82.

creating the "situations privilégiées" which might transform her existence.

This predilection has been frequently discussed by critics, but the object in her childhood which was the source of this attitude is rarely seen to be the work of art.[79] The engravings of her copy of Michelet's *Histoire de France* gave rise to Anny's contemplation of the events in history and in the life of an individual. In her reading Anny eagerly anticipated the works of art which appeared at great intervals in the history. Significantly they were never juxtaposed with the events of the text. Independent of the historical incident, these engravings representing "situations privilégiées" fixed the historical event in the rigid form of the art object. In no other painting has Anny ever found the rigorous unity of these illustrations. The artist's choice of subject matter receives even greater weight and importance from its stylistic rendering by the painter. Kings and the moment of death are linked in these events; all who witness the royal procession of Henri IV or the death of Henri II are affected by what is happening. The artist is the creator of the privileged quality that Anny finds so appealing. This artistic transformation of daily events becomes the goal of the child. She feels that she must eliminate from her own life all that is not stylistically compatible with the artistic vision. She accepted the challenge on the occasion of her father's death. She attempted to play her role by discovering "the required gestures." [80] However, her aunt and her mother ruined the occasion because they did not understand that the privileged moment required their participation in order that it be transformed into a work of art. Roquentin tries to understand the rules of the artistic game when he sums up what Anny has told him of the source of her own endeavors: "In each privileged situation, certain acts must be done, certain words must be said, certain attitudes must be taken—and other attitudes, other words are strictly forbidden." [81] Roquentin has finally realized that Anny, in her own way, was attempting to give her life the rigorous order of the work of art. The "situations

79. Only Hazel Barnes in her book, *Literature of Possibility*, comments on the source of Anny's *modus vivendi*, but she notes only that it arises from "the full-page illustrations in her books." P. 199.

80. "Les gestes qu'il fallait." *La Nausée*, p. 186.

81. "Dans chacune des situations privilégiées, il y a certains actes qu'il faut faire, des attitudes qu'il faut prendre, des paroles qu'il faut dire—et d'autres attitudes, d'autres paroles sont strictement défendues." *Ibid.*, p. 187.

privilégiées" of the illustrations in her Michelet became her own living of "moments parfaits."

During the course of his relationship with Anny, Roquentin has never fully understood the necessity of participating in her creative game. Now he is willing to try. His work on Rollebon has been permanently abandoned. He seizes upon the opportunity to transform his existence by Anny's device. Her "moments parfaits" might work where his own "aventures" have failed. His life might well achieve the hardness of the Khmer statue by her methods. Unfortunately Anny has arrived at the same point by another road. He should have understood it on entering her room. She is no longer faithful to her image. Gone is the portable décor which framed the illustrations that were her life. She no longer transforms her room with exotic Japanese masks and Spanish shawls. In acting out her life she discovers that there is always a flaw in her dramatic shaping of events. Just when he needs her technique the most, she reveals to him her conclusion that "there are no 'moments parfaits.' " [82]

The two of them commiserate over their rejected solutions to the problem of *being*. As in *Melencolia I* of Dürer with its central winged figure in the company of the tiny putto, Anny and Roquentin attempt to arrive at some solution by aesthetic means. Panofsky traces the source of Dürer's pair to illuminated manuscripts and calendars; however, the Dürer engraving "shows a deliberate contrast between the inaction of the Melancholia and the strenuous efforts of the scribbling putto." [83] Anny's active, dramatic approach and the more passive, reflective effort of Roquentin are both suggested in Dürer's work. As they chat briefly of their mutual disillusion, they discuss once again the aesthetic solutions they have tried. "Paintings, statues can't be used," Anny tells Roquentin before she irately responds to his suggestion of the theater with "Well, what about the theater? Do you want to enumerate all the fine arts?" [84] Perhaps acting succeeds only for the audience. On the other side of the footlights the "moments parfaits" may exist, but for Anny this is not success because the art of the play excludes them: that is, the spectators are not actors. They are not involved in the "situations privilégiées." She forsakes her career as an actress in hopes of achieving a mystical vision by bringing to mind a succession of

82. "Il n'y a pas de moments parfaits." *Ibid.,* p. 181.
83. *Albrecht Dürer*, 1: 160.
84. "Les tableaux, les statues, c'est inutilisable." "Eh bien quoi, au théâtre? Tu veux énumérer tous les beaux-arts?" *La Nausée,* p. 191.

almost perfect moments from their past. Anny does not divorce herself from a relationship with someone seeking an aesthetic solution. She has seized upon a German painter who is not like Roquentin or herself. At least, "not yet," she adds, because "he acts, he exerts himself." [85] In the course of their discussion Roquentin mentions the book he has tried to write, but Anny never permits him to elaborate on the "étrange bonheur" he receives from the ragtime music of an old phonograph record. They end their conversation and separate, but the haunting theme of the jazz tune remains in Roquentin's mind, and he returns to Bouville to prepare for his final departure from the provincial city.

Dürer's portrait of the artist's melancholy corresponds in many respects to that of Roquentin in his dejection.[86] As Roquentin reflects on his impotence and on the necessary economies that his income will oblige him to make in his life in Paris, we are reminded of the empty purse and keys that hang from the waist of Dürer's seated figure. Panofsky interprets these details as indicating a "temporary absence of wealth and power." [87] How to live with this melancholy is the problem. The traditional prescription suggested to those afflicted with the distressing humor of melancholy, as Panofsky notes, is "exercise, regular hours, a careful diet and music," [88] and in an aside the scholar mentions that Dürer himself recommends the "cheerful tunes of the lute." [89] Roquentin's own prescription for his condition, "Eat, sleep, sleep eat. Exist slowly, gently," [90] parallels that of the traditional program, and most strikingly in the consolation he receives from music. Roquentin has constantly been attracted by the brief jazz melody.[91] In all of his efforts to alleviate or

85. "Pas encore, il agit, celui-là, il se dépense." *Ibid.,* p. 192.

86. In an earlier discussion of the tradition of Dürer's engraving in French literature and art, our attention was focused on Michelet's *Histoire de France,* the source of Anny's frantic attempt to *be* like a work of art by imitating the book's illustrations.

87. *Albrecht Dürer,* 1: 164.

88. *Ibid.,* 165.

89. Quoted by Panofsky, *ibid.*

90. "Manger, dormir. Dormir, manger. Exister lentement, doucement." *La Nausée,* p. 197.

91. The jazz melody suggests the use of music in the work of Proust. Several articles discuss the parallels between the use of a musical theme by Sartre and Proust: Cohn, "Sartre's First Novel," pp. 62–65; Grubbs, "Sartre's Recapturing of Lost Time," 515–22; and Shattuck, "Making Time," pp. 248–63. Any future discussion of the theme should take into account Michel Butor's "Les Œuvres d'art imaginaires chez Proust," in his *Répertoire,* 2: 252–92.

attenuate his nausea, this melody, which he first heard whistled by American soldiers in 1917, comes to have first place. The quality that fascinated him was the inflexible, rigorous order of the succession of notes. In speaking of it for the first time in his diary he says that "there is another happiness—outside there is that band of steel, the brief span of music which traverses our time through and through, rejecting it, rending it with its dry little points; there is another time." [92] This other time, the inevitability of the procession of notes, is related as well to the magic square and a card game and its magic combinations. In terms almost identical with those he uses to describe the melody, "the event which so many notes have prepared, from so far away, dying that it might be born," [93] Roquentin admires the trump played in the card game: "Handsome king, come from so far away, prepared by so many combinations, by so many vanished gestures." [94] Like the end of a novel which prepares its beginning, the note of the jazz melody and the handsome king depend on all that precedes them. The song penetrates the superfluous existence of the man. He turns to this rigor when the existence he has discovered through his nausea becomes too heavy and dense for him: "The voice, deep and throaty, suddenly appears and the world vanishes, the world of existence." [95] The natural thing for him to do before leaving Bouville is to hear the record one more time.

Before returning to the café and the record, Roquentin visits the scene of his abortive attempt to justify his existence by writing the biography of the Marquis. He enters the library where he spent so many long hours in this artificial endeavor before his realization that "one 'existant' can never justify the existence of another 'existant.'" [96] At present he knows that it should have been another kind of book. The tools of his research surround him, as they do the Dürer angel; his measuring and

92. "Il y a un autre bonheur: au dehors, il y a cette bande d'acier, l'étroite durée de la musique, qui traverse notre temps de part en part, et le refuse et le déchire de ses sèches petites pointes; il y a un autre temps." *La Nausée,* p. 36.
93. "L'événement que tant de notes ont préparé, de si loin, en mourant pour qu'il naisse." *Ibid.,* p. 37.
94. "Beau roi, venu de si loin, préparé par tant de combinaisons, par tant de gestes disparus." *Ibid.,* p. 38.
95. "La voix, grave et rauque, apparaît brusquement et le monde s'évanouit, le monde des existences." *Ibid.,* p. 132.
96. "Jamais un existant ne peut justifier l'existence d'un autre existant." *Ibid.,* p. 222.

weighing of another's life with these devices are now revealed to be useless. He bids farewell to the statue of Impétraz, reflecting to himself, "*I* shall never see Impétraz's skull again, nor his top hat nor his morning coat." [97] In the library he considers whether he should walk the streets of Bouville, among them the Rue Tournebride dominated by the church of Sainte-Cécile, but he decides against it. His visit is marred only by the expulsion of an acquaintance from the library,[98] and finally Roquentin returns to the café and the jazz melody.

Freed from the tyranny of Rollebon, Roquentin exists. His experience in the public garden is the culmination of the spells of nausea. At the moment of this revelation, the *being* of works of art contrasts with *existence* in its gratuitousness, yet Roquentin continues to yearn for something beyond this world, something measurable, necessary, and fixed. He reaches out for another world where "circles and melodies retain their pure and rigid lines." [99] Dürer's angel rejects his practical mathematical and geometrical preoccupations, but he cannot lay down his compass. The need for an ideal mode of existence remains. In his final moments in Bouville, Roquentin has the same compulsion when he reflects in the café: "The truth is that I can't put down my pen—I think that I'm going to have Nausea and I have the impression that I'm delaying it by writing." [100] He believes he has rejected music and accepts only out of politeness when Made-

97. "Moi, je ne verrai plus le crâne d'Impétraz, ni son haut-de-forme ni sa redingote." *Ibid.*, p. 202.

98. This man, known as the autodidact, has not come into our discussion of art and the artist in this novel. His portrayal by Sartre does suggest, however, the central figure in the companion piece of the Dürer *Melencolia I*, that of *Saint Jerome in His Study* (Pl. 6). Panofsky informs us that the two works exist as a pair and were never given away singly (*Albrecht Dürer*, p. 156). Like the autodidact, Saint Jerome exists in the ordered world of books, that of his study, absorbed in his acquisition of knowledge. The contrast between Roquentin and the autodidact is shown by Sartre when, during a visit to Roquentin's room, the autodidact examines a postcard of a Saint Jerome on the cathedral at Burgos. Discussions of Roquentin's writing of a book, the autodidact's aesthetic insensitivity, and the import of the art of a previous century for man today are the subjects of several of their conversations in which the autodidact's ideas and attitudes are ridiculed by Sartre.

99. "Les cercles, les airs de musique gardent leurs lignes pures et rigides." *La Nausée*, p. 162.

100. "La vérité, c'est que je ne peux pas lâcher ma plume: je crois que je vais avoir la Nausée et j'ai l'impression de la retarder en écrivant." *Ibid.*, p. 216.

leine, the waitress, offers to play his favorite tune one last time. What he has refused is the consoling aspect of music for those who seek compassion in its beauty. To alleviate their affliction, people like his Aunt Bigeois turn to music because "they fancy that the captive sounds flow into them, sweet and nourishing, and that their sufferings become music." [101] The saxaphone begins and his position changes. His reaction to the music is one of shame. The deliverance from the consoling idea of the melody results from the understanding that it is beyond this world. His feeling of shame on hearing the jazz melody derives from the fact that "*it* doesn't exist because it has nothing 'de trop': it is all the rest which in relation to it is 'de trop.' It *is*." [102] It *is* in another time, another world; Roquentin, too, would like to *be*—not through his "adventures," not through Anny's "moments parfaits," not through the paintings of Renaudas, but, as Robert Campbell suggests, through "L'acte d'imagination." [103] Roquentin would like to forsake the world of existence in order to dwell in the world of the work of art "with the doges of Tintoretto, with the good Florentines of Gozzoli, behind the pages of books, with Fabrice del Dongo and Julien Sorel, behind the phonograph records with the long dry laments of jazz." [104] Roquentin unites the ordered, irreversible time of the novel, the hard quality of the jazz melody, and the ceramic-like flesh of the men in painting. Their *being,* which is imaginary like that of the circle and triangle contemplated by the Dürer figure, cuts through the fleshy superfluity of his own existence.

The jazz tune serves only to bring shame upon the listener. It is impossible to follow the music's advice to *be* like it, but the melody may have succeeded in justifying the existence of the composer and the singer. Roquentin sees their suffering embodied in the music. The error of his aunt was to have felt her suffering transformed into the music of Chopin when she sought consolation in her grief. For Roquentin, just as for Sartre, the work of art brings the spectator or listener back to the painter or compos-

101. "Ils se figurent que les sons captés coulent en eux, doux et nourrissants et que leurs souffrances deviennent musique." *Ibid.,* p. 217.

102. "*Elle* n'existe pas, puisqu'elle n'a rien de trop: c'est tout le reste qui est trop par rapport à elle. Elle *est.*" *Ibid.,* p. 218.

103. *Jean-Paul Sartre,* pp. 172–73.

104. "Avec les doges du Tintoret, avec les braves Florentins de Gozzoli, derrière les pages des livres, avec Fabrice del Dongo et Julien Sorel, derrière les disques de phono, avec les longues plaintes sèches des jazz." *La Nausée,"* p. 218.

er's suffering, but the suffering has become a thing. As Sartre says
in his *Qu'est-ce que la littérature?* concerning the work of Tintoretto, "It is an anguish become thing, an anguish which has
turned into yellow rent of sky, and which thereby is submerged
and impasted by the very qualities of things, by their imperme-
ability, their extension, their blind permanence." [105] From Roquentin's point of view the artist's existence may be justified
through the alchemy of the creative act. Roquentin is not certain,
but he hopes that this is the case. He will try again. The artist of
the Dürer engraving remains artist, but his temporary melancholy has permitted him to renew his art. Roquentin feels that
the Negress and the Jew are saved. They have been purified,
"washed of the sin of existing," [106] because they resemble the
heroes of novels. He speculates that he might take up his pen to
write the book, but in his eyes it would have to be a novel
capable of causing his readers to think of him as he has thought
of the composer and the singer of the jazz melody. In doing this
he might be able to accept himself, as he says, "in the past, only
in the past." [107] Some future reader will remember him. The
appropriateness of the words of the song seems clear.

> Some of these days
> You'll miss me honey.[108]

The sweat and suffering of his existence as man may possibly be
discovered by the reader of the novel he thinks of writing just as
he has found the composer "through the melody, through the
pure, acidulated sounds of the saxophone." [109] Through the creation of the work of art and, by extension, the myth of the author
who created it, someone may be moved by his life. He feels his
existence will become part of the myth of the artist who has

105. "C'est une angoisse faite chose, une angoisse qui a tourné en
déchirure jaune du ciel et qui, du coup, est submergée, empâtée par les
qualités propres des choses, par leur imperméabilité, par leur extension,
leur permanence aveugle." P. 61.
106. "Lavés du péché d'exister." *La Nausée*, p. 221.
107. "Au passé, rien qu'au passé." *Ibid.*
108. *Ibid.* Henry A. Grubbs, Philip Thody, and Hazel Barnes have
considered the source of the tune. Sartre is reproached by Grubbs and
Barnes for not quoting the words accurately. Thody "suspects" that
the details of the life of the composer and singer are invented by
Sartre, but seems to miss the point in saying that the most significant
thing about it is that "it was composed and performed by two outcasts
of bourgeois society." P. 13.
109. "A travers la mélodie, à travers les sons blancs et acidulés du
saxophone." *La Nausée*, p. 220.

brought the work of art into being, but this is a tenuous solution which is never pursued. The temptation of *being* seems finally to have been rejected by Roquentin. He writes no novel. Only the notebooks we have read reveal his rejection of the *being* of the work of art and the mythification of the artist that occurs for the creator in the past—only in the past.

In his notebooks the successive rejections of the false uses to which art is submitted are revealed. From the Khmer statue to the jazz melody, the reader follows Roquentin's agonizing search for the meaning of life and of art. Sartre begins with the experience before the statue as a means of suggesting the yet unformulated distinction between the crude material *being* of stone and its *being* as work of art in contrast to the gratuity of Roquentin's existence. By focusing on the ambivalence inherent in this object, the protagonist is led to a consideration of the justification of his own existence. The problem is not clearly stated in the beginning. It is formulated through a continuing referral to this starting point that provides the novelist with a touchstone for the aesthetic and ontological investigation of the artist-hero. This study has not treated the latter aspect except where it has touched upon the former.

The first group of art objects used in *La Nausée* is that criticized by Sartre in his "Portraits officiels." In relating this essay to the novel, I have discussed sculpture, architecture, and painting in one role that society frequently gives to art. In an attempt to establish the source of their own places in the universe, men create idols. Implied in the satire of seeking a rationale in these art objects is a criticism which in another age Sartre would have directed at the religious images of Christ and the Virgin Mary. The hierarchy of divinity provides man, the believer, with a fixed position. This security derived from having a precise role in the order of things is found in paintings and statues of kings and emperors. Sartre's disapproval of this use of art is more explicit in "Portraits officiels" when he deals with François I and Napoleon. Authoritarian social systems use the artist to maintain their control. Both the believer and the subject accept the aesthetic object as a presence of divinity or royalty. In *La Nausée* Sartre effectively employs the portrait of Philip II to eliminate the possibility of Roquentin's being seduced by the existing social order into accepting the moral values on which it is founded. The citizens of Bouville substitute their leaders for the monarchy, but Roquentin has always refused a role in society as father, professor, or industrial giant. The painting in its role of moral edification is linked to the creation of a continuing social hierarchy through the statues and portraits of the leader. Sartre's fictional *La Mort du célibataire* illustrates the use of art to terrify the individuals who would exist outside of society by not accepting the dominance of those who direct it. Terror in the form of art parallels the terrifying description of Hell used by the Marquis de Rollebon in order to bring about a deathbed conversion. The portrait of the Spanish monarch and the information provided by the satirical newspaper of this provincial city enable the protagonist to see the lie of art in this role and to reject it. Sartre's use of the statue of Impétraz, the church of Sainte-Cécile, and portraits in the museum of Bouville is an attempt to free the reader from their sorcery and witchcraft in the same way that Roquentin is freed from their spell. The artificial hierarchy held together by the artist's varnish melts before the eyes of the detached viewer, Roquentin. There is no answer for him in this falsely constructed justification of existence.

Afloat in a world that offers him no satisfying place and still in need of a reason for living, Roquentin reflects on a possible answer in the ordering of his life by "aventures." A second category of art dealt with by Sartre is that of the novel. Roquentin exists in the present; however, he needs to give form to the happenings of life as it is lived. Through his reading of *Eugénie Grandet* and *La Chartreuse de Parme,* he discovers the futility of imposing beginnings and ends on the events of his life. The banality of the fabric of continuing existence seems to have been overcome by specific incidents in his travels in exotic lands. The atmosphere of the night club, La Grotte bleue, is recaptured in a moment of reverie through the song *Blue Sky,* but unlike the hero of a novel he is forced to return to the time and space in which he is living at present. There are no beginnings in life because there are no ends. The author gives the novel its structure through the creation of his characters. Situated outside their lives, he places characters in meaningful sequence in which all things are relevant. Roquentin is unable to do this for his own life. The humdrum always outweighs the extraordinary. Recounting one's own life in the dramatic form of adventures, Sartre demonstrates, never disguises it from monotony and boredom. Only the unity of the novel accomplishes this in a fictional world where everything is significant. Adventures are in books, Roquentin learns, before he ceases to hope that he might resolve his dilemma through his aesthetic endeavor.

The illustrations from the *Histoire de France* of Michelet

provide yet another possible solution. Unlike Roquentin, whose attempt at ordering occurs through the remembered past, Anny, his former mistress, seeks to imitate in her life the theatrical character achieved by the artist in his depiction of significant moments of history. Her mistake, according to Sartre, is the error of those who would become a work of art by acting out their lives. In the same way that Roquentin realized that he became the fabricator of his adventures by being detached from them, Anny's instant drama forces her to be dramatist, director, and actress. She cannot be fully involved in her life as dramatic participant because she must see what is being created. The illustrator cannot be physically involved in his dry point or engraving. The gestures of the individual represented and their satisfactory aesthetic relation to the scene as a whole are imposed by the artist in the same way that the actions of the characters in the novel and their meaningful roles in the work depend on the writer. Sartre demonstrates that the inevitable awareness characterizing the attitude of the novelist or artist flaws the solutions of Anny and Roquentin in their desire to be like a work of art. Existence wins out over their pose and gesture. Biological existence cannot be clothed or costumed because the spectator-viewer role prevents man from achieving the *being* of the Khmer statue as work of art.

The jazz melody focuses the attention of the reader on the rejection by Roquentin of the use of the fine arts as a consoling factor in his life. The example of his Aunt Bigeois serves to criticize the position of the aesthete who uses his experience of the work as a means of changing his emotions into pigment, stone, or musical note, whose desire is to have himself absorbed by the symphony or painting simply by seeing or listening to what the artist has created. For Sartre the transformation cannot occur in this relation between perceiver and art object. Only when the individual takes the position of creator is there the slight possibility that the artist's life might be transformed in the *being* of the work of art—anguish become thing, as Sartre has suggested in relation to Tintoretto. However, the passive aesthetic experience is incomplete, and only through self-deception does the listener find help in the music of Chopin.

The qualities of fixity, stability, and permanence are represented by Sartre as having their parallels in the rigorous, determined order and inevitability of the work of art in the form of the syncopated ragtime melody. The game of cards serves as an intermediate step as the protagonist moves toward his final discovery through his reading of *Eugénie Grandet* and his listening to the record in the café. The appeal of the king of trump is found in the jazz melody. The creative solution is linked to precise ordering by reference to the fixed character of geometric forms. The abstract concept of the circle and the triangle leads to the characterization of the work of art as imaginary. The time and space of the melody or novel cannot be destroyed by the destruction of the record or book. The *being* of the hero of fiction is safe in his world as is the geometrical form. Roquentin is unable to create the triangle, but he is tempted by the measured rigor of time and space to propose to himself the writing of a work of fiction, which is subsequently rejected by implication for we are given only the diary of Roquentin—not the novel. In *La Nausée* the reader follows the progressive refusal of *being* in stone and the temptation of the imaginary *being* of the art object as Sartre has represented it in his philosophical study, *L'Imaginaire*. The latter form of *being* occurs only in the created work of art, not in the attempt to live one's life as a work of art, as both Anny and Roquentin have tried, or in the project of writing a novel. Antoine Roquentin becomes aware that the nausea of the experience of life in the flesh cannot be overcome in the present by any artistic project. The writer or artist only achieves *being* in connection with his own legend or myth as it becomes a part of the past.

Nothing happens in the novel. The action occurs in the intellectual contemplation of philosophical and artistic problems by the hero who refuses to become an artist. Consciously or unconsciously Sartre has used the work of Dürer as a basis for the construction of the novel. The change in title has perhaps obscured the presence of the artistic preoccupations of the hero. The seated artist of the Dürer engraving effectively summarizes the existence of Roquentin. Both of them are artists who reflect on two aspects of the human condition: man in the flesh and man in his creative capacity, which might be characterized as "la tentation de Saint Antoine." Sartre brilliantly unites philosophical and aesthetic problems in presenting the protagonist in his quest for a justification for his life. The melancholy atmosphere of the novel and the engraving is heightened by the representation of the artist seated near the sea of despair amidst the ineffectual tools he has rejected in his aesthetic endeavors, and by the frustrating attempt of the artist to give form to nature embodied in the enormous stone of the engraving. Dürer's artist found in the traditional device of music the means of relieving his temporary condition, and Sartre's hero, too, seeks consolation from the jazz melody as a possible means of overcoming his melancholy from the failure of his artistic project. Measuring and ordering the life of another and the external aspects of the world become the subjects of the artist and the writer, but both Dürer's seated angel and Roquentin meet defeat. Yet in creating a work of art, both Dürer and Sartre have provided a portrait of themselves as artists through the representation of the melancholy gloom that overtakes the creator when he is confronted with the search for a justification of human existence.

3

Art and the Drama

IN HIS THEATER Sartre initially shows the same preoccupations
with the work of art that we have seen in *La Nausée*. Music,
painting, architecture, and sculpture furnished rich material in
the creation of the novel. Roquentin's experience of these art
forms resulted in his forsaking being an artist as a means of
justifying his existence. The strong attraction of the work of art
in its use by religious or political authorities to create and
preserve an established hierarchy brings Sartre to use them in his
first play.[1] There are sculptural and architectural elements in *Les
Mouches* (*The Flies*) which Sartre uses in the same way as in *La
Nausée*. *Huis clos* (*No Exit*), his second dramatic work, shows a
different use of the statue in the action of the play. His subsequent dramatic production includes frequent examples of objects
of art, but in these plays and scenarios he focuses his attention
only briefly on a painting, a melody, a medallion, a style of
furniture, or the statue in relation to a secondary theme. The
examples of the work of art as a minor motif are drawn from *La
Putain respectueuse* (*The Respectful Prostitute*) and *Le Diable
et le bon Dieu* (*The Devil and the Good Lord*).

Sartre creates his play *Les Mouches* from the familiar Greek
myth of Orestes in the tradition of Aeschylus, Sophocles, and
Euripides, but the elements of the story—and in particular the art
objects—that he chooses for his purpose are characteristically
Sartrean. The palace of Agamemnon, the temple of Apollo, the

1. This, of course, does not include the play "Bariona," written for
his fellow prisoners while Sartre was a captive of the Germans. Simone
de Beauvoir insists in *Force de l'âge* that although its subject was the
birth of Christ it was, like *Les Mouches,* an invitation to resistance as
"le drame traitait de l'occupation de la Palestine par les Romains."
P. 499.

statues of the gods, and the sacrificial altars are available to him in the *Oresteia* of Aeschylus, yet more important than their appearance in the Greek plays is their presence in other forms in the experience of Roquentin. The church of Sainte-Cécile and the statue of Impétraz are the first steps along the road that leads the Sartrean hero to the square at Argos dominated by the terrifying statue of the god of the flies and death; to the temple at the cave of the dead; to the throne room with its bloody statue of Jupiter; and finally behind the bronze doors to the sacred image of Apollo. In readying the play for presentation to the public, the director, Charles Dullin, to whom the play is dedicated, understood the importance of the sets dominated by the presence of the statues and, according to Simone de Beauvoir, he turned to the artist Henri-Georges Adam for the creation of the masks, costumes, and sets: "The statues of Jupiter and Apollo played a large role in the play, so he decided to ask a sculptor to create the sets." [2] Adam designed the sets, masks, and statues in a style

2. "Les statues de Jupiter et d'Apollon tenaient une grande place dans l'action, aussi décida-t-il de s'adresser à un sculpteur." *Ibid.*, p. 553. Three of Adam's sketches for *Les Mouches* are used as illustrations for the deluxe edition of Sartre's *Théâtre* published by Gallimard in 1962. Simone de Beauvoir was impressed by "de grand corps de pierre (great bodies of stone)" when she visited the artist's studio, but a conflicting account of the decision to ask Adam to create the sets is given by Georges Boudaille in his article "Henri-Georges Adam," pp. 41–53. "En 1942, J.-P. Sartre qui connaissait et aimait ses gravures lui demande d'étudier des masques pour sa pièce *Les Mouches* que Dullin monte au Théâtre de l'Atelier." "In 1942, Sartre, who knew and liked his prints, asks him to study the problem of the masks to use in *Les Mouches* which was being staged by Dullin at the Théâtre de l'Atelier." P. 44. The artist's experience with the play is seen by Boudaille as the experience which caused Adam to become a sculptor. Boudaille recounts that "Adam se passionne pour ce problème de volumes, nouveau pour lui, et grâce à Sartre et Dullin, le voilà devenu sculpteur." "Adam developed a passionate interest in the problem of volume, something quite new to him, and thanks to Sartre and Dullin, became a sculptor." *Ibid.* Adam confirms Sartre's influence on his decision to become a sculptor in his brief article, *"Les Mouches,"* which appeared in *Cahiers Charles Dullin.* "C'est sans doute grâce à lui que je suis devenu sculpteur, en exécutant les statues de Jupiter, et d'Apollon, et les masques et costumes des acteurs dans des décors construits." "It is undoubtedly thanks to him that I became a sculptor, by creating the statues of Jupiter and Apollo, and the masks and costumes for the sets [for *Les Mouches*]," p. 6. Adam was fascinated by these statues and masks which he later assembled (Pl. 7) with a photograph of Charles Dullin in the role of Jupiter. The sculptor was pleased that Dullin came to him for advice about "le masque de Jupiter qu'il s'était composé," p. 6. Adam's photo-

which recalls the square dominated by the "sorcerer," Impétraz, as Sartre wrote of the statue in the novel (Pl. 7). The imposing appearance the bronze gave to the flesh of the scholar is continued in the opening scene of *Les Mouches* with the presence of the statue of Jupiter characterized by its vacant stare and blood-smeared head. As in the square at Bouville, the spell of this statue brings the insect-like old women of Argos briefly in contact with the magical power of the deity as they offer their libations before scampering away. The old woman of Bouville is fearful of the creature of bronze: "Suddenly she grows bolder, she scuttles across the courtyard as fast as her legs will move, stops for an instant before the statue, her mandibles quivering. Then she scurries off, black against the pink pavement, and disappears into a crack in the wall." [3] She becomes in *Les Mouches* a more active participant in the ritual required by the fierce god as the offerings are furtively made.

Sartre obliges Jupiter to confront his image in the statues in the successive acts of the drama (Pl. 7). Jupiter, in Sartre's reworking of the myth, is directly involved as a dramatic character in the play and must himself contend with the image created for him by the religion he has established. This separating of the model from his portrait in the work of art occurs elsewhere in the writings of Sartre. In his essay on the official portrait, previously discussed in conjunction with *La Nausée,* the distinction is made between the man and the king. The painter creates the presence of the monarch and sacrifices the weakness of the human to the portrayal of his divine right. One of the most striking experiences of Roquentin is his freeing himself from the talismanic power of the paintings of the leaders of Bouville by applying the knowledge of their lives that he has found in *Le Satirique Bouvillois.* Sartre once more presents the possibility of

---

graph illustrates the contrast between Jupiter and the statue of the god and also suggests the relation of the two to the guard's masks which served both to protect the sanctuary of Jupiter and to conceal the man's flesh.

3. "Elle s'enhardit soudain, elle traverse la cour de toute la vitesse de ses pattes et s'arrête un moment devant la statue en remuant les mandibules. Puis elle se sauve, noire sur le pavé rose, et disparaît dans une lézarde du mur." *La Nausée,* p. 44. Hazel Barnes, *Literature of Possibility,* comments on the portrayal of the people of Argos as insects and suggests as a source for this idea the works of Kafka and Dostoevski (p. 86), but she does not relate the coupling of statue and man as insect to the above-mentioned incident of the statue of Impétraz in *La Nausée.*

the comparison of the model with the image created by the artist in the tale of Orestes. Before the ritual effigy of the god, Sartre parades the god himself. Jupiter is characterized by the preceptor who accompanies Orestes as the bearded one. This stylistic trait of the representation of the god is remembered by the preceptor when he intuitively feels Jupiter's resemblance to the bronze statue of Jupiter Ahenobarbus that he has seen at Palermo. The Jupiter with the brazen or red beard provides the god with an essential aspect of his disguise, and in following the pair from Delphi to Argos, Jupiter "even then, aboard the ship, paraded his beard about." [4] The beard of the god in the play only disguises the man. Unlike the statues that represent him, the crimson blood of offering and the hair become sacred bronze have not transformed his person into a deity. He is conscious of his vulnerability and has taken an alias to move about in the world of men. He fears the possibility of a comparison with his created image as seen in the statue. When one of the old women of Argos questions him as to his identity, he quickly admonishes her: "Run along, you crazy old woman! Don't worry yourself about what I am; you'd be better off taking care of yourself, trying to earn forgiveness by repenting of your sins." [5] Jupiter has been obliged to participate actively in the world because he is threatened with the possibility of the destruction of the hierarchy his image has helped to create.

Electra, like Roquentin, has freed herself from the power of the god's image but for different reasons. Sartre dramatizes this fact in the confrontation of Electra and the statue of Jupiter in the presence of Orestes and his preceptor. She dares to look squarely into the face of the representation of the deity and defy its power, as Roquentin did in his passive contemplation of the portrait of Philip II in the library of the Escorial and of the paintings of the Bouvillois in their museum. In the eyes of the young girl the blood that sanctifies his image is only raspberry juice. Her gesture of defiance is expressed in her offering of garbage and ashes. She sees the statue for what it is, but is unable to destroy its power over the other citizens of Argos. The god is only a hollow image of wood covered with varnish and is

4. "Étalait déjà sa barbe sur le bateau." *Les Mouches* in *Théâtre* (1947), p. 15. Further quotations from this play will be from this edition.

5. "Va, va, folle! Ne te soucie pas de ce que je suis: tu feras mieux de t'occuper de toi-même et de gagner le pardon du Ciel par ton repentir." *Ibid.*, p. 20.

comparable to the ashy residue Roquentin revealed with his own scrutiny of other official portraits. In *La Nausée* the red-headed protagonist is not primarily concerned with revealing his discovery to others by destroying the power of the work of art and the myth of the religious and political order it helps to maintain. He has been more directly concerned with the nature of the work of art and its creation as a means to justify his own existence. Electra has been forced to participate in the creation of this order, but as a result of her backstage knowledge, she knows that she is not under the influence of its spell. She has been obliged to play a role in the ritual presentation of the order "when, once a year, the people require a portrait of our family life for their edification." [6] Her family, the family of kings, joins hands with the priesthood and the image of the god to manifest the hierarchy in which the people of Argos now have their place. She awaits the arrival of someone who would wrest the statue from its place and reveal its impotence to all who are limited and fixed by its sorcery. She calls for the destruction of the statue that she can only defy by gesture. She knows that Orestes will come one day: "And then he will draw his sabre, and split the statue from the head to foot, like this! Jupiter will topple, one half to the left, the other half to the right, and everyone will see that he is made of white pine." [7] Electra believes that if the statue were destroyed, the reign of terror consecrated by the blood of her father would come to an end. "The god of the dead is made of pine. The terror, the blood on his face, and the dark green of his eyes are only layers of varnish, aren't they?" The wooden presence of Jupiter would be consumed in flames leaving only ashes: "White pine! Good old white pine! How splendidly it burns." [8] She believes that the god of the dead would die with the statue because the power resides in the official portrait and not in his person.

After a long absence Orestes returns, on the most important day of the year. The celebration of the return of the dead from

6. "Une fois l'an, quand le peuple réclame un tableau de notre vie de famille pour son édification." *Ibid.,* p. 36.

7. "Et puis il tirera son sabre et fendra [la statue] de haut en bas, comme ça! Alors les deux moitiés de Jupiter dégringoleront, l'une à gauche, l'autre à droite, et tout le monde verra qu'il est en bois blanc." *Ibid.,* p. 30.

8. "Il est en bois tout blanc, le dieu des morts. L'horreur et le sang sur le visage et le vert sombre des yeux, ça n'est qu'un vernis, pas vrai? Du bois blanc! Du bon bois blanc: ça brûle bien." *Ibid.,* pp. 30–31.

the underworld [9] intensifies the remorse of the people of Argos
and solidifies the social order based on the worship of Jupiter and
his representative on earth, Aegisthus. Once a year the powerful
forces strengthen their hold on the citizens through the means of
a ritual return of the shades of relatives and friends. The most
important of these is Agamemnon whose death provided the
necessary event and the required blood for the consecration of
the hegemony. Agamemnon's rule was ineffective in the eyes of
Jupiter because "he had not permitted public executions." [10]
Because he had not cooperated in the joint effort of gods and
kings to subject men to their power, he became the sacrificial
victim. Sartre relates the dead king to the blood-smeared image
of Jupiter in the religion of the city whose believers conjure up
"the image of a great cadaver with a bloodied face." [11] Orestes
himself asks whether the blood and sacrifice which create insects
of terrorized men are the necessary accessories of the tyranny of
the god:

> These walls smeared with blood, these millions of flies, this
> stink of slaughter, this sweltering heat, these deserted
> streets, this god with the bloodied face, these terrorized
> larvae beating their breasts deep within their houses, and
> these screams, these unbearable screams—are these the
> things that fill Jupiter with delight? [12]

The anniversary of the murder of Agamemnon and the annual
celebration based on it become an extension of the powers of
Jupiter. The dominant elements of the stage set for the ceremony
in the play accentuate the relation between the sacred rock that
closes the mouth of the cave of the dead, the enormous temple

9. In her *Literature of Possibility,* Hazel Barnes notes that "Sartre
has combined the Christian concept of atonement for spiritual guilt
with the primitive idea that one must magically get rid of evil spirits."
P. 86. The magical aspect of the ceremony should be related as well
to the characterization of the work of art by Sartre as itself sorcery, as
he had done in writing of the statue of Impétraz, and to Jupiter's
frequent use of incantations to maintain the order threatened by Electra
and Orestes.

10. "Il n'avait pas permis que les exécutions capitales eussent lieu
en public." *Les Mouches,* p. 18.

11. "L'image d'un grand cadavre à la face éclatée." *Ibid.*

12. "Des murs barbouillés de sang, des millions de mouches, une
odeur de boucherie, une chaleur de cloporte, des rues désertes, un dieu
à face d'assassiné, des larves terrorisées qui se frappent la poitrine au
fond de leurs maisons—et ces cris, ces cris insupportables: est-ce là ce
qui plaît à Jupiter?" *Ibid.,* p. 21.

erected on this consecrated ground, and the magical strength of the god deriving from these objects of stone.[13] The gripping power of this supernatural place, this ritual, and those who perform it must be broken. The disappointment Electra has experienced in not discovering her brother in the person of Philebus causes her to attempt to destroy this spell at the very climax of the ceremony. The picture she has created in her own mind, of the hero who would arrive to split the statue in two, does not coincide with the aristocratic youth. Philebus has not yet become Orestes, and Electra, tired of waiting, makes her move. The most important religious day of the year is chosen as the occasion on which to attempt to free the citizens of Argos. The myth of the sacred day is attacked. In *La Nausée,* Sartre attempts to free men from superstition and from the accompanying feeling of well-being in repentance rooted in the myth of religion. Sunday dress and Sunday attitudes serve to fix men in a posture of fear and remorse. The superstitious people have dressed themselves in black to witness the ceremony of the return of the dead. The royal family and the high priest in elegant mourning clothes play the principal roles in this manifestation of the ruling order. Electra's efforts to break the spell of the myth are as theatrical as the ceremony is. She appears—not in the expected costume of black—but flaunts herself before the assembled crowd in her impious white gown to manifest her gaiety. The ineffectiveness of her confrontation is suggested in her earlier dramatic heaping of garbage and ashes on the statue when she wishes for a more effective means of attacking its powers—that is, for the return of Orestes. She is greeted by Aegisthus who demands, "Electra, answer me. What is the meaning of that costume?" [14] The nature of her affront is understood by the king immediately. It is through her choice of dress that she dares attempt to reveal to the people the means by which they are betrayed. Implicit in her choice of theatrical encounter is the very reason for her failure. Electra never took herself, and hence her challenge to Jupiter's

13. Sartre's use of the temple here in a way comparable to the use of the church of Sainte-Cécile is an accurate characterization of Greek sacred architecture and its site. Vincent Scully, in his book *Earth, the Temple and the Gods,* maintains that "the place is itself holy and, before the temple was built it embodied the whole of the deity as a recognized natural force. With the coming of the temple, housing its image within it and itself developed as a sculptural embodiment of the god's presence and character, the meaning becomes double, both of the deity as in nature and the god as imagined by men." Pp. 1–2.

14. "Electre, réponds, que signifie ce costume?" *Ibid.,* p. 56.

image and the extensions of his divine personage, seriously. She is ineffectual in her attempt to destroy the power of the statue and the order which it creates because she depends on theatrics to destroy what is essentially theatrical. She would remove the illusion of the theater by revealing backstage secrets. In her abortive confrontation she uses an inappropriate weapon rather than the cold steel she has previously suggested as the required means for breaking the spell by splitting the statue in two. Jupiter meets Electra's threat by his displacement, with his incantations, of the *papier-mâché* stone from the cave of the dead to the steps of his temple. Electra realizes her mistake when she confesses her self-deception to Philebus: "I imagined that I could heal the people here with words." She finally understands "that they must be healed by violence," [15] but instead she seeks her salvation in the myth of the gods' power in another aspect when she rushes to the statue-dominated sanctuary guarded by a companion deity, Apollo. The safety guaranteed her by the temple depends on the continuing functioning of a myth, a belief in the protection of the magic that resides in the god's image.

Orestes has freed himself from statuary and the myths that depend upon it through his extensive travels and his study of the fine arts. The temples and god images he has confronted are similar to the royal portraits encountered by Roquentin in his travels. This experience frees Orestes and Roquentin from the supernatural power created by the work of art. By means of the miracle of theatrical lighting, recalling his familiar thunderbolt, Jupiter attempts to convince the young man of the prevailing power of his order. But just as the artificially created atmosphere of power embodied in the Bouville museum fails to work on Roquentin, the god's sleight of hand fails to convince Orestes. The red-headed bachelor is separated from Bouville. Orestes rejects the city of Argos. There is no place for either of them in these hierarchies because the tricks of the prestidigitator are wasted on them. The threat of the painting depicting the death of the bachelor and the magical illumination of the rock before the cave of the dead are ineffective. But Orestes, unlike Roquentin, will himself become the means by which the power of the gods will be broken. Orestes initially is tempted to turn on the city in order to destroy its complicity in hiding man from himself:

15. "J'ai voulu croire que je pourrais guérir les gens d'ici par des paroles. C'est par la violence qu'il faut les guérir." *Ibid.*, p. 63.

I will be an axe and split apart these obstinate walls, I will cut open the bellies of these bigoted houses and from these wounds will rise the stench of offerings and incense; I will be a blade and drive myself into the heart of this city like an axe struck into the heart of an oak.[16]

This theatrical splitting asunder of the city continues the theme suggested by Electra's earlier appeal for the rending of the statue, but Orestes forsakes this course of action when he decides to murder his mother and her consort. He envisions his action in terms of flesh and blood under the knife rather than in terms of the wood of the statues and houses beneath his axe. Roquentin discovers the vulnerability of the flesh through the satirical newspaper and destroys the magic of the portraits by a knowledge of the man. Because of Orestes's similar museum experience, he applies his axe-become-knife not to the statue or canvas but to the flesh of Aegisthus and Clytemnestra on which these portraits are based.

Significantly, the murder takes place in the palace in the presence of the work of art. The architecture of royalty focuses on the palace of the king with the symbolic coupling of state and religion in the form of the throne and the terrifying and bloody representation of the deity. The vast throne room and its accessories, which frighten the masked soldiers who guard them, are reminiscent of the museum at Bouville and of the conversation of the old couple who, like the soldiers, are under the spell of these works of art. Even Aegisthus is caught in the magic of the myth which he has helped to create. Clytemnestra reminds him of this by asking, "Have you forgotten that it was you who invented these fables for the people?" [17] Alone before the statue he addresses the image of the god and characterizes himself as the representation of that god in flesh and blood: "I parade my great and terrifying mien everywhere, and all those who catch a glimpse of me feel their guilt within their very bones." [18] But the comparison with the statue is further extended when he speaks of

16. Je deviendrai hache et je fendrai en deux ces murailles obstinées, j'ouvrirai le ventre de ces maisons bigotes, elles exhaleront par leurs plaies béantes une odeur de mangeaille et d'encens; je deviendrai cognée et je m'enfoncerai dans le cœur de cette ville comme la cognée dans le cœur d'un chêne." *Ibid.,* p. 71.

17. "Est-ce que vous avez oublié que vous-même inventâtes ces fables pour le peuple?" *Ibid.,* p. 78.

18. "Je promène partout ma grande apparence terrible, et ceux qui m'aperçoivent se sentent coupables jusqu'aux moelles." *Ibid.,* p. 79.

his emptiness. He, too, is hollow like the towering figure of Jupiter in the first act. Jupiter enters in person and Sartre emphasizes once again the opposition between the god and his image. The king does not recognize the god, for he does not coincide with the image created for him. Jupiter himself resorts to his tricks of thunder and lightning in order to cloak the weakness of his person and thus to convince Aegisthus.

Their discussion begins with Jupiter reflecting on the immense and terrible statue. Incredulously he asks: "So that's supposed to be me? That's how they picture me in their worship, these citizens of Argos?" [19] The confrontation of a god with his own image is, as he comments, a rare experience. The threat that hangs over the order which he has created is the impending destruction of the person of the king. Jupiter has entered the action in order to save his earthly representative from the hand of Orestes. Jupiter is dependent on the presence of the king, who, as he says, is created in his own image: "A king is a God on earth, majestic and ominous as a God." [20] Aegisthus does not find these qualities in either Jupiter or in himself. He understands that the representations of the god and the king are in no way like the Jupiter and Aegisthus who are now discussing the function of the work of art in this hierarchy of fear. The painful secret of kings and gods is that men are free and that if this were known the statues and the images in whatever form would be destroyed. Aegisthus bursts forth: "You can bet that if they knew it, they'd burn my palace to the ground." [21] Since his accession to the throne, all of his acts and gestures have had only one goal. The image had to be created, and the result has been to hide Aegisthus from himself and to substitute the hideous but fascinating mask for the person. The complaint of Aegisthus that he is nothing but the fear of others created by this mask causes the god to reply violently by indicating the statue of Jupiter: "I, too, have my image. Don't you think it doesn't make me dizzy?" [22] These terrifying masks and statues that create the order under which men live must be maintained as long as there are men.

19. "C'est moi, ça? C'est ainsi qu'ils me voient quand ils prient, les habitants d'Argos?" *Ibid.*, p. 80.

20. "Un roi, c'est un Dieu sur la terre, noble et sinistre comme un Dieu." *Ibid.*, p. 84.

21. "Parbleu, s'ils le savaient, ils mettraient le feu aux quatre coins de mon palais." *Ibid.*

22. "Moi aussi, j'ai mon image. Crois-tu qu'elle ne me donne pas le vertige?" *Ibid.*, p. 85.

Jupiter's attempt to guarantee this hierarchy is threatened by Orestes's knowledge that man is free. The king hears the god's counsel but asks him to leave, for he cannot bear the god's presence, which recalls the disparity between Jupiter and his statue, and by extension, between himself and his image.

The lengthy discussion concerning the projection of the kingly and the godly into the world to create an order, which disguises the true nature of men from themselves, reveals a distinction between Jupiter and Aegisthus. Jupiter's image in statue and temple differs from the ceremonial nature of the king's image. The latter requires Aegisthus to wear the mask and thus to perform in the setting of the city, the palace, and the throne room—a role Jupiter is not obliged to take. Jupiter's scheme of things requires the presence of Aegisthus to act the role of the king. Orestes will not accept Electra's proposed destruction of the statue of the god. His awareness of the distinction between the king and the god is stressed in the meeting between Jupiter and Aegisthus. Orestes will strike the incarnation of order in the very person of the king. His purpose will be achieved by destroying the personage on whom the people of Argos depend in order to play their own roles. He will render powerless the terrifying aspect of the god who is only an image guaranteed by the mask worn by man in the flesh. The death of Aegisthus and Clytemnestra is an attack on the complicity of man in the sacred drama of remorse.

At his request Orestes is led to the temple of Apollo by Electra, for he has yet another step to take before the myth of the power of the gods is destroyed. He has brought down the statue of Jupiter not by destroying its physical structure but by destroying its accomplices in the person of the king and queen. The ceremonial masks have fallen from the ravaged flesh of the rulers, and their bleeding wounds reveal the failure of the sceptre and throne to disguise the man and the woman. Yet Electra will not be freed. She believes in the power of sanctuary at the feet of the statue of Apollo. Orestes returns with Electra to this place closed behind the protective bronze doors of the temple. Here he takes the final step to free the people of Argos from the spell of the work of art in its role of establishing the order desired by the gods. That men are free of the power of the statue, whether it be felicitous or malevolent, must be demonstrated by Orestes, who has destroyed Aegisthus the man in his complicity in the role of the monarch. Orestes carries his blasphemy to the temple of the benevolent Apollo. He has exposed the existence of flesh behind the mask of ceremony and the wood and bronze of the artist to reveal the freedom of men in "their existence, their obscene, insipid existence, given to them for nothing." [23] What Orestes has brought into the light is the flesh men would avoid. Men bleed but statues do not. The blood of statues is, as Electra knows, only raspberry juice. She cannot accept the vulnerability of man in his freedom, and she returns characteristically to the gods in the dramatic form of their physical manifestation on earth. She begs the god to protect her from her existence and offers her repentance for the acts of Orestes: "I will obey your law, I will be your slave and your thing. I will embrace your knees and feet." [24] She offers her freedom in exchange for sanctuary at the feet of the god. Orestes would free her from all gods, both Jupiter and Apollo. In flaunting his freedom from the sanctuary before the people of Argos by his act of leaving the temple, he would take with him the talismanic power that separates them from their fleshy existence. As he steps down from the pedestal of the statue of Apollo, forsaking the temple and the statue, he takes with him the magic with which the sculptor and architect have endowed these objects. [25] Electra chooses to be deceived by their power and by the resultant power of gods, but just as Roquentin leaves the museum Orestes leaves the temple and the city of Argos. However, whereas Roquentin freed only himself from their power, Orestes attempts to free all the men of Argos, leaving them with this advice: "Farewell, men, try to live. Everything is new here, everything must begin anew." [26] Man must reject the work of art when it is used by the hegemony to provide a model for his life. Orestes has gone one step further than Roquentin because he tries to demonstrate to others what Sartre believes to be the negative character of the work of art as it is used to create a privileged establishment.

In representing the human form in stone or bronze, the sculp-

23. "Leur existence, leur obscène et fade existence, qui leur est donnée pour rien." *Ibid.*, p. 114.

24. "Je suivrai ta loi, je serai ton esclave et ta chose, j'embrasserai tes pieds et tes genoux." *Ibid.*, p. 116.

25. Orestes leaves the protective pedestal of the god by recounting the tale of a flute player who rids the citizens of Scyros of the rats infesting their city and then in like manner draws the flies away from Argos. The flute brings to mind the jazz melody and its consoling powers over Roquentin's nausea, but the piper here actually removes the leprosy by disappearing with the flies forever.

26. "Adieu, mes hommes, tentez de vivre: tout est neuf ici, tout est à commencer." *Les Mouches*, p. 120.

tor creates a basis for the myth of hierarchy. The portrait of the king and the image of the god considered by Sartre in his attack on this myth of right and privilege are not treated for their aesthetic merit. Nor is artistic quality of concern to him when he uses the statue as a symbol of *being*. The stone that imprisons man is an even more striking symbol of *being* than the stone alone, and it is in relation to the project of *being* that Sartre returns in *Huis clos* to the anthropomorphic sculpture. This use of the work of art is appropriate in a play that is not concerned either with men fixed on a particular level of society or with the search for meaning in freedom from a religious or social order. The three characters are fixed in death by their inability to change their lives through any action. In life they were both subject and object and undertook to control the opinions of others concerning the object they each were. In their death they gradually become aware in their experience of one another that they can no longer create the object they would become. They have no control over the objects placed at their disposal; they are forced to suffer psychologically from their inability to use these objects and from their awareness of the use to which these objects were put in life.

Critics of *Huis clos* refer to the furnishings and the Barbedienne bronze only to dismiss them as unimportant. Oleg Koefoed is typical when he writes, "As for the infernal décor, it was dictated by physical, rather than literary, requirements." [27] The exception is Robert Campbell who asserts that "like the hero, we gradually become concerned with the naïve replies of the bellboy, with the presence of the Barbedienne bronze, with unusual objects and familiar things which we are assured have no meaning." [28] It may be argued that these objects are examples of the minor arts and can hardly be placed in the same category as the paintings in the Bouville museum or the statues of the gods in *Les Mouches,* but the furnishings and the bronze reproduction are effective extensions of the art objects seen in earlier works. They have been chosen for a reason, and their appropriateness becomes apparent in the course of the play.

The Second Empire furniture is the first thing that Garcin

27. "Quant au décor infernal, il a été dicté par des exigences matérielles plutôt que d'ordre littéraire." "L'œuvre littéraire de Jean-Paul Sartre," p. 67.

28. "Nous sommes amenés à nous inquiéter, en même temps que le héros lui-même, des réponses naïves du garçon d'étage, de la présence de ce bronze de Barbedienne, de ces objets insolites, de ces ustensiles précis que l'on nous avère sans signification." *Jean-Paul Sartre,* p. 138.

notices when he enters the room, and he questions the boy about it. The boy informs him that the clients of the establishment are many and implies that the décor suitable for Garcin would hardly be appropriate for a Hindu. Garcin believes that he can become accustomed to any furniture in death, just as in life he had lived "a sham in a Louis-Philippe dining room." [29] The center of the stage is dominated by the large mirror over the fireplace mantel on which the bronze rests. He is disturbed by the mirror, which no longer gives him a reassuring image of himself, but the statue holds his attention.

> And why should one want to look at oneself in mirrors? But the bronze, well, I suppose there will be moments when I'll look at it without blinking. Staring at it, you understand? All right, there's nothing to hide. I assure you that I am fully aware of my position. Do you want me to tell you how it happens? There he is, suffocating, sinking, drowning, only his eyes are above water and what does he see? A Barbedienne bronze. What a nightmare. [30]

In life Garcin refused to accept the *being* of a chance object, but the spectator knows that here in Hell Garcin is no longer able to act on objects or to force his desired *being* on the others who join him. Garcin is unaware of this and attempts to do so by recounting his story—creating an image of his being as he would have others see it—to Estelle and Inès. The relationship of the three characters forces him gradually to accept his inability to control his image. The complicity of a couple who would lie to one another about a desired image of beauty or heroism is destroyed by the look of a third person who sees them as they are. Garcin attempts to carve an image of himself for the two women by asserting that he lived his life according to principles: "I was editing a pacifist newspaper. War broke out. What should I have done? They were all staring at me. 'Will he dare do it?' Well, I

29. "Une situation fausse dans une salle à manger Louis-Philippe." *Huis clos* in *Théâtre* (1947), p. 128. Further quotations from this play will be from this edition.

30. "Et pourquoi se regarderait-on dans les glaces? Tandis que le bronze, à la bonne heure. . . . J'imagine qu'il y a de certains moments où je regarderai de tous mes yeux. De tous mes yeux, hein? Allons, allons, il n'y a rien à cacher; je vous dis que je n'ignore rien de ma position. Voulez-vous que je vous raconte comment cela se passe? Le type suffoque, il s'enfonce, il se noie, seul son regard est hors de l'eau et qu'est-ce qu'il voit? Un bronze de Barbedienne. Quel cauchemar!" *Ibid.*, p. 129.

did. I folded my arms, and they shot me. What's wrong with that? What's wrong with that?" "There's nothing wrong with that. You are. . . ," but it is swiftly destroyed by Inès who ironically concludes Estelle's sentence, "A Hero." [31] Garcin does not give up easily and subsequently refers to his clothes riddled with twelve bullets as "a museum piece, a historical jacket." [32] He pursues this idea to the end by attempting to force Estelle to tell him that he is not a coward. She accedes to his wish, but Inès makes Garcin aware that Estelle does not believe it when Estelle tells him: "For thirty years you dreamed that you were courageous: you were permitted a thousand little weaknesses because heroes are permitted anything." [33] Inès destroys the image he has chosen to force others to see by her insistence that only acts would have proven that his project for *being* was not a dream. The look of the two women eats away the substance of this dream of *being,* and he turns from them to caress the statue: "Well, here's the moment of truth. The bronze is there. I contemplate it and am aware that I am in hell. I tell you everything was carefully planned. They intended for me to stand before this mantel, pressing my hand on this bronze, with all eyes upon me. All those devouring looks." [34] He is now aware that he is unable to act upon the objects that surround him or to create the object he wishes to be. He can only look at the statue, which represents *being* unaffected by the eroding look of another person.

Inès is aware from the beginning that it is not by chance that the statue is there. The reply given by Sartre to a question concerning "the philosophical meaning of the bronze statue" was that "it seemed [to him] that in hell one ought not to have anything but an ugly object to look at." [35] When seen in the light

31. "Je dirigeais un journal pacifiste. La guerre éclate. Que faire? Ils avaient tous les yeux fixés sur moi. 'Osera-t-il?' Eh bien, j'ai osé. Je me suis croisé les bras et ils m'ont fusillés. Où est la faute? Où est la faute? Il n'y a pas de faute. Vous êtes. . . Un Héros." *Ibid.,* p. 145.

32. "Une pièce de musée, un veston historique." *Ibid.,* p. 155.

33. "Tu as rêvé trente ans que tu avais du cœur; et tu te passais mille petites faiblesses parce que tout est permis aux héros." *Ibid.,* p. 179.

34. "Eh bien, voici le moment. Le bronze est là, je le contemple et je comprends que je suis en enfer. Je vous dis que tout était prévu. Ils avaient prévu que je me tiendrais devant cette cheminée, pressant ma main sur ce bronze, avec tous ces regards sur moi. Tous ces regards qui me mangent." *Ibid.,* p. 181.

35. "Il [lui] paraissait bien qu'en enfer un homme n'ait rien où poser son regard qu'un objet laid." "Jean-Paul Sartre répond à la critique," p. 4.

of the play, the answer is clearly ironic. The bronze is another example of Sartre's use of the sculptor's art to represent *being*. Garcin finally realizes his failure to model his acts upon the image he has chosen. In death the statue reminds him that he has achieved *being* in a form other than what he desired. He can only suffer from his awareness that although he can no longer act upon objects, he is tormented by what they represent. In the case of the Barbedienne bronze, it is the ugliness of *being*—quite unlike the *being* he would like to have achieved. In this Second Empire Hell, the myth of being is used to reveal that man becomes what he does. Unless the acts of life add up to the beauty of the attempted myth of the hero, the man attains only the ugly *being* represented by the statue. The dramatic device of the suffering from the disparity between the two effectively illustrates Sartre's recourse to the art object to reveal that man is in death what he did in life.

In Sartre's first two dramas, the work of art—most conspicuously a statue—is central both as a literary device and as an object having a major role in the dramatic action. These plays date from the period of the Second World War, and extensions of attitudes toward the work of art expressed in *La Nausée* are seen in them. The second of these plays, *Huis clos,* does not attack the art object as an element contributing to the power of a religious or social hierarchy. The Barbedienne bronze as a symbol of *being* recalls that Jupiter is bound to his statue as Garcin is to his solidified life. In his subsequent dramatic efforts Sartre does not return to the use of the work of art as a dominant element; sculpture, architecture, and other works of art gradually become marginal elements in his plays and scenarios. One can only speculate on why this occurs. Perhaps it is due to his preference for treating the problem of the artist in his novel, *Les Chemins de la liberté, (Roads to Freedom)* and in the critical essays on the art of painters and sculptors, such as Calder, Giacometti, and Hare, which he begins at this time. Whatever the reason may be, the occasional references to the work of art are subordinate to the major themes of the later dramatic works. Nevertheless, Sartre draws from time to time on the fine arts to enrich his plays.

One example is to be found in *La Putain respectueuse.* Sartre uses an art object to comment ironically on the girl's life when she expresses the desire to hang an engraving of a painting, *La Cruche cassée (The Broken Pitcher)* (Pl. 8), in her room. She always carries the picture with her in a trunk. Although she greatly admires the portrait of the unfortunate young girl who has broken her pitcher, the prostitute fails to understand the allegory of the painting. The meaning of the girl's "accident"—her tragic ruptured innocence—is obvious to the spectator who knows the Greuze painting, but it escapes Lizzie entirely. Sartre makes clear Lizzie's elective affinity with the girl in the portrait, and we are delighted and amused by the girl's naïve choice. The terrifying first step towards whoredom is now bathed in the gentle light of Greuze's portrait of lost innocence. She describes a second engraving she would like to acquire, a portrait of an elderly grandmother quietly knitting while she tells a story to her grandchildren. Sartre uses this print to reveal the yearning of the prostitute for the comfortable bourgeois life she will never have. The two paintings represent the unfortunate accident of her youth and the eternally happy grandmother she would like to be.

Another example of the work of art in the drama of Sartre is present in the confrontation of Goetz, the hero of *Le Diable et le bon Dieu*, with the sculptural representation of Christ. The event cannot be characterized as minor, yet the role of the statue is lost in the enormity of the vision of the play. The complex plot is laid in Germany at the end of the Middle Ages. By killing his mother and the king, Orestes destroys the basis of power of the hierarchy, but Goetz uses another method when he assumes the magical powers of the image of Christ. Catherine, Goetz's mistress, is dying; and both a priest, who has sided with the people in revolt, and Nasty, their leader, refuse to absolve the woman from her sins. Goetz has been converted from the service of evil to the service of good. He would like to free Catherine, who is caught in the spell of belief in her own sins. The setting—the empty church now forsaken by its priests—is used by Sartre to suggest the hollowness of this structure erected to the glory of God.

The theme of the stripping of the poor by the bishop, God's representative, in order to create the sacred images prepares us for the scene with the crucifix. Nasty, the leader of the revolt, has said earlier in speaking of the bishop that "there are gems and gold in his churches. He caused the death of all those who died of hunger at the feet of his marble Christs and ivory virgins." [36] By appealing to Goetz's choice of destruction as his reason for existing, Nasty later tempts the hero to join the people in their fight to escape their suffering. Nasty proposes that Goetz's capac-

36. "Il y a de l'or et des pierreries dans ses églises. Tous ceux qui sont morts de faim au pied de ses Christ de marbre et de ses vierges d'ivoire, je dis qu'il les a fait mourir." *Le Diable et le bon Dieu*, p. 40.

ity for destruction should be turned on the architectural and sculptural representations of power that the church has built with the gold and silver stolen from the poor and on the books that spread its doctrines: "If you really want to destroy, destroy the palaces and the cathedrals built by Satan, destroy the obscene, pagan statues." [37] Electra's appeal to her brother to pull the statue of Jupiter from its pedestal and split it in two in order to reveal its true nature would achieve the same results as Nasty's proposal. Neither Orestes nor Goetz undertakes the destruction of the statue with its magic powers. Goetz instead gives away his lands and seeks to do good, but his attempt fails to unite him with the people.

Then the dying Catherine provides the occasion for Goetz's encounter with the crucifix. Goetz is fully aware of the powers the statues possess. He is tormented by the people's belief in plaster saints and by the sale of indulgences, which is always accompanied by the magic flute—a motif seen previously in Sartre's works. The spell cast over the people by the sculptural representations of Christ is not simply a medieval enchantment, and Sartre was fascinated to feel its presence in the audience when the play was performed for the first time. "The first night, which was a performance before the critics, the audience was afraid. In the stigmata scene, when Goetz apostrophizes the crucifix, the spectators wondered if He were going to strike him dead." [38] Goetz calls upon the figure of the dying Christ to inflict his body with physical manifestations of his sins in order to free the dying Catherine, but the silent god-figure retains its immutability. The incident reveals to Goetz that God helps those who help themselves. He takes a page from the magician's book in order to share the power of this amulet, the Christ-figure, and inflicts upon his own body the sacred detail of the statue. The blood from Goetz's wounds is represented to the people as the blood of the hanging Christ-figure and the talismanic powers seem, to those present, to flow from the crucifix to Goetz's body. [39]

37. "Si tu veux détruire pour de bon, raser les palais et les cathédrales édifiés par Satan, briser les statues obscènes des païens." *Ibid.,* p. 103.

38. "Le premier jour, qui était une représentation avant les critiques, la salle avait peur. Dans la scène des stigmates, lorsque Goetz apostrophe le Christ en croix, le public se demandait s'il allait le frapper." "Jean-Paul Sartre répond à la critique," p. 4.

39. A discussion of the evolution of this theme in the work of Sartre by Kenneth Douglas in "Sartre and the Self-Inflicted Wound," pp. 123–31, recounts this incident but does not relate it to the crucifix and the statue motif.

His theatrics depend on the powers of the statue. His gesture relates him to the power of the spell felt even by the contemporary French audience. He becomes the living, walking statue with the same powers over the people that the awesome Christ-figure has. Goetz cries out to Catherine and to the crowd that "the blood of Christ, my brothers, flows from my hands. Fear nothing, my love. I touch your brow, your eyes, your mouth with the blood of our Saviour." [40] And the love that the people have reserved for the crucifix is shared by Goetz. This taking on of the powers of the Christ-figure temporarily solves his dilemma, but the role of the priest-actor-prophet proves to be unsatisfactory. This incident, however, is one more example of Sartre's use of the art object in his theater.

Les Mouches illustrates the way in which Sartre uses sculpture and architecture as major elements with which the individuals involved in the situation of the drama are confronted. In this play the art object has a central place in the action and functions as a focal point through which the attitudes of the characters may evolve. From the characterization of the work of art as an enslaving element used by the religious and political hegemony, he moves to the device of the Barbedienne bronze in the play Huis clos to construct his mythical Hell in a Second Empire setting. The statue in this instance is clearly more than an ugly detail of the inferno; it is a symbol for the frustrated project of being which resulted in a being other than that Garcin would have liked. In the works that follow these two plays, the minor but intriguing role Sartre gives to the art object has been examined in examples from La Putain respectueuse and Le Diable et le bon Dieu. The Greuze painting and the crucifix illustrate aspects of Sartre's treatment of art in his dramatic works. Although their role is less important than in Les Mouches and in Huis clos, they remind us of Sartre's continuing preoccupation with the artist and the objects he creates.

40. "Le sang du Christ, mes frères, ruisselle de mes mains. Ne crains plus rien, mon amour. Je touche ton front, tes yeux et ta bouche avec le sang de notre Jésus." Le Diable et le bon Dieu, p. 193.

4

The Artist and the Road to Freedom

IN HIS WORK *Les Chemins de la liberté* (*Roads to Freedom*) [1] Sartre does not focus on art and the artist as he did in *La Nausée;* his criticism of the work of art used to create the myth of the power of privileged beings is here subordinated to the presentation of Mathieu Delarue's search for freedom in the years preceding the fall of France. From June of 1938 to the catastrophic events that lead to his capture and imprisonment as a member of the French Army, this work recounts his search for authentic existence. But if the central concern in these novels is the journey down the road to freedom, Sartre does not forsake the artistic preoccuptions of his first novel and his plays. The existence of the artist is examined in the life of the painter, Gomez, who turns from his creative work to become involved in the Spanish Civil War. In Mathieu Delarue's own struggle to be free, he is confronted not only with Gomez, the artist become general, but also with an ancient Chinese pot, the work of Gauguin, and diverse aspects of the sculpture and architecture that surround him in Paris. The theme of the disturbing confrontation of the *being* of an object—particularly a statue of stone or bronze—which has been traced from its first appearance in the form of the Khmer statue in *La Nausée*, is continued here in the portrayal of several of the characters. Sartre first satirized youthful imitators of Baudelaire and Rimbaud in his short story "L'Enfance d'un chef" ("The Childhood of a Leader").[2] The temptation to be a poet is again derided by Sartre in his portrait of young Philippe Grésigne. Sartre weaves these incidents and motifs that relate to

1. Of this projected work, *L'Age de raison, Le Sursis,* and *La Mort dans l'âme* have been published. A fragment of the fourth volume, "Drôle d'amitié," appeared in *Les Temps modernes.*
2. In *Le Mur.*

the theme of art and the artist into his yet unfinished novel in many different ways.

In studies of this trilogy the painter, Gomez, has been neglected. When the complex action of the novel is discussed, Gomez is lost in the summaries of plot or overshadowed by the characters of Brunet, the Communist, or Daniel Sereno, the homosexual. The significance of the artist's role in Mathieu's life is overlooked by those who would characterize Gomez as a form of political commitment rejected by Mathieu[3] or simply as "a Spanish republican in New York, who represents the attitude of some of the European refugees in America."[4] From the beginning of the novel, the Spanish Civil War—the event uppermost in the minds of the European intellectuals in the years immediately preceding the Second World War—plagues Mathieu. A fortuitous encounter with a beggar inspires the beggar to reward Mathieu's generosity with the gift of a Spanish stamp. This stamp on a letter to the Comité anarcho-syndicaliste from the combatants in Madrid introduces the theme of the absence of the painter from Paris and, therefore, the guilt Mathieu feels for not having gone to the aid of the Spanish Republicans. From beginning to end, the novel is filled with Mathieu's desire to go to Spain. His inability to travel this road is emphasized by those objects in Paris, such as the stamp, that force him to be aware of the absent painter and, by implication, his own absence from the conflict in Spain.

Mathieu turns from his chance encounter with the beggar and, with the stamp in his possession, enters the shell-like security of the room of his mistress, only to receive the jolting news of her pregnancy. The problem is immediate and personal. Mathieu's futile search for someone to perform an abortion causes him eventually to approach Gomez's wife, Sarah, for help. In turning to her, he is again confronted with the artist's decision to forsake his painting for a role in the Spanish conflict. In the painter's studio Mathieu reflects on his friend's immediate departure for Spain on learning of the fall of Irun. He winces as he remembers his meeting with the beggar the night before. Sartre here introduces the artist who turns to action and leaves behind his unfinished works in order to participate in the violence of the flesh-and-blood conflict of men. The unfinished works in the studio abandoned by the painter intensify Mathieu's shame at not hav-

3. Brée and Guiton, *French Novel,* pp. 211–12.
4. Peyre, *Contemporary French Novel,* p. 232.

ing been able to take the same step: "The room remained exactly as he had left it: an unfinished canvas on the easel, a half-etched copperplate on the table, surrounded by phials of acid." [5] The irritating absence of Gomez leads Mathieu to reflect on the nude portrait and etching of "mistress" Stimson. He attempts to justify his inability to go to the aid of the Spanish by condemning Gomez's conduct towards his wife. Mathieu also tries to convince himself that Gomez was not seriously involved in his painting.

Sartre uses the artist who forsakes his painting in order to commit himself as a contrast to Mathieu and his trivial personal problems. Gomez's action was decisive, virile, and in total opposition to the ineffective procrastination of Mathieu. Sartre does not depict Gomez's actions in Spain as Malraux did for his heroic artists in L'Espoir (Man's Hope), but he effectively suggests the succesful involvement of Gomez with other men in their fight as the painter rose rapidly through the ranks to the grade of general. Throughout the first volume, Gomez is very much present in Mathieu's Paris. Even the empty studio serves the cause because it is here that the Communists meet the messengers sent from Spain by Gomez. Sartre transforms the place of creativity into a place of involvement, just as he shows Gomez choosing commitment through involvement in the lives of men. Spain and Gomez return to Mathieu's thoughts frequently, and never more strongly than in his subsequent discussion with Brunet. His continuing inability to commit himself brings Delarue back to thoughts of the beggar who, like himself, wanders aimlessly in the streets of Paris far from the bombings beyond the Pyrenees. He asks himself disgustedly, "Why am I here in this loathsome world of the sensational, with its surgical instruments and its clandestine trips by taxi, this world without Spain? Why am I not in the thick of it, with Gomez, with Brunet? Why don't I want to go and fight?" [6]

The personal problem of Mathieu is set against the background of the threat of war into which Mathieu and the whole of Europe are drawn. In the second volume of Les Chemins de la liberté, Mathieu's pleasant vacation interlude is interrupted by

5. "La pièce était restée dans l'état où il l'avait laissée: une toile inachevée sur le chevalet, une plaque de cuivre à demi gravée sur la table, au milieu des fioles d'acides." L'Age de raison, p. 45.

6. "Pourquoi suis-je dans ce monde dégueulasse de tapages, d'instruments chirurgicaux, de pelotages sournois dans les taxis, dans ce monde sans Espagne? Pourquoi ne suis-je pas dans le bain, avec Gomez, avec Brunet? Pourquoi n'ai-je pas eu envie d'aller me battre?" Ibid., p. 121.

mobilization. Before his departure he accepts an invitation to meet Gomez, who is on leave from the war in Spain. Their meeting between trains only underlines Mathieu's uneasiness in the presence of the artist who has chosen to give his life meaning through participation in the war in Spain. The distance that separates them is greater than ever, and the physical presence of Gomez makes Mathieu as ashamed of his position as his absence had in Paris. Mathieu again tries to justify himself and feebly offers the excuse of the difficulty of the transition from peace to war. He receives an answer to the question he asked himself in Paris. "I did it in an hour. Do you think I wasn't caught up in my painting?" [7] Confronted with the physical presence of the general, Mathieu feels intensely the experience of Gomez in which he has not shared. Sartre depicts this former artist as a man who has lived with no regrets—not even for the painting he left behind. No attempt on the part of Mathieu to praise the handsome paintings of the period before the departure for Spain will make Gomez regret his decision to leave for Spain and the war, even though his participation has forever destroyed for him the possibility of creating. As he himself says, "I'll never be able to paint again." [8] The artist has given up his painting, but it is not the glory of war he is seeking, for he knows that the cause for which he fights is on the point of defeat. Like so many of the characters on the road to freedom his efforts lead to naught. But in turning from art he has not remained suspended in the purgatory of uncommitted existence. When Mathieu asks what will become of him, he answers, "What difference does it make? I'll have lived." [9]

Sartre might well have left Gomez in Spain after having created the portrait of the artist who found that the arts are not sufficient and who turned instead to action. However, the author does not leave him on the battlefield in defeat. As I have suggested above, it is not only as a refugee from the war in Europe that Gomez later finds himself in New York. In *La Mort dans l'âme* (*Death in the Soul*) Sartre turns to other artistic problems that the painter discovers in exile. In Manhattan the experience of the extraordinary brightness of the sun intimidates him because of its effect on the colors of the external world. His initial reaction to the colors of the American city is negative. In

7. "Je l'ai fait en une heure, dit Gomez. Croyez-vous que je ne tenais pas à ma peinture?" *Le Sursis,* p. 212.
8. "Je ne pourrai plus jamais peindre." *Ibid.,* p. 221.
9. "Qu'est-ce que ça fait? J'aurai vécu." *Ibid.*

depicting this experience, Sartre draws upon Masson, who found that American cities are not conducive to painting. Sartre explains his reason for this in his essay on "Les Villes d'Amérique": "It is due in part to the fact that American cities are already painted. They don't have the half-hearted colors of our cities. What can you do with these hues that are already in themselves art, or at least artifice? Leave them right where they are." [10] Gomez begins by withdrawing from the problem of the intensity of light as it reveals the colors. "He looked hard at the shrieks of all these colors: even if I had the time, even if I took it into my head to do it, how could you 'paint' with this light?" [11] But inside the Museum of Modern Art he discovers that this light reawakens the desire to paint. His reaction to the colors is just the opposite of Masson's. His past in which he believed himself to be a painter is contrasted with the revelation he experiences before the emerald green of the grass in the garden. Now in this light he realizes that even after Picasso he knows what still must be done in painting. He experiences the explosive effect Sartre will praise in his essays on painting, particularly in his essay on Lapoujade. The painter sees the world as if cataracts have been removed from his eyes:

> All these colors had suddenly burst into life and fêted him, like 1929 with its balls, the Redoute, the Carnaval, the Fantasia; people and objects became flushed; a violet dress turned to purple, the red door of a drugstore turned to crimson, colors raced hard through all things like a pulse gone wild; stabbing pain, vibration swelled to the point of explosion; objects were going to burst or fall down in an apoplectic fit, and the whole thing shrieked, it swore, it was carnival.[12]

10. "C'est en partie, je crois, parce que les villes sont déjà peintes. Elles n'ont pas les couleurs hésitantes des nôtres. Que faire de ces teintes qui sont déjà de l'art ou, du moins, de l'artifice? Les laisser où elles sont." *Situations,* 3: 102.

11. "Il regardait crier toutes ces couleurs: même si j'en avais le temps, même si j'en avais la tête, comment voulez-vous 'peindre' avec cette lumière?" *La Mort dans l'âme,* p. 10.

12. "Toutes les couleurs s'étaient allumées en même temps et lui faisaient fête, comme en 29, c'était le bal de la Redoute, le Carnaval, la Fantasia; les gens et les objets s'étaient congestionnés; le violet d'une robe se violaçait, la porte rouge d'un drugstore tournait au cramoisi, les couleurs battaient à grands coups dans les choses, comme des pouls affolés; c'étaient des élancements, des vibrations qui s'enflaient jusqu'à l'explosion; les objets allaient se rompre ou tomber d'apoplexie et ça criait, ça jurait ensemble, c'était la foire." *Ibid.,* p. 25.

But it is too late. Colors have been given back to him only after he has ceased to believe he is destined to paint. The painter's experience in the war has changed all possibility of painting because, as Mathieu observed, "He has fought. Behind him lie scorched cities, stripped ridges, whirlwinds of red dust, flares that do not even shine in his eyes." [13] Here in New York he knows what to do, how to create with these colors and this light, but after Spain it is too late. Another will have to do what he is no longer able to do. These eyes, which have seen exploding bombs, are assaulted by the green of the grass beyond the windows of the museum, but he cannot bring himself to transfer it to canvas. He would have transformed it by making it incandescent, but now he resigns himself to giving up painting forever.

Gomez has accepted the position of art critic. No longer a creator, he must forgo the important questions asked by the reality of the grass and by the world of human experience. In exile in America he is portrayed by Satre as further disenchanted by art when he experiences painting in the service of an ideology ensconced in a clinical setting. Sartre returns to his rejection of a museum as a place in which those art objects that help to create a particular myth are housed. In *La Nausée* he writes of the galleries in which the works of Renaudas, Bordurin, and Séverand are displayed. Sartre creates an antipathetical portrait of the museum of Bouville in its use as a receptacle for the ideas of the powerful elite. In *La Mort dans l'âme* he deals with the Museum of Modern Art in the same way. For Sartre the ideals of American society are embodied in the collection of severely abstract paintings installed behind glass walls that separate art from life. No passionate experience of life could survive in the germ-free, air-conditioned setting. The wing in which Gomez finds himself contains "fifty canvases by Maudrian on the white walls of this clinic: sterilized Painting in an air-conditioned room; nothing suspect; here one is protected from microbes and human passions." [14] What the American public seeks most from art is reassurance. Ritchie, the American who has helped Gomez to obtain a job as an art critic, expounds on the function of art in the United States. It is to be an angelic art for people who live

13. "Il s'est battu. Il y a derrière lui des villes roussies, des tourbillons de poussière rouge, des croupes pelées, des explosions de fusées qui ne brillent même pas dans ses yeux." *Le Sursis*, p. 213.

14. "Cinquante toiles de Maudrian aux murs blancs de cette clinique: de la Peinture stérilisée dans une salle climatisée; rien de suspect; on était à l'abri des microbes et des passions." *La Mort dans l'âme*, p. 26.

under the provisions of a Constitution that idolizes the pursuit of happiness. "It's seraphic," as he says; "we Americans want painting for happy people or at least for those who try to be happy." [15] Above all Ritchie seeks innocence in a painting. Certainly no embarrassing questions should be touched upon by the artist. Abstract painting for Ritchie represents an ideal of happiness in which there is no place for sweat, blood, suffering, or dying. According to the American created by Sartre, art should not confront the individual with a portrait that publicly investigates personal, private problems. That is a job for the psychiatrist. Painting should rise above uneasiness and anxiety. Sartre attacks the American for his naïve idealism and for his innocent optimism. The leaders of Bouvillois society required the painter to eliminate their deformities and inadequacies in representing them on canvas in order to avoid looking at themselves as they really were. The American expects art to embody the ideal of an ordered world in which "questions concerning sex or the meaning of life or poverty are never asked." [16] Sartre satirizes the charming, deodorized American who closes his eyes to the problems of the world when he enters the sanctuary of the gallery or museum. Ritchie requires the reassurance of the kind of art he describes in order to live without discovering his own fleshly existence. As Ritchie himself says, "I *have* to go to all the exhibitions: it's a must."[17]

Gomez represents the same threat for Ritchie and the Americans that Sartre showed Roquentin to be for the citizens of Bouville. There is no portrait of a dying bachelor to serve as a warning, but Gomez's excessive perspiration and untidy thoughts are confronted by air-conditioning and ordered painting. The order that does not exist in the world is created in art to challenge the untidiness of life in the flesh. Sartre needles those who turn to such paintings by distorting the name of the painter Piet Mondrian to the richly suggestive Maudrian.[18] The danger-

15. "C'est séraphique. Nous autres, Américains, nous voulons de la peinture pour gens heureux ou qui essaient de l'être." *Ibid.*, p. 27.

16. "Des questions sur la sexualité ou le sens de la vie ou le paupérisme." *Ibid.*

17. "Il faut que j'aille à toutes les expositions: C'est un besoin." *Ibid.*, p. 28.

18. Sartre maintains his "Maudrian" with its suggestion of "le mal" in all editions published in French, but the English translation unfortunately substitutes "Mondrian" for the name of the evil "Maudrian." Sartre's attention to the names of the artists whom he has included in the discussions of painting in his novels can be seen in a change he

ous implications of the aesthetic described by Ritchie are clear. Sartre attacks it when in his description of one of the paintings of the American ideal he wittily—and perhaps maliciously—introduces a blue disk into the purity of linear equilibrium. Mondrian's art requires the encounter of verticals and horizontals in order to achieve the desired equilibrium (Pl. 9).[19] Hired to be an art critic, but in fact expected to praise these works, which give comforting reassurance to the citizens, Gomez is to be feared for his experience in Spain. His first assigned article has as its subject Maudrian. Ritchie suddenly feels ill at ease when he sees Gomez before the canvas because he understands that the abstract works of the painter who has become the god of the Americans may be attacked. When Ritchie intuits the portent of the Spaniard's hesitant reaction to the work of Maudrian, he desperately tries to explain that the god is not to be criticized adversely. He echoes Sartre's opinion on the American way to succeed[20] when he

made for the 1949 Gallimard edition of *La Mort dans l'âme*. When this part of the novel was published in *Les Temps modernes* no. 39 (Dec. 1948–Jan. 1949): 1–45, his list of painters "who ask embarrassing questions" included Klee, Rouault, and the Fauve painter Othon Friesz (p. 21). In subsequent editions Sartre has substituted Picasso for Friesz. Sartre is not alone in his attack on Piet Mondrian through distortions of his name. Salvador Dali in his *Les Cocus* includes a painting in Mondrian's style whose title is *Piet Niet*. Dali then cleverly mocks Mondrian by repeating his given name and by playing with it maliciously. "Et l'on entendra le Piet, Piet, Piet des nouveaux académiciens modernes . . . . Des critiques complètement crétins ont employé pendant plusieurs années le nom de Piet Mondrian comme s'il représentait le 'summum' de toute activité spirituelle. Ils le citaient à tout propos. Piet pour l'architecture, Piet pour la poésie, Piet pour la philosophie, les blancs de Piet, les jaunes de Piet, Piet, Piet, Piet, . . . Piet, Piet, Piet, Piépie, Pitié, Piet. Eh bien! Piet, c'est moi Salvador qui vous le dis, avec un 'i' de moins, ce n'eût été qu'un pet." Pp. 83–85.

19. Compare Mondrian's own statement published in *Plastic Art*, "Art has to attain an exact equilibrium through the creation of pure plastic means composed in absolute oppositions. In this way, the two oppositions (vertical and horizontal) are in equivalence, that is to say, of the same value: a prime necessity for equilibrium. By means of abstraction, art has interiorized form and color and brought the curved line to its maximum tension: the straight line, using the rectangular opposition—the constant relationship—established the universal individual duality: unity." Pp. 31–32.

20. "And you have to succeed because only then can you stand before the crowd as somebody. Take American newspapers, for example; as long as you haven't made it, it is foolish to expect that your articles will be published the way you submitted them." "Et puis on doit réussir parce que, seulement alors, on pourra se poser, en face de la foule,

advises Gomez on writing for the public: "Be cautious. . . .
Don't begin with an attack. . . . Above all, the public doesn't
want to be startled. Start out by making a name for yourself; say
simple, sensible things, and say them nicely." [21] The followers of
Maudrian, who inherit a puritanical zeal from their ancestors, are
prepared to deal with the nonbeliever who dares threaten the
order Maudrian's paintings have created. Sartre cleverly relates
Ritchie and the American in their role as cherubims and sera-
phims in the service of Maudrian to those Puritan forefathers
who destroy in the name of Good. "No question about it, Ritchie
was an angel; in his eyes you could read the obstinacy of angels;
his great-grandparents, who were angels too, had burned witches
on the squares of Boston." [22] It is not only the articles he might
write criticizing the works of Maudrian, but it is the very presence of a man in the flesh who suffers and has seen death that
threatens the values enshrined in the Museum of Modern Art.
Ritchie is used to warn Gomez of the stake that is prepared for
him. This warning closely parallels the painting of *La Mort du
célibataire* protecting the portraits of the leaders of Bouville
from the unbelieving eye of Roquentin. Sartre once again criticizes art that eliminates man's existence in the flesh by manifest-
ing values of purity and serenity on canvas. Gomez's awareness
of his body and his resistance to the values expressed in this art
bring him to reflect on his position. "I sweat, I'm poor, I have
suspicious ideas, European ideas; the handsome angels of America will end up by burning me too." [23] After the events in which
he has participated in Spain, he cannot be assuaged by the
artificial world of the abstract art of Maudrian.

But Sartre does not limit his criticism to the portraiture of the
hegemony or representation of values in abstract painting. In the

---

comme une personne. Voyez les journaux américains; tant que vous
n'avez pas réussi, il est vain d'espérer que vos articles paraîtront comme
vous les avez remis." *Situations*, 3: 86.

21. "Sois prudent, dit Ritchie. Ne commence pas par un éreintement.
. . . Il ne veut surtout pas qu'on l'effraye. Commence par te faire un
nom: dis des choses simples et de bon sens, et dis-les agréablement."
La Mort dans l'âme, p. 27.

22. "Ritchie, c'était un ange, bien entendu; on pouvait lire dans ses
yeux clairs l'obstination des anges; ses arrière-grands-parents, qui
étaient aussi des anges, avaient brûlé des sorciers sur les places de
Boston." *Ibid.*, p. 29.

23. "Je sue, je suis pauvre, j'ai des pensées louches, des pensées
d'Europe; les beaux anges d'Amérique finiront bien par me brûler."
Ibid.

course of their discussion, Ritchie and Gomez touch on revolutionary art, and the latter expresses an opinion Sartre will reiterate in his essays on art: he confesses that he never believed in revolutionary art to any great extent. Sartre now uses Gomez to characterize art as essentially optimistic because it justifies human suffering by transforming it into a thing of beauty. Unlike Titian, Gomez cannot try to justify the torn flesh that he has seen, because "one can never paint Evil." [24] Sartre explains this in "Le Peintre sans privilèges":

> Actually, if an attempt has been made, up until now, to depict the evil that men do to one another, an unpleasant alternative has suddenly been revealed: betraying painting without benefiting Morals, or, if the paintings are beautiful, betraying the rage and suffering of men for Beauty. Betrayal everywhere. [25]

With this realization Gomez returns to the position he took in his discussion with Mathieu and refuses to paint ever again. Yet he is reluctant to leave it behind. With a certain nostalgia he remembers the paintings of Picasso, which ask those unbearable questions Ritchie avoids: " 'They' [the paintings] had been lucky enough to come off. They had been blown up, breathed full of life, pushed to their very limits, and had fulfilled their destiny." [26] But his involvement with men in their corporeal existence renders art negligible in the balance because "if painting isn't 'everything,' it's just a bad joke." [27] The anguish he feels on leaving the museum is like what he felt on leaving his unfinished works in the studio forever behind him. The light of day is too intense. He turns from it to the consolation of the artificial light of a cocktail lounge, where he experiences the pain of his forsaken project of being an artist:

> Gomez put his head between his hands and stared at the wall; how clearly he could see the etching he had left un-

24. "On ne peut pas peindre le Mal." *Ibid.*
25. "De fait, si l'on essayait, jusqu'ici, de montrer le mal que des hommes font à d'autres hommes, on se trouvait, tout d'un coup, devant cette déplaisante alternative: trahir la peinture sans grand profit pour la Morale, ou, si l'œuvre, en dépit de tout, paraissait belle, trahir pour la Beauté la colère ou la peine des hommes. Trahison partout." *Situations,* 4: 366.
26. "Elles avaient eu la chance d'aboutir, celles-là, on les avait gonflées, soufflées, poussées à l'extrême limite d'elles-mêmes, et elles avaient accompli leur destin." *La Mort dans l'âme,* p. 26.
27. "Si la peinture n'est pas 'tout,' c'est une rigolade." *Ibid.,* p. 29.

finished on the table. A dark mass on the left would have been enough to balance it. A shrub, perhaps. Yes, a shrub. He could see it all very clearly, the etching, the table, the big window—and he began to cry.[28]

In *La Mort dans l'âme,* Gomez progresses from the secondary role in the life of Mathieu to become important in his own right with his artistic dilemma. Gomez moves from art to involvement, but his almost inevitable failure and resultant exile bring regret for the artistic project left behind.

Mathieu also experiences the influence of the art object. It is necessary to recall Roquentin who begins his struggle with an experience which centers on a Khmer figure in stone. Representing two aspects of *being* for the Sartrean hero, the work of art in stone is similar to an ancient Chinese pot of fired earth in *Les Chemins de la liberté.* Sartre brings the character Mathieu Delarue into contact with art objects and, as has been seen, with the artist himself in the person of Gomez. The obsession that has dominated Mathieu's life is the desire to be free. In order to achieve this he feels he cannot go to Spain and he cannot marry his mistress. The accidental pregnancy threatens to bring this project of freedom to an irrevocable end. On leaving Gomez's studio, he feels despair at becoming fixed as husband and father. Sartre again depicts the encounter of his heroes with the statue, which represents the frozen, static qualities of eternity. A proliferation of statues seen in the intense light of the Luxembourg gardens continues the pattern we have seen earlier in the depiction of the statues of Jupiter, Impétraz, and Velléda either in bright light or surrounded by the green of nature. The solidity of *being,* which Mathieu so frantically avoids, fills the atmosphere when he imagines the animosity of the figures in stone: "The lawn rippled back and forth at his feet, a statue offered its youthful stone ass to him, the pigeons cooed, birds of stone." [29] Seated in the gardens, he reflects on his existence as it is being transformed by circumstance into the fixity of the statues around him. The *being* of

28. "Gomez se mit la tête dans les mains et regarda le mur; il revoyait nettement la gravure qu'il avait laissée sur la table. Il aurait fallu une masse sombre sur la gauche pour équilibrer. Un buisson, peut-être. Oui, un buisson. Il revit la gravure, la table, la grande fenêtre et se mit à pleurer." *Ibid.,* p. 37.

29. "Le gazon moutonnait jusqu'à ses pieds, une statue lui tendait son jeune cul de pierre, les pigeons roucoulaient, oiseaux de pierre." *L'Age de raison,* p. 53.

these art objects is contrasted with the *being* of the trees in nature experienced by Roquentin in *La Nausée.* "There '*it*' was: these children scampering, the same for a hundred years, this same sunlight on broken-fingered plaster queens, and all these trees." [30] His stubborn determination not to *be,* like these petrified creatures before him, brings him to reflect on his own childhood and that first moment in which he conceived of the project of freedom.

In the presence of the eternal art object—an ancient Chinese vase—he feels his dough-like existence intensified. The vase, too, was formless earth before it was transformed into the hard, impassive object it became.

> On the table, there was . . . a fine Chinese vase, green and gray, with parrot's claws for handles; Uncle Jules had told him that the vase was three thousand years old. Mathieu had gone up to the vase, his hands behind his back, shifting his feet nervously, and looked at it. It was frightening, in this venerable oven-browned world, to be a little dough ball of bread faced with an impassive vase three thousand years old. [31]

The work of art demonstrates to the boy his inability to win at the game of ceasing to exist. He discovers that although he may succeed in emptying his head of his thought he cannot empty his body of himself. His taste remains, and the fired earth become ancient art object has a weight and density superior to his own. The boy, Mathieu, has neither the past nor the hardness of this fine gray and green object justifiable in itself. Young Mathieu feels himself trapped in the confines of his existence as defined by his family and the world about him. The child attempts to forget the vase and the questions he is forced to ask himself when confronted with its *being,* and he turns to playing a comedy before a mirror. At once creator of

30. "Il y avait ça: ces enfants qui couraient en désordre, les mêmes depuis cent ans, ce même soleil sur les reines de plâtre aux doigts cassés et tous ces arbres." *Ibid.,* p. 54.

31. "Sur la table, il y avait . . . un beau vase de Chine, vert et gris, avec des anses commes des serres de perroquet; l'oncle Jules lui avait dit que ce vase avait trois mille ans. Mathieu s'etait approché du vase, les mains derrière le dos, et l'avait regardé en se dandinant avec inquiétude: c'était effrayant d'être une petite boulette de mie de pain, dans ce vieux monde rissolé, en face d'un impassible vase de trois mille ans." *Ibid.*

his playful image and spectator, he cannot forget himself in his theatrics, and he returns to the problematical vase.

Orestes was tempted to bring about the destruction of the hollow statues of the gods; Roquentin stared down the gaze of the Bouvillois in their portraits; Mathieu, as a child, resorts to a more direct form of action: "Suddenly, he had gone back to the table, he had lifted up the vase, which was extremely heavy, and hurled it to the floor: it had happened just like that, and immediately afterward, he had felt as light as gossamer." [32] His bid for freedom is made through the physical destruction of the art object which respresents *being* in all its compactness and density. Fired by the intense heat of the kiln, the mud and liquid glaze had become a thing of beauty. As a man Mathieu will always feel shame before objects of beauty, which remind him of his own ugliness and his viscous existence, but in that moment he triumphs over the vase—over the work of art in all its hardness of ceramic, stone, or bronze. On surveying the destruction he has wrought, he is aware of the superiority of an act over an object: "He had felt quite proud, freed from the world, without ties, without relatives, without origins, an obstinate little excrescence that had burst the terrestrial crust." [33] This piercing of the symbolic crust, which contained *being* like the Bouville portraits, lets his liberty burst forth from behind the dam that locked it in. This feeling of lightness that comes with the act of breaking the containing vessel represents the freedom that he so jealously guards before the facts of the war in Spain and Marcelle's pregnancy. Sartre uses the Luxembourg gardens as the setting for Mathieu's reflection on his youthful destruction of the vase representing *being*. In this way, the statues in stone must bear witness to Mathieu's continuing refusal to yield to the temptation of *being*. Delarue is drawn to these works only to reject their fixity.

He will return to the body as it is represented in the work of art in the paintings of Gauguin, but again he will free himself from their spell. Immediately after his reflections in the Luxembourg gardens, Mathieu awaits the arrival of Ivich, the sister

32. "Tout à coup, il était revenu près de la table, il avait soulevé le vase, qui était fort lourd, et il l'avait jeté sur le parquet: ça lui était venu comme ça, et, tout de suite après, il s'était senti léger comme un fil de la Vierge." *Ibid.,* p. 55.

33. "Il s'était senti fier, libéré du monde et sans attaches, sans famille, sans origines, un petit surgissement têtu qui avait crevé la croûte terrestre." *Ibid.*

of one of his students. In his relations with Ivich, Mathieu has gone to great lengths to meet her in the presence of works of art: "He liked to show her beautiful paintings, beautiful films, beautiful objects, because he was not; it was a way of apologizing for himself." [34] This subterfuge does not work because he knows full well that her experience of the painting increases her distance from him rather than drawing her closer. Ivich is drawn to the beauty of a painting because in it she finds an inspiration for her own desire to be beautiful. Mathieu realizes this when he thinks of her in Proustian fashion, "painted and varnished, like a Tahitian woman on a canvas by Gauguin, unutilizable." [35] This very quality of being unattainable, of appearing to be as a work of art outside the realm of the pragmatic world of daily life, provides an answer to Mathieu's perplexity as to what he wants from her. Ivich is not unlike Anny in her desire to construct an image of herself. Like Mallarmé's Hérodiade, Mathieu's young friend cannot bear to be touched and has a gnawing fear of interference by others who praise her appearance at a particular moment. Compliments are offensive to her because she experiences them as awkward hatchet blows on the block of marble she herself is chiseling with perfection into a thing of beauty. She becomes totally absorbed in the work of art because she uses it to create her image. Ivich does not look at other people, Mathieu notes, but prefers to observe her own body as she prepares a self-portrait to be enshrined in her imagination, as she had actually done in venerating one of her Chinese-red fingernails. Her excessive fascination with beauty draws her into moods of solitary concentration in which she is as unattainable as the Tahitian woman of Gauguin. In this state Mathieu feels strongly attracted to her. As he himself confesses, "It was in these moments that he was most drawn towards her, when her charming, almost delicate little body was inhabited by a distressing force, a passionate, disturbing, unprepossessing love of beauty." [36] On these occasions and particularly when she is lost

34. "Il aimait lui montrer de beaux tableaux, de beaux films, de beaux objets parce qu'il n'était pas beau, c'était une manière de s'excuser." *Ibid.,* p. 57.

35. "Peinte et vernie, comme une Tahitienne sur une toile de Gauguin, inutilisable." *Ibid.,* p. 58.

36. "C'était dans ces moments-là qu'il tenait le plus à elle, lorsque son petit corps charmant et presque mignard était habité par une force douloureuse, par un amour ardent et trouble, disgracié, pour la beauté." *Ibid.,* p. 66.

in contemplation of an art object, Mathieu is strongly attracted to her, but he is, as well, fully aware of his separation from her. Nevertheless, by his proposed visits to museums and galleries he repeatedly gives her the opportunity to use paintings as a basis for her attempts to create her own *being*.

It is on the occasion of their visit to an exhibition of Gauguin's painting that Sartre portrays disenchantment with the gallery setting for the work of art. The Galerie des Beaux-Arts in the chic snobbery of its location in the Rue du Faubourg Saint-Honoré joins Sartre's portraits of the museum at Bouville and the Museum of Modern Art. All the weight of officialdom is brought to the gallery setting of the works of a French painter. The atmosphere of discreet, inoffensive beige walls bathed in gray light eliminates the passionate life of the artist and evokes the mood of a shrine dedicated not to the painter and his paintings but to *l'esprit français.* Sartre satirizes the setting in which "one is supposed to whisper, not to touch the objects on exhibit, to exercise one's critical abilities with moderation, but decisively, and not under any circumstance to forget the most French of all the virtues, Relevance." [37] He attacks the civic responsibility that the gallery apotheosizes by again giving us the portrait of visitors to the shrines of hieratic values first depicted in *La Nausée.* The elderly couple of the Bouville museum become in *L'Age de raison* the worthy frequenters of the exhibitions of the chosen saints of the French Republic. Their presence at this and other showings arranged under the auspices of the state is related to their position in society. On this stage set for their benefit and convenience, the intellectual elite are able to display their right to criticize the creations of a renegade painter who condemns their existence. The atmosphere permits them to judge the life of Gauguin. The inane comments of one of these eternally youthful couples attending the exhibition are the object of Sartre's criticism; for instance, the comment of the man—a recipient of the Legion of Honor—that the true Gauguin is Gauguin the decorator. Like Ritchie in the Museum of Modern Art, this couple rejects the questions the paintings ask. The installation of these works in the gallery setting is designed to reassure the Frenchman of his intellectual capacity and discriminating critical

37. "Il convenait de parler bas, de ne pas toucher aux objets exposés, d'exercer avec modération, mais fermeté, son esprit critique, de n'oublier en aucun cas la plus française des vertus, la Pertinence." *Ibid.,* p. 77.

ability. Sartre's presentation of the experience of this couple in the atmosphere of an official exhibition effectively damns them, as they are drowned in their "bath of 'esprit français.' " [38]

The presence of the couple and the official tone in the gallery are too distracting for Mathieu. Here Sartre illustrates his thesis that the work of art requires the active participation of the viewer for the aesthetic experience. Catherine Rau, in her article on Sartre's aesthetics, cites this episode as an example of "the necessity of a spectator for the occurrence of the work of art." [39] She does not, however, relate this to Mathieu's reaction to the gallery's atmosphere which stifles the experience of the art object. This setting obscures the painter's struggle in the creation of his canvases. For Sartre the work of art depends on the viewer in order to *be*. As Mathieu says, "Paintings don't get you, . . . they propose themselves to you; it's up to me whether they exist or not; standing before them I am free." [40] This second visit to the exhibition affects Mathieu in the same way as Roquentin's return visit to the Bouville museum, and he is unwilling to bring the imaginary work of art into being. "The paintings had burned out, and it seemed monstrous, in this bath of relevance, that there could have been people who painted, who depicted nonexistent objects on canvas." [41] The presence and conversation of the couple interrupts Ivich in her contemplation of the paintings, and she exclaims with irritation that exhibitions should not be open to the public.

The pursuit of beauty as a model for her own life causes Ivich to give primacy to the created object. For her, paintings exist in their own right quite apart from the artist with whom she feels no relation. Mathieu is shocked by this because of his interest in how the painter represents the body as an object. The means by which the flesh is transformed into a thing characterized by *being* continues to intrigue him, and he regrets her unwillingness to look at the one painting that still fascinates him (Pl. 10): "Two women walking over the pink

38. "Bain d'esprit français." *Ibid.*
39. "Aesthetic Views of Jean-Paul Sartre," p. 140.
40. "Les tableaux, ça ne vous prend pas . . . ça se propose; ça dépend de moi qu'ils existent ou non, je suis libre en face d'eux." *L'Age de raison*, p. 77.
41. "Les tableaux s'étaient éteints et ça paraissait monstrueux, au fond de ce petit bain de pertinence, qu'il se fût trouvé des gens pour peindre, pour figurer sur des toiles des objets inexistants." *Ibid.*, p. 78.

grass in their bare feet; one of them was wearing a cowl, she
was a sorceress; the other was stretching forth her arm in
prophetic stillness. They were not quite alive. They seemed to
have been caught in the act of being metamorphosed into
things." [42] The spell this painting casts over Mathieu is characteristically Sartrean. Like Mathieu, Sartre is fascinated with the
way in which this transformation into *being* occurs; he takes it
up again in his analysis of the paintings of Giacometti. Sartre's
interest in this transformation always centers on the human
body. Gauguin, the man, intrigues Mathieu because he sees the
painter's attempt to represent the human body—particularly
his own body as the painter would have it seen by others—by
substituting pigment for flesh. Gauguin is an appropriate
choice; his artistic career was characterized by flight from the
responsibilities of social existence. Mathieu's precious freedom
is confronted by the paintings of an artist who turned away
from wife and children and his banker's existence in pursuit of
a justification of his life. The Sunday painter who breaks from
his fixed position in society and commits himself fully to his art
is just what Mathieu is unable to be. Mockingly he compares
himself to Gauguin in his activities as a Sunday writer and
suggests the possibility that he too might do as Gauguin did
and leave for Tahiti. Mathieu is fascinated by the artist's
self-portraits. For him Gauguin's great achievement, revealed
in his self-portrait, was to have sought the loss of human
dignity in the solitude and pride of his creative life. The
portrait reveals Gauguin's concept of himself as a Christ who
sacrificed his body for his art (Pl. 11). He represents his
gratuitous fleshly existence by making his body "a lush, overripe tropical fruit with pockets full of water." [43] But through
the act of painting Gauguin is able to redeem his flesh by using
it to create a *thing* of beauty capable of moving Mathieu by its
terrible and obscene *being* in the work of art. Unlike Mathieu,
who is drawn to a portrait of the soft, ravaged flesh of Gauguin late in his career, Ivich admires the hardness of the
handsome, youthful face of an early self-portrait. In the latter

42. "Deux femmes foulaient une herbe rose de leurs pieds nus.
L'une d'elles portait un capuchon, c'était une sorcière. L'autre étendait
le bras avec une tranquillité prophétique. Elles n'étaient pas tout à fait
vivantes. Il semblait qu'on les eût surprises en train de se méta-
morphoser en choses." *Ibid.*, p. 79.

43. "Un fruit gras et mou des tropiques avec des poches pleines
d'eau." *Ibid.*, p. 78.

there is a model of beauty that coincides with her own project, but she is irritated by the distance that separates her from the paintings. She cannot touch them or possess them; therefore, she rejects them. Beside Ivich before these bodies, "Mathieu felt ashamed. He was 'de trop': a great garbage heap at the foot of the wall." [44] His flesh does not have the rigorous necessity of the jazz melody described by Roquentin, and he feels the sense of anguish before the corporeal existence of Gauguin which was changed by metamorphosis into a thing. His inability to use the freedom he felt on destroying the Chinese vase is heightened by the artist's work as well as by Gomez's departure for Spain. He resists the temptation to be fixed like an object in the work of art—whether it be in ceramic, stone, or pigment. Sartre uses the body frozen for all to see by the act of the artist in order to dramatize Mathieu's choice to remain free. But the same temptation to be fixed—particularly as a statue of stone—will haunt his friend Daniel throughout the novel.

Sartre moves directly from the exhibition of Gauguin's painting to the presentation of Daniel Sereno. The Gauguin portrait created by the artist with the use of a mirror is a narcissistic act fixed by the painter's brush and pigment in the work of art. Daniel is first discovered by the reader shaving before his mirror in the same stance, stripped to the waist like the Gauguin self-portrait. Daniel waits to spring the trap he has set for a young girl whose admiration for this inordinately handsome man causes her to leave flowers for him each morning. Both Gauguin and Daniel are preoccupied with the body. In examining his image in the mirror, Daniel is delighted by the shock that his naked torso will have on the young girl. The pride in the image of his flesh recalls what Mathieu found in Gauguin's portrait of himself as Christ (Pl. 11). Daniel is careful with his weight and conscious of his handsome face, to the point of carefully avoiding nicking his flesh with his razor. His attitude toward his body is ambivalent, however; he also sees in it the possibility of controlling his image by marring his face through a masochistic act. He deliberately cuts the head of a pimple in order to challenge those who would fix him in their minds as always handsome. Both Daniel and Ivich fear the categorizing of the individual unless they can control the

44. "Mathieu avait honte de lui-même. Il était de trop: une grosse immondice au pied du mur." *Ibid.*

image created. There is this difference: Ivich would be fixed in an image of beauty, as evidenced in her admiration for the handsome early portrait of Gauguin. Daniel would prefer the painting in which the body is represented as ugly flesh. He prefers to force the spectator to view him on his own terms and deliberately chooses an ugly tie and a heavy jacket that will cause his body to sweat profusely. This decision constitutes an appeal to be seen as he would like to *be*.

Daniel plays the game of seeing himself as he would have others see him. He would prefer to avoid being aware of his body except as an object seen by them. This desire closely parallels Gauguin's project in painting his body for a viewer who is forced to see the image he has created of himself, but Daniel is no painter and can only imagine the effect he has on an imaginary viewer: "He watched himself coming along, hobbling a little under his burden, clumsy, already bathed in sweat; he saw himself come, he was nothing more than pure look." [45] His imagined picture of himself is destroyed by his reflection seen in a shop window. The revulsion he would oblige others to feel is negated by the image of his body as it is. His project is to fix his body in an attitude that will evoke violent hatred in those who view him. This is the motive for his plan of self-castration, which would render his body in death a *thing* of disgust. This gesture would be his means of creating once and for all the picture he would give to the world. His imagination conjures his flesh transformed by his act into the *corpus delicti:* "I'll be lying on the floor, inert, my trousers open and sticky, the razor will be on the floor, red, jagged, inert." [46] This picture of his body finally become object has certain parallels with the painting, *La Mort du célibataire,* described by Sartre in *La Nausée.* The bachelor of the painting (like the Gauguin self-portrait) is naked to the waist, but the painter, Richard Séverand, created the picture of the corpse, green in death, as a warning of the ruling citizens to the museum visitor who might threaten the established order. Daniel would use his own body as Gauguin did, in order to freeze himself in a desired image. His razor dipped in red would replace Gauguin's brush and his flesh and blood would

45. "Il se regardait venir, boitillant un peu à cause de son fardeau, emprunté, déjà en nage; il se voyait venir, il n'était plus qu'un pur regard." *Ibid.,* p. 94.
46. "Je serai couché par terre, inerte, le pantalon ouvert et poisseux; le rasoir sera par terre, rouge, ébréché, inerte." *Ibid.,* p. 275.

replace the oils and canvas. "This terrible and obscene flesh" [47] of the Gauguin portrait would be his own. His body would become an affront to bourgeois morality—the opposite of the intention of the Séverand painting. But before he can become this imagined *thing,* he must first accomplish the act. He is unable to do it and is instead fixed only in his mind's eye in a frozen gesture reminiscent of the numerous statues Sartre has used previously in his works: "A body, lifelike and warm, with an arm of stone. The enormous arm of a statue, inert, frozen, with a razor at the end of it." [48] This abortive attempt to *be* leads Daniel to another means of self-torture. In marrying Marcelle, Mathieu's pregnant mistress, he will substitute one gesture for another.

Daniel's project to fix himself for eternity in the eyes of others by carving his own body brings to mind Sartre's characterization of the sculptor as a creator of dead bodies. In his essay "La Recherche de l'absolu" ("Search for the Absolute"), on the sculpture of Giacometti, Sartre writes that "for three thousand years sculptors have only been carving cadavers." [49] The activity of the sculptor recurs frequently in Daniel's project to *be.* The homosexual Daniel's experience of the human body brings him inevitably to an admiration for a hardness which might be imparted by modeling the flesh. Sitting beside his bride, Marcelle, he is conscious of the flabby, rubbery quality of a woman's body representing the antithesis of the hard, muscular quality of the male—and a statue. Women lack the armature that a sculpture and a male body share in Daniel's mind. Death, which would have given his own body a rigidity for eternity, is present in his reflection on fleshly experience. Daniel admires the body of a lad who is stripped to the waist digging a dog's grave. The well-formed back makes him want to run his hand over this flesh as the sculptor fashions his clay: "That handsome body called for the caresses of a sculptor, it ought to be modeled." [50]

In the presence of this young god, as Daniel calls him, Sartre brings Daniel once again to his project of achieving density of

47. "Cette chair obscène et terrible." *Ibid.,* p. 78.

48. "Un corps vivant et chaud avec un bras de pierre. Un énorme bras de statue, inerte, glacé, avec un rasoir au bout." *Ibid.,* p. 275.

49. "Depuis trois mille ans, on ne sculpte que des cadavres." *Situations,* 3: 292.

50. "Ce beau corps-là, il appelait des caresses de sculpteur, il faudrait le modeler." *Le Sursis,* p. 106.

being. Roquentin's reflection on the superfluity of his own existence on hearing the jazz melody results from his awareness of the music's *being* which he conceives of as ordered hardness devoid of the gratuitousness of the flesh. This passage in *La Nausée* is echoed in Daniel's reflection on his existence as the notes of a polonaise are introduced as accompaniment. Daniel does not reflect on the work of art as music, as Roquentin had. His concern is to find a means to transform his body into a statue of stone, in order to achieve the twofold *being* suggested by the Khmer statuette—that of crude existence and the imaginary work of art. He would like to be able to force his existence outside of himself, beyond that of his flesh transformed into *being:* "to be of stone, immobile, insensate, no sound, no movement, blind and deaf, flies, earwigs, ladybirds would be crawling up and down my body, a ferocious statue with an empty stare, without a worry." [51] He speculates that if he were able to bring this about he might finally coincide with himself and be "the pure object of [his] hatred." [52] This *being* as a thing implies the need for the look of the Other. This necessity for the spectator, which Sartre emphasized in his discussion of the *being* of the work of art in the case of the Gauguin paintings, has its parallel in Daniel's requirement of the glance of another person in order for him to be fixed as the object of evil he would like to be for eternity. His pondering leads to a rejection of this means because he cannot depend upon the look of Mathieu or any one else for any length of time. His own narcissistic glance continually separates him from that state as an object. Like Anny he cannot be both actor and spectator in his little drama. He is led to find a solution in the pure look of the ideal spectator, the eye of God. This omnipresent gaze might achieve the transformation of his flesh into the *being* of stone that he failed to bring about with the razor. The stare will strike as a knife into his fleshly existence.

> He was the *object* of a look. A look which peered deep into him, pierced him with knife thrusts, and was not his look; an opaque look, night in person, waiting for him

51. "Etre de pierre, immobile, insensible, pas un geste, pas un bruit, aveugle et sourd, les mouches, les perce-oreilles, les coccinelles monteraient et descendraient sur mon corps, une statue farouche aux yeux blancs sans un souci." *Ibid.,* p. 107.
52. "L'objet pur de [sa] haine." *Ibid.*

there deep within him, condemning him to be himself, coward, hypocrite, pederast for all eternity.[53]

Daniel requires the glance of Medusa, which would change his body into a statue of stone.

His resolution to become this object brings him to the church on Sunday. Sartre again depicts the attempts of men to find justification for their existence by creating for themselves a place in a hierarchy dominated by the eye of God. Daniel turns to a Romanesque church in hopes of experiencing this perfect look. His scheme to be fixed in stone is dramatically underlined by his fascination with the recumbent tomb figures in one of the side chapels of the church. Daniel would like to achieve the same repose as that human form in stone. To *be* an oak or a stone is clearly insufficient, for he seeks a specific image of himself and for that reason requires his body as basis for his projected *being*. He must remain recognizable as Daniel, but a monstrous Daniel—the embodiment of cowardice and homosexuality. He joins the congregation in their joy at being seen as sinners. The church is represented by Sartre as a place created for the experience of being seen in Sunday masks. The light of the stained glass creates the setting of silence and mystery and sets the stage for the experience in which "the look will fall on him from the stained glass windows; they all go in order to be seen; half of humanity lives under a look." [54] And the reassuring gaze that fixes each man in the mask he has chosen becomes "the look of Medusa," described as "petrifying." [55] The look of the eye of God brings repose in a world of virtues and vices of stone. Daniel begins to realize his own project to become "a monument of iniquity" as he kneels in the violet light and endeavors to present his body in order that it might be petrified, by the glance of God, as the mask of Cain. Daniel permits himself to believe that the weight and density of *being* descend on him. He attempts to guarantee this

53. "Il était l'*objet* d'un regard. Un regard qui le fouillait jusqu'au fond, qui le pénétrait à coups de couteau et qui n'était pas son regard; un regard opaque, la nuit en personne, qui l'attendait là, au fond de lui, et qui le condamnait à être lui-même, lâche, hypocrite, pédéraste pour l'éternité." *Ibid.*, p. 109.

54. "Le regard tombera sur lui des verrières et des vitraux; ils vont tous se faire voir; la moitié de l'humanité vit sous regard." *Ibid.*, p. 157.

55. "Le regard de Méduse, tombera d'en haut, pétrifiant." *Ibid.*, p. 158.

state by putting the experience on paper in the form of a letter to Mathieu. In writing of the event he creates his new-found *being* by giving literary form to the myth he has deliberately imposed on his fleshly existence. Daniel has sought to be like a statue of stone, but he requires his account of it in order to perpetrate the myth of *being*. He prefaced his prayer for transformation with a line from Mallarmé's "Le Tombeau d'Edgar Poe" ("The Tomb of Edgar Poe"): "Such as into Himself eternity at last changes him," [56] and he is conscious of the use of the myth of *being* as it is found in the works of the poet. He attempts to convince himself that he has become in life what the poet only achieved in his death. Daniel needs to feel his *being* as if he himself were the recumbent figure ornamenting the tomb. Daniel's conviction that he has been frozen by the eye of God in the posture of evil depends on the existence of another person who sees what he is. He tries to force Mathieu to see him in this stance by describing his new state in a letter. But it is only through self-deception that he can believe himself to be immutably fixed. Only a sculptor or a poet can use his existence to create *being,* and this is clearly not sufficient for Daniel because, as Roquentin discovered, *being* is only in the past. Daniel requires it here and now.

After this failure, Daniel welcomes the occupation of Paris because it achieves for the city the fixity he desires for himself. The victory of the Germans transforms the city into an eternal object of stone. Like the "eternity of statue" experienced by Mathieu who sees not only himself but his fellow soldiers as "statufied," the living city of Paris is changed into the immutability of stone by "the eternal and gorgonizing look of history." [57] In this mineral atmosphere Daniel sees the city now fixed like Rome and Egypt in a historical past. In this landscape of "stone confections made from the sugars of history," [58] he observes the pigeons, "immemorial birds become stones by dint of feeding on statues." [59] Like the pigeons in relation to the statues, he sees himself petrified by his contact with the age of stone as embodied in the temples, the triumphal arches, and the

---

56. "Tel qu'en Lui-même enfin l'éternité le change." *Mallarmé, Œuvres complètes,* eds. Mondor and Jean-Aubry, p. 70.

57. "Le regard éternel et médusant de l'histoire." *La Mort dans l'âme,* p. 69.

58. "De la pierre confite dans les sucres de l'histoire." *Ibid.,* p. 115.

59. "Oiseaux immémoriaux devenus pierres à force de se nourrir de statues." *Ibid.,* p. 116.

obelisk, which he describes as a "knife of stone." Yet there is still a distance between his *existence* and the *being* he continues to seek. Fortuitously he discovers an adolescent contemplating suicide and the temptation of the beauty of flesh replaces his revel in the historicity of the defeated city. Daniel turns from his preoccupation with the *being* of the stern block of stone tomb figures. Narcissus, in the form of Philippe Grésigne, draws Daniel towards what he calls "Beauty, my Destiny." [60]

Several themes of the poetry of Mallarmé have provided Daniel with material on which he has endeavored to base his project for *being*. Sartre uses Mallarmé's preoccupation with suicide, mirrors, and the calm repose found in the stone of the poets' tombs, which he takes up in his essay on this poet,[61] to create the character of Daniel in *Les Chemins de la liberté*. Young Philippe Grésigne, too, has attempted to use the poet and poetry to aid him in his search for a meaning with which to endow his existence. Sartre shows the misapplication of the myth of Baudelaire and Rimbaud to the life of the protagonist of his short story "L'Enfance d'un chef." His other short stories do not touch on the work of art as a major element, but in creating the character Lucien Fleurier he draws upon the oedipal relation of Baudelaire with his mother and upon the life and works of Rimbaud.

In *Les Chemins de la liberté,* Sartre again draws the portrait of the adolescent who discovers in his readings of the poets a mode of conduct for his own life. In the company of his mother and stepfather, Philippe cannot justify his existence. He feels himself transparent as glass: "a jolting window-pane on a glazier's back." [62] In an attempt to give meaning to his life he turns to writing poetry. One of his poems is accepted by a pacifist review, and encouraged by this he gradually permits himself the luxury of conceiving himself a poet. As the stepson of a general his affiliation with a pacifistic movement adds weight to his revolt as a budding poet. His inflated idea of his own importance leads to a break with the editor of the review, Pitteaux. Philippe hopes to find substance in the eyes of others by running away from home. In order to make certain that his act is interpreted correctly, he leaves a note in which he

60. "Beauté, mon Destin." *Ibid.,* p. 117.
61. In his "Mallarmé," *Les Ecrivains célèbres,* ed. Queneau, 3: 148–51.
62. "Une vitre cahotante sur le dos d'un vitrier." *Le Sursis,* pp. 136–37.

attempts to demonstrate the meaning of his flight by allusions
to the poets Verlaine and Rimbaud. The meaning of Verlaine's
"Laetus et errabundus" completely escapes his mother, but
Philippe believes he finds the opacity he sought in his vagabond-
age through her anguish. He imagines himself as the cause of
his mother's torment: "Now I am opaque like a dead body. She
is asking: 'Where is he? What is he doing? Is he thinking of
me?' " [63]

In his undertaking he draws upon the poetry he has read. He
plays out his little drama of being a poet by acting out the
events that will create his own myth. He prepares his image as
"future poet, yesterday, yesterday, yesterday forever." [64] Philippe takes a shabby room while waiting for a forged passport.
Here he sees the hotel transformed into a literary shrine of the
future: "One day they will place a marble plaque on the wall
of this hotel: Here Philippe Grésigne spent the night of Sep-
tember 24–25, 1938." [65] He draws upon Lautréamont and Rimbaud for inspiration in this nocturnal reverie, but he discovers,
as Roquentin had before him, that a poet can only *be* in the
future when he is dead. Thus, as he lies in bed the vagaries of
his imagination lead him to a vision of himself as a martyr of
peace: "Martyr, lying on his back, like a recumbent effigy of
stone, with two sorrowing angels at his head." [66] In this he
shares the predilection for the *being* of the recumbent tomb
figures with Daniel. He is delighted to discover that the couple
in the adjoining room are members of the proletariat caught in
the machine of war. His overtures of friendship are rejected
by the lovers. He is thrown out of their room and seeks
consolation in his *vade mecum,* a volume of Rimbaud's
poetry.

Sartre continues his caricature of the young man's search to
justify his existence by attempting to live his life in the manner
of the myth of the poet Rimbaud. Philippe's comical "dérèglement des sens" (disordering of the senses) leads him to the
bottle. Intoxication helps to put him in a poetic frame of mind.

63. "A présent je suis opaque comme un mort; elle se demande:
'Où est-il? Qu'est-ce qu'il fait? Est-ce qu'il pense tout de même à
moi?' " *Ibid.,* p. 136.

64. "Poète d'avenir, hier, hier, hier pour toujours." *Ibid.,* p. 146.

65. "Plus tard ils mettront une plaque de marbre sur le mur de cet
hôtel, ici Philippe Grésigne passa la nuit de 24 au 25 septembre 1938."
Ibid.

66. "Le martyr, couché sur le dos, comme un gisant de pierre et deux
anges tristes à son chevet, avec des palmes." *Ibid.,* p. 148.

Sartre satirizes his encounter with himself before the mirror of the bar. In attempting to fix himself for eternity, he contemplates the frozen reflection of the martyr. He would tear this image from the prison of the mirror world "like a dead skin, like scales from an eye." [67] He attempts to transform this moment by poetic means with several versions of the event:

Mirrors operated for cataract . . .
Cataracts of light
In mirrors operated for cataract
Daylight sinks in cataract in the mirror operated for cataract
Niagara of light in cataract in the mirror operated for cataract.[68]

Like Daniel in his attempt to freeze his mirror image in the tradition of the painter's self-portrait, Philippe is unable to hold his pose for very long. What is temporarily frozen must return to the world of the war. He is inspired to flip a coin to decide his fate in the tradition of the purity of chance found in the poetry of Mallarmé: "A throw of dice! Ding, never, ding, ding, will a throw, ding, of dice, ding, abol, ding, ding, ish, ding, ding, chance. Ding!" [69] He breaks himself free from his mirror and embarks on his adventure. Philippe does not get far; to his dismay he has forgotten his suitcase.

Before bringing this vagabond poet into the hands of his Verlaine, Sartre submits him to a Baudelairean experience. Philippe encounters his "Malabaraise" and explains to her that "the world is full of signs. Everything is a sign. One must know how to decipher them." [70] The young Orpheus seeks his first night of love before taking his own life. It is at the moment of contemplated suicide that Daniel finds his destiny

67. "Comme une peau morte, comme une taie à un œil." *Ibid.*, p. 217.
68. "Les glaces opérées de la cataracte . . .
Cataractes du jour.
Dans les glaces opérées de la cataracte
Le jour s'engouffre en cataracte dans la glace opérée de la cataracte
Niagara du jour en cataracte dans la glace opérée de la cataracte." *Ibid.*
69. "Un coup de dés! Ding, jamais, ding, ding, un coup, ding, de dés, ding, n'abo, ding, ding, lira, ding, ding, l'hasard. Ding!" *Ibid.*, p. 218.
70. "Le monde est plein de signes. Tout est signe. Il faut savoir les déchiffrer." *Ibid.*, p. 226.

in the beauty of this flesh. Daniel serves as Philippe's guide in the "dérèglement systématique des sens" of Rimbaud. The pair disappear from the novel in the arms of one another.

Inspired by the myth of *being* as they found it in painting, sculpture, and poetry, each of them has sought this justification but neither attains it. This failure is underscored by Sartre when he places Philippe before a portrait of a dead child in Daniel's collection.

> Philippe gazed in ecstasy at the portrait of this handsome child, so pale, so disdainful, who was staring back at him from the heart of the nether world with the self-sufficiency and seriousness of an initiate. They resemble one another, thought Daniel. Fair, both of them, both of them insolent and sallow, one on this side of the picture and the other on that side, the boy who had wanted to die and the boy who was dead for good were looking at each other; death was what separated them: nothing, the smooth surface of the canvas.[71]

Nothing. But this invisible barrier between *existence* and *being* which has consumed Daniel and Philippe—and Roquentin before them—can only be destroyed by the artist who represents flesh in imaginary *being*. Mathieu's fascination with Gauguin's self-portrait introduced the myth of the painter's life characterized by flight from society and the attempt to redeem fleshly existence by the creative act of the artist. The work of art must not serve as a model for a man's life, as Sartre repeatedly demonstrates in his fiction. It can only serve to show the impossibility of *being* in life and become the basis on which a new myth might be created in stone, pigment, or words. And this can occur, as Sartre has shown in *La Nausée* and in *Les Chemins de la liberté,* only when the man becomes a part of the past.

71. "Philippe regardait avec extase le portrait de ce bel enfant pâle et dédaigneux qui lui retournait son regard du sein de la mort avec la suffisance et le sérieux d'un initié. Ils se ressemblent, pensa Daniel. Blonds tous les deux, tous les deux insolents et blêmes, l'un de ce côté-ci du tableau et l'autre de l'autre côté, l'enfant qui avait voulu mourir et l'enfant qui était mort pour de bon se regardaient; la mort, c'était ce qui les séparait: rien, la surface plate de la toile." *La Mort dans l'âme,* p. 126.

5

Sculpture and Sculptors

FOR SARTRE the work of art—especially sculpture—represents *being*. In the novels and plays the statue is characterized by the dual aspect of its *being* as an object of stone or bronze and its *being* as a work of art. The Khmer statue in *La Nausée* is the first instance of the human body portrayed in stone, and it is significant that this work is anthropomorphic in character. The idea of man fixed for eternity as an object is consistently rejected by Sartre. The immobility that the sculptor endeavors to overcome by suggesting movement nevertheless remains a dead object. The human body that serves as a model for the object loses the capacity to act, and despite the cunning of the sculptor only a world of corpses is created. These corpses deny man his freedom to act because the sculptor has traditionally been involved in the creation of a myth in one form or another. In his creative works Sartre criticizes the statue not so much as an aesthetic object but as an element of the myth of power it creates. The sculptor endows the inanimate object with divinity by giving an eternal form to the human body. The statue becomes a carrier of values that gives to men a fixed place in a religious or political myth. Jupiter, Impétraz, and Henri IV are official portraits that permit the believer or the subject to accept a definition of himself in a hierarchy. These statues are reassuring because they hide the individual from the gratuitousness of human existence. The human figure is used to create a visible manifestation of an ideal of monarchy, divinity, or bourgeois morality. Sartre attacks sculpture in its use as a magical object in the perpetration of a myth.

In his desire to destroy the politico-religious myths, Sartre has attacked the sculptor's art. His view of sculpture as a three-thousand-year-old tradition of complicity in the creation of hierarchies changes only through his contact with the contemporary artist. Sartre's prejudice against the sculptor breaks down when he examines closely the work of his acquaintances. In the works of Calder, Hare, and Giacometti he discovers that sculpture has undergone a profound change. No longer does it represent the human form idealized in fixed movement. The techniques of these sculptors help them to free themselves from the tyranny of the ideal human figure. They break with the tradition of the human body as a basis for the creation of the myths of gods, leaders, and kings whose rights and powers derive to a large extent from the image created by the sculptor. The sculptural tradition that Sartre has characterized in his creative works as contributing to the establishment of false values is rejected by these artists. In their works Sartre comes to see sculpture in a role he believes to be different from the creation of "a dead man on a dead horse"[1] in order to protect "a rigorous hierarchy of worth and power."[2]

ALEXANDER CALDER

During a visit to the United States following the Second World War, Sartre met the sculptor Alexander Calder. Simone de Beauvoir describes in *La Force des choses* the works that charmed Sartre into writing an essay on them for an exhibition in Paris. For the occasion the Galerie Louis Carré published a handsome catalogue, *Alexander Calder: Mobiles, stabiles, constellations.*[3] Calder's wit and charm had been known in Paris since his participation in the Paris Salon des Humoristes in 1927. Through his miniature circus he came to know artists such as Miró, Pascin, Léger, and Mondrian. The now famous visit to Mondrian's studio was the impetus for his mobiles. Calder recounts the impact of Mondrian's paintings and tells of his desire to impart movement to them, but indicates that "Mondrian himself did not approve of this idea of all."[4] How-

1. "Un mort sur un cheval mort." "La Recherche de l'absolu," *Situations,* 3: 292.
2. "Une rigoureuse hiérarchie de mérites et de pouvoirs." *Les Mots,* p. 23.
3. 1946. This essay, "Les Mobiles de Calder," was reprinted by Sartre in *Situations,* 3: 307–11. Calder recounts his introduction to Sartre by André Masson and reproduces the catalogue, including the first page of Sartre's essay for the exhibition, in his autobiography, *Calder,* pp. 188–91.
4. "Mobiles," in *Painter's Object,* ed. Evans, p. 63.

ever, Calder pursued this interest, which resulted in the mobiles Sartre saw in 1945 on his trip to America.

The essay he wrote on Calder was the consequence of this timely encounter—timely because the elements which appealed to Sartre's sensibility had only recently become dominant in Calder's art. Calder temporarily put aside—but did not reject—the electric motors he used in his work. The constructions to which Sartre responded are mobiles, which "react to the wind and are like a sailing vessel in that they react best to one kind of breeze." [5] This fortuitous meeting caused Sartre to rethink his attitude toward the art of sculpture. He proceeded to disassociate Calder from the concept of sculpture that had forced him to Roquentin's position. When the *autodidacte* of *La Nausée* comments that in painting "aesthetic pleasure is foreign to me," Roquentin replies that for him "the same thing is true for sculpture." [6] Sartre was not certain of a definition of sculpture when he began his essay, because Calder's work does not fall into the category of sculpture that aims to impart movement to the inanimate. He does not suggest motion by having recourse to the human figure, which by contamination with the material is forever entombed. The materials Calder works with appeal to Sartre because zinc, tin, and bone do not carry the stigma of the sacred. The anthropomorphism of the sculptor's art is avoided by Calder in materials as well as in form. Sartre is pleased to find that movement is not to be enshrined "in bronze or gold, those glorious and idiotic materials, doomed by nature to immobility." [7] Motion is not eternalized through the use of a privileged element; rather, through materials ephemeral in nature, a trap is set for a momentary encounter. Sartre responds to an event—not to a created object. The transformation of the human form into a dead object in order to give the sculpture an aspect of mobility belongs to the Greeks. Calder's aim in sculpture, according to Sartre, is the antithesis of the sculptural tradition that creates such objects. In his choice of materials and structure, Calder avoids the creation of an anthropomorphic object characterized by subservience to the materials which give it fixity and to a hierarchy of values which it embodies.

In addition to approving of Calder's choice of material and

5. *Ibid.*, p. 67.
6. "Le plaisir esthétique m'est étranger." "C'est pareil pour la sculpture." P. 139.
7. "Dans le bronze ou dans l'or, ces matériaux glorieux et stupides, voués par nature à l'immobilité." *Situations*, 3:307.

his rejection of the human body as a means of formal organization, Sartre discovers that aesthetic pleasure is possible from Calder's sculptures. "Their movements which have no aim except our delight, an enchantment for our eyes," [8] are related to a jazz tune. They fulfill Sartre's requirement that the work of art be imaginary and exist nowhere outside of the experience of it. The jazz melody that temporarily relieves "l'épaisseur" (the density) of Roquentin's existence is similar to Sartre's experience of the mobile as "a tiny local 'fête,' an object defined by its movement and beyond which it does not exist. . . , a pure play of movement, like a pure play of light." [9] Calder's creation is linked with the idea of the "fête" defined by Simone de Beauvoir in her *La Force de l'âge* (*Prime of Life*) as "above all a passionate apotheosis of the present, while confronting the uncertainty of the future. A calm succession of happy days will never give rise to a 'fête': but if, in the midst of a misfortune, hope sparks forth again, if you tighten your grip on the world and time, suddenly the moment burns brightly, you leap into it and are consumed— that is a 'fête.' " [10] The mobile and the jazz melody penetrate the humdrum of day-to-day existence as a kind of "fête" which hours and days of patient watching or listening prepare, whose only reason for being is to please for some brief moment. The melody and the mobile *are*. In them there is nothing superfluous. They have a life of their own as imaginary objects brought into being by the patient viewer or listener. In speaking of a mobile of Calder, Sartre observes that

> each of its evolutions is an inspiration of the moment; the general theme with which its creator endowed it can be recognized, but the mobile embroiders a thousand personal variations on it; it is a little tune of hot jazz, unique and ephemeral, like the sky, like the morning; if you miss it, you lose it forever. . . . It is not enough to give it a

8. "Ces mouvements qui ne visent qu'à plaire, qu'à enchanter nos yeux." *Ibid.,* p. 309.

9. "Une petite fête locale, un objet défini par son mouvement et qui n'existe pas en dehors de lui. . .un jeu pur de mouvement comme il y a de purs jeux de lumière." *Ibid.,* p. 308.

10. "Avant tout une ardente apothéose du présent, en face de l'inquiétude de l'avenir; un calme écoulement de jours heureux ne suscite pas de fête: mais si, au sein du malheur, l'espoir renaît, si l'on retrouve une prise sur le monde et sur le temps, alors l'instant se met à flamber, on peut s'y enfermer et se consumer en lui: c'est fête." Pp. 588–89.

passing glance; you have to live with it and fall under its spell. Then the imagination rejoices in its pure forms as they are interchanged—forms that are at the same time free and regulated.[11]

The "fête," the jazz melody, and the mobile are sources of pleasure, but the anticipation and the unpredictability that unite them are joined most significantly in their ephemerality. Sartre describes the mobile, for example, as "a flower that wilts as soon as it stops"[12] (Pl. 12). The evanescence of the *being* of the music and the mobile as works of art contrast with the density of crude *being* of stone used to create a statue. Sartre's refusal to experience sculpture as a work of art—that is, an aesthetic object—is forgotten when he discovers these mobiles that have "a life of their own. . . halfway between matter and life."[13]

What Sartre delights in finding in these works is the absence of content. Unlike the Impétraz, the Jupiter, and the Henri IV, these works are not intended to suggest anything. There are no references beyond themselves to a world of meaning. Sartre insists on this aspect of the sculptor's work when he writes that "Calder suggests nothing: he traps real movements alive and shapes them. His mobiles signify nothing, refer to nothing but themselves; they *are,* they are absolutes."[14] They do not seek the source of their slightest movement in the world of the human. The gesticulation of the mechanical toy, with anthropomorphic reference to human existence, imitates human gesture with false precision in the same way that older sculpture imitated man's gestures and betrayed him. For Sartre, Calder's constructions escape from the "blind, ruthless rigor of purely

11. "Chacune de ses évolutions est une inspiration du moment; on y discerne le thème composé par son auteur, mais le mobile brode dessus mille variations personnelles; c'est un petit air de jazz-hot, unique et éphémère, comme le ciel, comme le matin; si vous l'avez manqué, vous l'avez perdu pour toujours. . . . Il ne s'agit pas d'y jeter un coup d'œil en passant; il faut vivre dans son commerce et se fasciner sur lui. Alors l'imagination se réjouit de ces formes pures qui s'échangent, à la fois libres et réglées." *Situations, 3:* 309.
12. "Une fleur qui se fane dès qu'elle s'arrête." *Ibid.,* p. 308.
13. "Une vie propre. . . à mi-chemin entre la matière et la vie." *Ibid.,* pp. 310–11.
14. "Calder ne suggère rien: il attrape de vrais mouvements vivants et les façonne. Ses mobiles ne signifient rien, ne renvoient à rien qu'à eux-mêmes: ils sont, voilà tout; ce sont des absolus." *Ibid.,* p. 308.

mechanical translations." [15] Because these works avoid the use of the human figure to embody abstract concepts, Sartre can delight in the aesthetic pleasure of them in a way comparable to Roquentin's experience of the jazz melody.

Sartre responded to the elements in Calder's sculpture that reinforced his own ideas. It should not be overlooked that, although the works in the exhibition were predominantly mobiles, stabiles and constellations were present. Calder had not entirely forsaken the motorized element so alien to Sartre. As he wrote in "Mobiles," "I still like the idea, because you can produce a positive instead of a fitful movement." [16] But Sartre makes Calder his own, and at the same time he makes discoveries about contemporary sculpture which he will pursue in writing of the work of David Hare and Alberto Giacometti.

Sartre's first foray into the field of art criticism was very successful. The essay and an English translation were published in *Style en France*,[17] and English versions appeared twice in the United States within one year.[18] Whenever someone turns to the work of Calder, it is inevitable that he return to Sartre's short essay and share the nuggets contained in it with others.[19] Perhaps the most delightful event in relation to this essay is the transformation of the first paragraph into a poem in the form of a mobile published in *Art présent*.[20] Most important in this encounter is the beginning of Sartre's interest in contemporary sculpture and sculptors, to be followed by his association with the Galerie Maeght's *Derrière le miroir*.

DAVID HARE

The director of the Galerie Maeght brought artists and writers into contact and published the poems and essays that the sculptures and paintings inspired. In October of 1947 a four-page unnumbered insert was included in *Derrière le miroir*. These pages were part of a recurring series in the periodical

15. "Impitoyable et aveugle rigueur des translations purement mécaniques." *Ibid.*, p. 310.

16. *Painter's Object*, ed. Evans, p. 57.

17. No. 5 (Apr. 15, 1947): 7–11.

18. "Existentialist on Mobilist," pp. 22–23, 55–56, and in the catalogue of the sculptor's show at the Bucholz Gallery, "Calder's Mobiles," *Alexander Calder.*

19. Cf. Sweeney, *Alexander Calder.*

20. "Poème," no. 3 (1947): 45.

called "Les Mains èblouies." It was in this series of essays that
Sartre published his second article on sculpture, "Sculptures à
'n' dimensions" ("N-Dimensional Sculpture") about the works
of David Hare.[21] Calder's works were among the pieces offered
for sale by the Galerie Maeght, and it may well have been
through Calder that Sartre met another young American
sculptor, David Hare.[22]

In beginning this essay, he returns to the elementary problem of the artist's choice of materials. In writing of Calder,
Sartre revealed his delight in the contemporary artist's rejection of privileged materials such as bronze and stone in favor
of tin, zinc, and iron. In the work of David Hare he again
criticizes stone as a material in which the human body is
rendered eternal by the sculptor. The stone or marble imparts
to human flesh an apparent substantiality that hides the tenuous
existence of man, but these materials, Sartre points out, depend
on the unity of the human face or body to belie their own
ephemerality. Just as the eternal, in Sartre's thought, no longer
plays an important role in man's existence as a historical being,
the traditional materials of the sculptor are found to be fragile
as well: "Marble suddenly reveals its defects: inalterable in
appearance, a secret crumbling gnaws at it; this pure hardening
of space is made up of separable parts." [23] The act of the
sculptor chiseling in order to create an external image of
eternity reveals the weakness of the materials with which he
works. On close examination the marble of the sculptor's studio is seen to be in the process of decomposition or fragmenta-
tion. The technique of carving forces the sculptor to proceed
gradually from one part of the anatomy to another and in so
doing fragments his conception of the finished work in the
accomplishment of the individual detail. Each of the parts of
the body reproduced by the artist in stone exists in its own
right as a fragment that predicts the work as a whole. This

21. I have numbered the pages of this insert one to four and will
refer to these pages when quoting from this essay.

22. Simone de Beauvoir is silent on this matter in her apparently
encyclopedic record of Sartre's acquaintances and activities. Sartre himself has omitted the essay on Hare's sculpture from the seven volumes
of *Situations* published thus far. Whatever Sartre's reasons are, his
omission of this article in no way detracts from its importance in his
growing interest in contemporary painting and sculpture.

23. "Le marbre révèle soudain son défaut: inaltérable en apparence,
un effondrement secret le ronge, ce pur durcissement de l'espace est fait
de parties séparables." "Sculptures à 'n' dimensions," p. 1.

predictability depends on the unity of the human form, which he recreates in a material that is itself divisible. The concept of the work and the marble itself are by their very nature capable of being broken down. The classical sculptures, to which Sartre refers, frequently come down to us in pieces, but the head severed from the body or the incomplete torso exist independent of the work as a whole. This predictability leads the viewer back to the wholeness of the concept of the god or ruler represented because of the sculptor's dependency on the anatomy of the human form. For Sartre, the sculptor's technique and choice of materials have caused the sculptor of the past to avoid representing the ambiguity of human experience.

Hare avoids the separating of the elements of the physiognomy by which the face can be reconstructed in a clear and logical manner. His own approach depends on his awareness of the wholeness of psychological experience. Sartre attributes to Hare the realization that "animals and men are ambiguous realities: indefinitely divisible when they are cadavers, but when alive, indecomposable presences." [24] Hare understands the opposition between the representational, which leads to the corpses Sartre detests, and the psychological unity, which permits a break from such a tradition in order to create a new sculpture. The difficulty of constructing a sculpture that embodies this conception of human experience is resolved by Hare in the works included in the exhibition at the Galerie Maeght. In writing on Hare's solution of this problem, Sartre traces the path the sculptor followed in his rejection of the purely representational. Sartre turns to Hare's first sculpture, a young girl whose sex figured as a kind of keyhole-rattrap. Hare is aware of the temptation of symbolism; he warns that "there is a great danger in the use of symbols; besides being an escape from the real, they tend to make out of a work of art an anecdote. That is to say, in the mind of the observer the symbol is translated back into the object, the object back into the work, and the whole becomes literature." [25] This is precisely what happens in Hare's early works, and Sartre used them to contrast with those which he had before him in 1947. These later works succeed because they do not have meaning

24. "Les animaux et les hommes sont des réalités ambiguës: indéfiniment divisibles en tant que cadavres, et quand ils vivent, présences indécomposables." *Ibid.*
25. "Spaces of the Mind," p. 49.

frozen into the work. They are psychological attitudes before they are analyzed and translated by the sculptor into a symbol. Sartre finds that the same problem is encountered in Tintoretto's painting. The artist did not choose a particular color in order to mean anguish or to provoke anguish, but in order to *be* anguish for the observer. "Tintoretto did not choose that yellow rent in the sky above Golgotha in order to 'signify' or to 'provoke' it, it 'is' anguish and yellow sky at the same time." [26] Hare accomplishes in sculpture what Sartre admires in painting. This sculptor analyzes and observes, not in order to recreate a facsimile of the object that causes the emotion, but rather to create in sculpture that emotion itself. Hare's sculpture for Sartre is not the experience of horror, anguish, or pity. It is the encounter with an object which is itself those emotions. Sartre does not use the term prereflective in connection with these sculptures, but he emphasizes that they are not subject to being analyzed or observed as a composite of multitudinous particles. The thing is there before the viewer has time to reflect upon it and no subsequent experience of the work will add to what has suddenly been revealed. Its wholeness cannot be disturbed by dividing it into parts or translating it into words. As Sartre says, "It is there, without parts, impenetrable, mysterious, fully lighted, delivered in its entirety, but delivered as a whole without your being able to do anything about it." [27]

A major aspect of classical sculpture for Sartre consists of the human body frozen in movement. He dwells on the idea of motion in the work of Calder because the mobile does not imitate man's gesture or actions. The athlete in stone imitates the displacement of the human body in space by suggesting the moment that precedes and follows it. To portray the body fixed in a particular action is to separate it from the sequence and therefore to give the viewer a single fragment of the whole. The experience of the viewer in Greek or Renaissance sculpture is the acceptance of the figure in the space which the viewer inhabits. The action of the figure occurs in the environment of the spectator and tricks him into a complicity through experience of that

26. "Cette déchirure jaune du ciel au-dessus du Golgotha, le Tintoret ne l'a pas choisie pour 'signifier' l'angoisse, ni non plus pour la 'provoquer,' elle 'est' angoisse, et ciel jaune en même temps." *Situations,* 2: 61.
27. "Elle est là, sans parties, impénétrable, mystérieuse, en pleine lumière, toute donnée, mais donnée d'ensemble et sans que vous en puissiez rien faire." "Sculptures à 'n' dimensions," p. 2.

momentary movement. Sartre relates this kind of representation of movement to the pointing figure of wax in the Musée Grévin, whose gesture appears so realistic that the visitor is tricked into believing he is real. Its imitative and artificial impact is only momentarily effective. The observer submits to and then escapes from its spell. Hare's approach to motion is quite different. Sartre is drawn to his figures because they are not realistic representations of movement. Hare's solution to this problem is to remove the figure from the space in which the viewer exists. Like the painter he must cause the world of his sculpture to become self-contained and indivisible. The sculpture is endowed with an inner life by combining in plastic form the associations of the mind that relate to a total experience of the action of the figure. No single gesture is reproduced. The movement is suggested by sculptural elements in an unreal manner. Sartre discusses individual works in an attempt to show that "Hare wants the gesture locked into the statue, he wants the work to have a space of its own, distinct from any other space and imaginary." [28] Through the creation of this imaginary space in which the figure exists, the viewer does not move to and from the sculpture but seizes it in its totality without reference to a concept of duration. This creation of a form that intensifies the human experience through what Hare calls the "spaces of the mind" is to Sartre superior to a statue that depends on the analytical and fragmentary reproduction of human gesture.

To achieve this synthesis, Hare is led to integrate the environment in which the figure exists into the sculptural whole as in *Homme à la batterie* (*Man with Drums*) (Pl. 13). We find Sartre's own objection to classical sculpture in what he suggests Hare's concept of those works would be: "He considers, I imagine, classical statuary to be an abstract art because it isolates its model from the world of the human and from real time." [29]

28. "Hare veut que le geste se referme sur la statue, que l'œuvre ait son espace propre, distinct d'une autre et manifestement imaginaire." *Ibid.*, p. 3.
29. "Il considère, je suppose, la statuaire classique comme un art abstrait puisqu'elle isole son modèle de l'univers humain et de la durée vraie." *Ibid.* Here Sartre is attributing his own ideas to Hare. Sartre's discussion of the work of art in *L'Imaginaire* includes no examples of sculpture and the painting on which he focuses his attention is a minor official portrait. The examples of sculpture given by Sartre elsewhere in *L'Imaginaire*—the *Venus de Milo* and the *David* of Michelangelo—are treated in relation to the historical period to which they belong and not as sculptural objects. The difficulty in following Sartre in his dis-

Hare's project of portraying the individual in his own landscape, in the very process of evolution and change, appeals to Sartre, who agrees that "if it is a question of representing this concrete totality, man in 'situation,' he must be surrounded with his real landscape." [30] The viewer must find a barrier between himself and the space in which the sculptural figure exists, or he will experience the statue in his own environment, limited and momentary as the classical statue. The superiority of Hare's work, according to Sartre, is his ability to create figures that exclude the viewer from the environment of the imaginary object. The observer must experience them from outside. In order for Hare's sculptures to be successful, in Sartre's eyes, each of them must be "an event, that is a living form moving in a time-space in which time functions as a unification of space." [31] In this way Hare will be able to force the viewer to experience the unity or wholeness which he inscribes in his works from the outside. If not, he will fall into the tradition of classical sculpture, which Sartre characterizes as showing man from within. Sartre uses a distinction between comedy and tragedy in order to demonstrate the contrast between the work of Hare and that of the traditional sculptor. "Indeed, it should be understood that classical statuary is connected with tragedy because it is an accomplice of our passions and aims at provoking them; a statue of Praxiteles or Donatello looms up from the 'inside' of the human world." [32] Hare's figures derive their power to free the viewer from desire or horror by capturing these emotions in bronze, just as comedy rids the

---

cussion of David Hare is that he implies here that the figure of the classical statue is abstracted from its own environment and consequently is viewed by the observer not as an imaginary object but as a part of the viewer's own space. Hare, unlike Michelangelo, will create a truly imaginary object by representing the figure in the hodological space of modern psychology: "Chaque figure aura sécrété sa coquille, un espace vivant et personnel qui la protégera contre notre espace." "Each figure will have secreted its own shell, a living and personal space which will protect it from our own space." "Sculptures à 'n' dimensions," p. 3.

30. "S'il s'agit de présenter cette totalité concrète: l'homme en situation, il faut l'entourer de son paysage vrai." *Ibid.*

31. "Un événement, c'est-à-dire une forme vivante en mouvement dans un espace-temps où le temps fonctionne comme unification de l'espace." *Ibid.*

32. "Comprenons, en effet, que la statuaire classique s'apparente à la tragédie parce qu'elle est complice de nos passions et vise à les provoquer: une statue de Praxitèle ou de Donatello surgit à l'intérieur du monde humain." *Ibid.*, p. 4.

spectator of hypocrisy or stinginess by forcing him to view the world in which they exist from outside. For Sartre, tragedy invites experience from within, comedy from without. Hare's project of creating a figure in its own landscape from which the spectator is excluded forces Sartre to a new relationship with sculpture.

David Hare's works differ from the marble men so repugnant to Sartre, because the American's sculptures are self-contained creatures in their own private worlds. The imitative character of classic sculpture in which the role of the artist is more difficult to discern has never attracted Sartre. In the works of Hare he is fascinated by a creative imagination he can accept and integrate into his own ideas. In the ambiguity of these figures which are neither gods, kings, nor the idealized human figure in movement, Sartre can experience the magic of sculpture. For him these works are rooted in human experience but escape from the limitations of reproducing what is seen in the world, through the use of suggestion and ambivalence. He takes pleasure in them as events with humorous and magical qualities, which intimate that "man is always in advance of himself and that the world is both totally given to him and totally to be made." [33] In them the human body is not fixed and limited for eternity, but exists in a work of the imagination that achieves true mobility in its own imaginary landscape.

ALBERTO GIACOMETTI

Shortly after writing "Sculptures à 'n' dimensions" for *Derrière le miroir,* Sartre turned to the work of a Swiss sculptor. Alberto Giacometti was a familiar face in the cafés for a long period after Fernando Gerassi had pointed him out to Sartre and Simone de Beauvoir. When Sartre returned to Paris after being released from a German prison camp, he and Simone de Beauvoir were introduced to Giacometti by a mutual friend. So, in the successive steps Sartre took toward an understanding of the sculpture of his contemporaries, he finally arrived, by way of Calder and Hare, at the work of a sculptor who remains closer to the traditional representation of the human figure. By that time, Sartre had reflected a good deal on older sculpture and had begun to formulate his objections to the classical works in a clearer man-

---

33. "L'homme est toujours en avant de lui-même et que le monde est, à la fois, tout donné et tout à faire." *Ibid.*

ner. At the end of 1947 he had conversed frequently with Giacometti, as Simone de Beauvoir recounts in her *La Force de l'âge*. In the first issue of *Les Temps modernes* for 1948, he published his essay on Giacometti's sculpture, which was translated into English for the exhibition at the Pierre Matisse Gallery in New York that same month. This essay, "La Recherche de l'absolu ("Search for the Absolute"),[34] appeared in the catalogue for the show (January 10 to February 14).[35]

In dealing with the work of Calder and Hare, Sartre felt obliged to characterize the task of the sculptor in the history of art. He does this again in order to show in what way Giacometti participated in the revolution observed in the works of the two Americans. Materials, motion, and the idea of unity serve once more to set the modern sculptor in opposition to the creator of statues that embody *being* for Sartre. None of the three artists through whom Sartre discovers contemporary sculpture works in stone, yet he feels forced to begin with a rejection of the sculptor who carves an image of man in rock. Stone gives the figure the weight of eternity, and for Sartre, it is used to represent man "in order to cure us of the sickness of having a body." [36] Those statues described by Sartre in *La Nausée* and *Les Chemins de la liberté,* Impétraz and the privileged figures of the Luxembourg gardens, derive their *being* from stone. The beauty and healthful appearance of these household gods look down reassuringly on childhood games and bourgeois ideals. "In the gardens they bear witness to the idea that the world is without risks, that nothing happens to anyone, hence nothing has happened to them except to die at birth." [37] As guardians of these ideals they are endowed with a power to flaunt their weighty being by the stone in which they are carved. "The eternity of stone is synonymous with inertia; it is a present forever fixed." [38] And Sartre rejects this material because man's existence is fragile and ephemeral. Only in death does the body stiffen and harden into *being*. In Sartre's eyes this is exactly what has happened throughout the history of sculpture. Carving in this material defeats the sculptor's effort to represent a man.

34. This essay was reprinted in *Situations,* 3: 289–305.
35. *Alberto Giacometti.*
36. "Pour nous guérir du mal d'avoir un corps." *Situations,* 3: 302.
37. "Ils témoignent dans les jardins que le monde est sans risques, qu'il n'arrive rien à personne et, par le fait, il ne leur est rien arrivé que de mourir à leur naissance." *Ibid.*
38. "L'éternité de la pierre est synonyme d'inertie; c'est un présent figé pour toujours." *Ibid.,* p. 294.

Giacometti is praised as much for his antipathy to stone as for his conscious choice of a material that represents its opposite. Simone de Beauvoir has recorded Giacometti's distrust of the sculptor's materials because of their opposition to the unity of the human face: "Inert matter, marble, bronze, or plaster, . . . is subject to infinite subdivision; each particle separates from, contradicts the whole, and destroys it." [39] Sartre rejects marble and bronze as privileged materials, which are divisible, but separates plaster, which he has often seen in Giacometti's studio, from the former elements: "The sculptor chose a weightless material, the most ductile, perishable and spiritual—plaster. He hardly feels it at the tips of his fingers; it is the impalpable counterpart of his movements." [40] In his essay on Hare, Sartre discussed at length the divisibility of marble and its effect on the sculptor's concept of the human figure. Instead of breaking down the marble block by carving a figure, he sees Giacometti using a material without weight to form a momentary agglomeration (Pl. 14). This flour is for him "la poussière d'espace" ("the dust of space") with which the sculptor works in a tentative manner, creating "the nebulous beings in the process of perpetual metamorphosis." [41] Describing the plaster in this way, Sartre is able to contrast it with the materials that symbolize *being* for him, and to take pleasure from the plaster statues as the epitome of his concept of man. He confesses that "it is true that these personages, because they were destined to perish on the very night they were born, are the only ones [he] knows to hold the unforgettable charm of seeming to be perishable. Never was matter less eternal, more fragile, closer to being human." [42] Like the trap Calder sets with his tin and zinc, Giacometti's scarecrow of wet dough and rusted wire effectively stands for the transiency of man's existence.

This ephemerality is caught not only in the nature of the substance with which the sculptures are made, but also in the

39. "La matière inerte, marbre, bronze ou plâtre, se divise . . . à l'infini; chaque parcelle s'isole, contredit l'ensemble, le détruit." *Force de l'age,* p. 501.

40. "Il s'est choisi une matière sans poids, la plus ductile, la plus périssable, la plus spirituelle: le plâtre. Il le sent à peine au bout de ses doigts, c'est l'envers impalpable de ses mouvements." *Situations,* 3: 294.

41. "Ces nébuleuses en perpétuelle métamorphose." *Ibid.*

42. "Il est vrai que ses personnages, pour avoir été destinés à périr dans la nuit même où ils sont nés, sont seuls à garder, entre toutes les sculptures que je connais, la grâce inouïe de sembler périssables. Jamais la matière ne fut moins éternelle, plus fragile, plus près d'être humaine." *Ibid.*

way the sculptor comes to grips with the problem of motion.
From the time of his essay on Calder, Sartre has defined the
sculptor's task as one of infusing man's movement into an object
that is completely immobile. Older sculpture has failed to come
alive: "These arms pretend to move, but they hang there supported from one end to the other by iron rods: these frozen
figures are hardly able to contain infinite dispersion within their
contours." [43] He finds the deception of the creatures that populate
the museums and gardens extremely irritating. In an essay on the
human face written years before the study on Giacometti's sculpture, Sartre described the stone men created by sculptors of the
past as doric columns totally lacking the passionate existence of
the men of flesh he encountered in his own life. "A society
composed of statues would be deadly dull, but in it you would
live under reason and justice: statues are bodies without faces;
blind and deaf bodies, without fear and without anger, uniquely
concerned with obeying righteous laws, that is to say those of
equilibrium and movement." [44] Donatello and Praxiteles failed
to understand the difference between the movement of men and
the movement of things. Classical sculpture always retains the
being of stone by imparting the volume of stone or bronze to
fleshly existence. This results in an image of an idealized human
body, constructed through the use of stylistic conventions that
contain contradictions in themselves. There are irreconcilable
differences between what the sculptor sees in his model and what
he represents in his work. He is unable to forgo his knowledge of
human anatomy when he carves his nude in stone. The detail of
the body as he knows it is in conflict with its appearance. This
results in an inconsistent image in his work; the burden is placed
on the observer. "It is the imagination of the viewer, mystified by
a crude resemblance, which lends movement, warmth, and life to
the eternal ponderosity of matter." [45] Sartre sees movement and
gesture in the unity of man, but these classical sculptures cannot

43. "Ces bras prétendent bouger, mais ils flottent, soutenus entre
haut et bas par des tiges de fer; ces formes figées ont peine à contenir
en elles un éparpillement infini." *Ibid.,* p. 292.
44. "Dans une société de statues on s'ennuierait ferme, mais on y
vivrait selon la justice et la raison: les statues sont des corps sans visages: des corps aveugles et sourds, sans peur et sans colère, uniquement
soucieux d'obéir aux lois du juste, c'est-à-dire de l'équilibre et du
mouvement." *Visages,* p. 23.
45. "C'est l'imagination du spectateur, mystifié par une grossière
ressemblance, qui prête le mouvement, la chaleur, la vie à l'éternel
affaissement de la matière." *Situations,* 3: 292.

reveal man as an "indissoluble unity and the absolute source of his movements." [46] The erratic movement of the observer between the ideal space in which the statue should exist and the observer's own actual space destroys the possibility of seeing man as the source of his movement. Paradoxically, it is in the true mobility of consistent imaginary space that man's mobility can be portrayed, and not in the imitation of reality that tricks the observer into believing the wax guard in the Musée Grévin is alive. In Sartre's eyes, Giacometti has created consistent imaginary space by creating the figure he sculpts in that figure's own space and not that of the spectator (Pl. 15). Rather than reproducing the human figure according to laws of proportion appropriate to objects, he stylizes the body in order to achieve the experience of man seen in his environment by other men.

Sartre sees the source of Giacometti's stylization in painting. The imaginary space of a painting is created in sculpture by compressing the space that surrounds the figure by the stylistic device of elongation and by fragmenting the surface of the plaster. This results in the fabrication of a figure that is fixed in its own space. No movement toward it will permit the viewer to enter that space because, in the process of elongating the figure and breaking its edge, Giacometti gives up the detail of the body retained by classical sculpture. Parts of the anatomy of the figure remain obscured and thus permit a unity of impression which cannot be fragmented by closer observation. The resulting distance from the figure creates an experience of a whole person viewed from the outside. Exteriority characterizes the work of Giacometti just as it does that of David Hare. Because we must view their figures from outside as one must in a painting, Sartre suggests that their works are significant representations of man *en situation*. For him Giacometti's, and hence the contemporary sculptor's, attempt to create "movement in total immobility, unity in infinite multiplicity, the absolute in pure relativity, the future in the eternal present" [47] has been successful.

In Giacometti's works Sartre experiences the unity he felt to be absent in traditional sculpture. Through sensitive, attentive viewing of the plaster works which represent one stage in Giacometti's career, Sartre discovers him to be an exponent of

46. "L'unité indissoluble et la source absolue de ses mouvements." *Ibid.*, p. 290.

47. "Le mouvement dans la totale immobilité, l'unité dans la multiplicité infinie, l'absolu dans la relativité pure, l'avenir dans le présent éternel." *Ibid.*

1. *Melencolia I,* by Albrecht Dürer
1514, engraving, 9¼ x 6⅝ in.
Kunstinstitutum, Marburg
(Art Reference Bureau, Marburg)

2. *Seated Buddha,* Khmer, Soen Tho (Tra Vinh)
VI–VII century, sandstone, 12¾ in.
Musée Guimet, Paris

3. *Louis XIV,* by Hyacinthe Rigaud
1701, oil on canvas, 110 x 93¾ in.
Louvre, Paris
(Art Reference Bureau, Alinari)

4. *Francis I,* by Jean Clouet
C. 1525–30, oil on panel, 37¾ x 29 in.
Louvre, Paris
(Art Reference Bureau, Alinari)

5. *Philip II,* by Pantoja de la Cruz
1598, oil on canvas, 79 x 41$\frac{11}{12}$ in.
El Escorial
(Art Reference Bureau, Mas)

6. *St. Jerome in His Cell,* by Albrecht Dürer
1514, engraving, 9⅓ x 6½ in.
Stadt Kunstmuseum, Dusseldorf
(Art Reference Bureau, Marburg)

7. Statue of Jupiter and Guard's Mask
Created for the original production of *Les Mouches* in 1943
(Henri-Georges Adam)

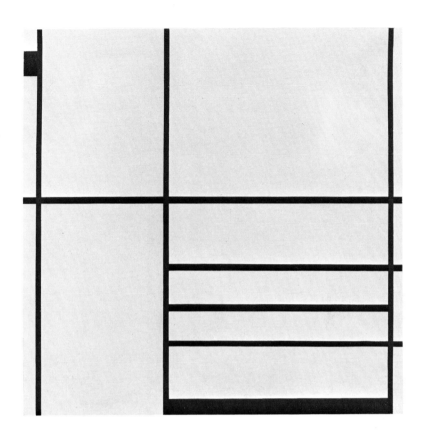

8. *The Broken Pitcher,* by Jean-Baptiste Greuze
C. 1770, oil on canvas, 42½ x 33⅞ in.
Louvre, Paris
(Art Reference Bureau, Alinari)

9. *Composition in White, Black, and Red,* by Piet Mondrian
1936, oil on canvas, 40¼ x 41 in.
Museum of Modern Art, New York

10. *The Call,* by Paul Gauguin
1902, oil on canvas, 51¼ x 35¼ in.
The Cleveland Museum of Art, Gift of Hanna Fund and Leonard C. Hanna, Jr.

11. *Self-portrait before the Yellow Christ,* by Paul Gauguin
1889, oil on canvas, 15 x 17¾ in.
Collection Maurice Denis, Saint-Germain-en-Laye
(Giraudon)

12. *Red Petals,* by Alexander Calder
1942, sheet steel and wire, sheet aluminum, 110 in.
The Arts Club of Chicago

13. *Man with Drums,* by David Hare
1947, bronze, 23 in.
Collection Alice Baber Jenkins, New York
(David Hare)

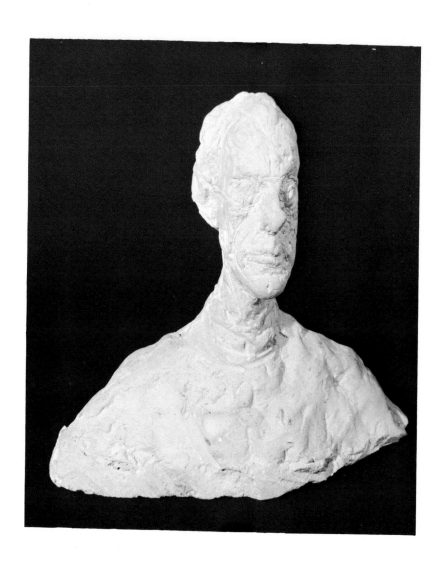

14. *Bust of Diego,* by Alberto Giacometti
1955, white plaster, 7½ x 8½ in.
Collection Mr. and Mrs. James W. Alsdorf, Winnetka, Illinois

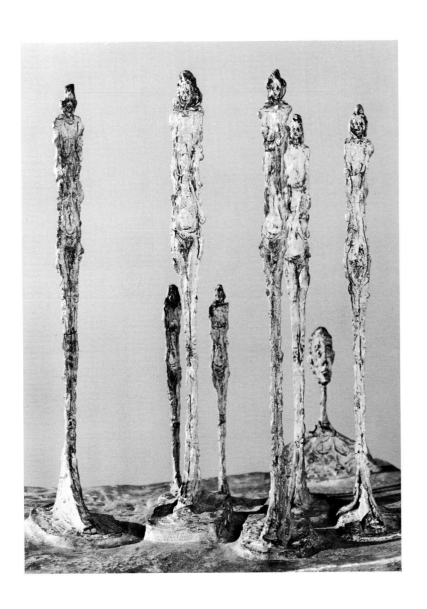

15. *Composition with Seven Figures and a Head (The Forest)*, by
Alberto Giacometti
1950, painted bronze, 22 in.
Collection Mrs. Albert H. Newman, Chicago
(Herbert Matter)

16. *Annette, Portrait of the Artist's Wife,* by Alberto Giacometti
1954, oil on canvas, 25½ x 21 in.
Collection Mr. and Mrs. Arnold Maremont, Winnetka, Illinois

17. *Summer,* by Giuseppe Arcimboldo
1563, oil on canvas, 29¼ x 24 in.
Kunsthistorisches Museum, Vienna
(Art Reference Bureau, Bruckmann)

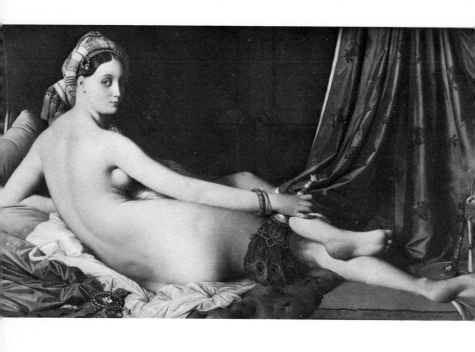

18. *Odalisque,* by Jean-Auguste–Dominique Ingres
1814, oil on canvas, 64 x 36 in.
Louvre, Paris
(Art Reference Bureau, Alinari)

19. *Avignon Pietà,* School of Avignon
C. 1470, oil on panel, 63¾ x 85¾ in.
Louvre, Paris
(Art Reference Bureau, Alinari)

20. *Isenheim Altarpiece,* by Matthias Grünewald
Center panel (closed), c. 1512–15, oil on panel, 106 x 121 in.
Musée d'Unterlinden, Colmar
(Art Reference Bureau, Marburg)

21. *Assumption of the Virgin,* by Titian
1516–18, oil on canvas, 271 x 142 in.
Santa Maria dei Frari, Venice
(Art Reference Bureau, Alinari)

22. *The Miracle of the Slave,* by Tintoretto
1548, oil on canvas, 164 x 215 in.
Accademia, Venice
(Art Reference Bureau, Alinari)

23. *Crucifixion,* by Tintoretto
1565, oil on canvas, 211⅝₁₆ x 482¾ in.
Scuola San Rocco, Venice
(Art Reference Bureau, Alinari)

24. *Guernica,* by Pablo Picasso
1937, oil on canvas, mural, 138 x 308 in.
Collection of the artist, on extended loan to the
Museum of Modern Art, New York

25. *Campo San Zanipolo,* by Francesco Guardi
1782, oil on canvas, 14¾ x 12⅜ in.
National Gallery of Art, Washington, D.C., Samuel H. Kress
Collection

26. *A View in Venice,* by Antonio Canaletto
Oil on canvas
Accademia, Venice
(Art Reference Bureau, Alinari)

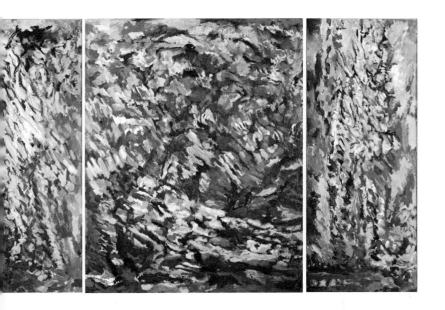

27. *Triptych on Torture: Homage to Djamila Boupacha and Henri Alleg,* by Robert Lapoujade
1961, oil on canvas, 75 x 137 in.
Galerie Pierre Domec, Paris
(André Causse)

28. *Paysage de la Martinique,* by André Masson
1941, pen and ink
Private collection
(French Reproduction Rights, Inc., SPADEM 1969)

29. *Winged Men Caught in Icy Rocks Freeing Themselves from This Himalaya of Polyhedrons Only at the Cost of Their Skins,* by André Masson
1947, lithograph, 18½ x 14 in.
Collection Deering Library, Northwestern University
(French Reproduction Rights, Inc., SPADEM 1969)

30. *Torrential Self-Portrait,* by André Masson
1945, pen and ink, 18⅞ x 24 in.
Private collection
(Galerie Louise Leiris)

31. Frontispiece for *Visages,* by Wols
1947, dry point, 7½ x 5 in.
Private collection
(French Reproduction Rights, Inc., SPADEM 1969)

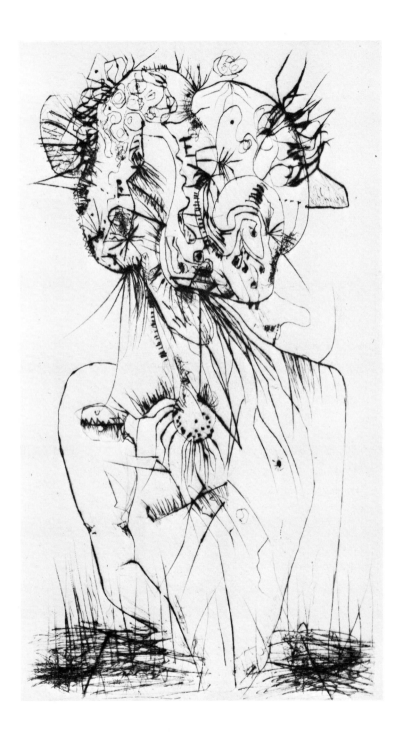

32. *The Great Burning Barrier,* by Wols
C. 1943–44, watercolor, 8⅝ x 6¼ in.
Collection Mme. Henri-Pierre Roché, Meudon
(French Reproduction Rights, Inc., SPADEM 1969)

existential attitudes. In writing of his sculpture, Sartre has observed closely, and come to know intimately, these elongated figures in the setting of Giacometti's studio and the adjoining Paris streets. Before bronze, before exhibitions, he observes and writes of these creatures, praising them highly because "each of them present to us the truth that man is not at first in order to be seen afterwards, but that he is the being whose essence is to exist for others." [48] From the time of the publication of his essay, these haunting figures join the mobiles of Alexander Calder as part of the popular myth of existentialism. In the works of Calder, Hare, and Giacometti, he has found sculpture representing ideas with which he is sympathetic. The new and different attitudes towards the human body represented in them delight Sartre, as they speak to his own concept of human existence. They center upon the human body and its activities as tenuous, ephemeral, and vulnerable. Man is seen not in stone but in the midst of "the astonishing adventure of the flesh." For Sartre, fixing the image of the human body in stone limits man by presenting a fixed being, and thus creates a lie behind which the gratuitousness of fleshly existence is hidden. In the mobiles of Calder, the contemporary sculptor is praised for having turned from the representation of the human body. Giacometti's elongation of forms and the ambiguous creatures of David Hare relate more closely to body imagery, and Sartre is forced to consider two of the stylistic devices that free them from conventional representations of the anatomy. Sartre selects from their endeavors the characteristics he admires. He enlightens us as to their problems, their goals, and their accomplishments. His essays, sensitive and at times lyrical appraisals of the works of Calder, Hare, and Giacometti, impel the reader to return to the sculptures to reflect on the accuracy of Sartre's observations.

Sartre is quite effective as an art critic; our experience of the sculpture of these men has been immeasurably enriched. But the reader has also become aware of the extent to which Sartre has made these artists his own. A new myth has been created. For the myth of *being* criticized in older sculpture Sartre has substituted his own. Each of these men is caught up in the existential world by contact with Sartre and especially through the essays he writes on their sculpture. I have indicated earlier in discussing Calder's work that Sartre has chosen only one aspect of that sculptor's art.

48. "Chacune nous livre cette vérité que l'homme n'est pas d'abord pour être vu après, mais qu'il est l'être dont l'essence est d'exister pour autrui." *Ibid.*

The mobiles are separated from the whole of Calder's undertaking. The same is true of the work of Hare, whose sensitive, more symbolic representations of the human body and early surrealistic sculptures are dominated by the presentation of the ambiguous figures in their own landscapes. Hilton Kramer has noted that the whole series of essays and books inspired by Sartre's writings has obscured the first twenty years of Giacometti's career. Sartre and those who have followed in his wake have created the myth of Giacometti as an existential saint. Kramer complains that

> this notion of Giacometti as exemplar of the Existentialist predicament, at once the victim of all the uncertainties that plague the modern mind and the hero who redeems them through a decisive action—in this case, an aesthetic action —has now formed the basis, more ideological than philosophic, of the two most ambitious monographs devoted to the artist's work. In them, the elevation of Giacometti to Existential sainthood has been achieved.[49]

Sartre's influence on Ponge, Genet, Dupin, Bucarelli, and Tardieu has been extraordinary [50] and shows the degree to which his ideas on Giacometti are abroad in the world.

49. "Giacometti," p. 52.
50. Ponge, "Réflexions sur Alberto Giacometti"; Genet, L'Atelier d'Alberto Giacometti; Dupin, Alberto Giacometti; Bucarelli, Giacometti; Tardieu, "Giacometti et la solitude."

6

Painting and Painters

IN *La Nausée,* Sartre's criticism of painting relates to its content and to its form. The visit to the museum at Bouville is the occasion to satirize painting as official portraiture. The use of the human figure to embody the rights of an elite group of society is rejected. The painter conveys merit or worth through the portrayal of the sitter's role in a social hierarchy. The members of the ruling class offer themselves as the subject of the painting. Creating the myth of privilege is only the pretext for painting each member of that group. Implied in this choice of abstract subject is the re-creation of the social or political distance which separates these leaders from other men. In his essay, "Portraits officiels," Sartre focuses on the same complicity of the artist in his portrayal of emperors and monarchs. The head of state or the ecclesiastical prince offers the painter an opportunity to represent on canvas idealized human figures that will create the myth of divine right. The superiority of a select minority is the didactic content of the paintings created by these artists. Sartre condemns this choice of subject in both *La Nausée* and "Portraits officiels."

His attack on official portraiture is not limited to subject matter. Sartre treats numerous aspects of the technique of the painter in his representation and transformation of the human body in the service of the hegemony. The artist's participation in the creation of the privileged hierarchy depends on the means of representation he uses. His conception of the figure in relation to the background serves to create a scale worthy of the concept to be portrayed. The standard of merit is applied to the body of the man. He is surrounded by accessories that will create the impression of stature appropriate for a man of his rank. In the case of Olivier-Martial Blévigne, the painter "Bordurin, with jealous care, had surrounded him with objects that ran no risk of dwarfing him; a hassock, a squat armchair, a shelf with a few small books, a little Persian pedestal table." [1] The accessories chosen for size and for their implied values—books, writing instruments, and scepters—distract the viewer from the sitter as man. The use of pigment to imitate precisely fine morocco bindings, materials of velvet, or the textures of *trompe-l'œil* reality is extended to the representation of the human body. Through the use of pigment the artist lends to flesh the hardness of fired ceramic, and the representation of the hands as porcelain instead of flesh tricks the viewer into a belief in their great worth. "At the ends of those trappings appear hands, handsome and insignificant hands, symbols, too, like the gilt hand of the scepter." [2] The figure is clothed in rich materials; the flesh is depicted with the smoothness of fine china; the space of the painting is crammed with objects representing the wealth of the elite. Only then are the details of likeness added. The handsome nose, brilliant eyes, and healthy cheeks create a privileged mode of *being* and successfully separate the viewer from the man whose fleshly existence the artist has disguised. The contours contain the *being* and the power of the ruling class. The created space is stuffed with symbolic objects and a china man. There is no room for the man of flesh. "They had been painted with great exactitude; and yet, under the brush, their faces had been stripped of the mysterious weakness of men's faces." [3] Space, line, and color in these paintings are used to create a vessel in the shape of the human body. This container for didactic concepts and official presences becomes the vehicle for creation of the myth of privileged *being.* These representations of the human body contribute to the establishment of merit and worth and thus, for Sartre, betray the meaning of the fleshly existence of man.

Simone de Beauvoir in *La Force de l'âge* confirms Sartre's rejection of the technique of the court painter. She also chides Sartre for his admiration of the works of Guido Reni but concedes that "the *Pietà* of Avignon and Grünewald's *Crucifixion* (Pl. 19, 20) were also among his favorites." [4] In these works the

1. "Bordurin, avec un soin jaloux, l'avait entouré de ces objets qui ne risquent point de rapetisser; un pouf, un fauteuil bas, une étagère avec quelques in-douze, un petit guéridon persan." *La Nausée,* p. 121.

2. "Au bout de ces étoffes paraissent des mains, belles et quelconques, symboles aussi comme la main dorée du sceptre." *Visages,* p. 16.

3. "On les avait peints très exactement; et pourtant, sous le pinceau, leurs visages avaient dépouillé la mystérieuse faiblesse des visages d'hommes." *La Nausée,* p. 117.

4. "Il aimait aussi avec prédilection, la *Pietà* d'Avignon et la *Crucifixion* de Grünewald." P. 117.

techniques of the artist are used to portray the tragedy of fleshly existence and the sorrow of the men and women who witness it. The solitude and suffering of the individuals depicted in these religious paintings are also found in the canvases of Gauguin. The subject of the crucifixion is the occasion for the nineteenth-century painter to portray himself as the Christ figure in order to suggest the artist's experience of suffering and isolation. In his friend Giacometti, Sartre discovers a painter who rejects official portraiture and whose subject matter and technique stand opposed to the work of Bordurin, Renaudas, Titian, Rigaud, and all those painters who have concealed men behind abstract concepts of right and privilege. His interest in painters and painting brings him to focus his attention in essays on the works of his friends, Giacometti, Lapoujade, Masson, and Wols, and to consider the art of Tintoretto, in whose works he finds the qualities he admires.

ALBERTO GIACOMETTI

Sartre's attempt to characterize Giacometti's experiment in sculptural representation in his essay "La Recherche de l'absolu" [5] begins with a consideration of the depicting of the human body in painting. Sartre convincingly demonstrates that Giacometti comes to his sculptural portrayal of the individual in space through his reflections on aesthetic problems peculiar to painting. In his first essay on the art of painting, [6] Sartre returns to the relation of painting to sculpture, which he first considered in his essay on Giacometti's sculpture. He approaches Giacometti's painting through his sculpture. The elongated figures of men and women link the sculptor to the painter. Sartre seizes on the works that are anthropomorphic in character. Portraits are uppermost in his mind. Still life and landscape are excluded from his consideration, because in art he is primarily concerned with human experience, as portrayed through the human body. Giacometti's work on canvas is examined in Sartre's continuing preoccupation with images of man. In this essay he focuses on the way Giacometti has used his technique to reveal each man as solitary, distant, but above all to avoid representing the human body in the fixity of *being*.

The space in which the figure exists in a painting is used by

5. *Situations,* 3: 289–305.
6. "Peintures de Giacometti."

Giacometti in his sculpture to create, through stylization, a space that emanates from the statue. Sartre notes this problem in his discussion of Giacometti's early experimentation with the creation of spatial limits through box or cage devices, as in his sculptures *Cage, Palais de quatre heures* (*The Palace at 4 A.M.*), and *Figurine dans une boîte* (*Between Two Houses*). Giacometti finally achieves this sense of space or emptiness without recourse to the cage, by building up the body image of his plaster men and women so that they are separated from the space of the viewer. Sartre characterizes this technique as the creating of emptiness from fullness. In reaction to the painting of official portraits crammed with symbolic objects, Sartre welcomes the spare, barren atmosphere of his friend's canvases. Giacometti treats the surface of the canvas and its frame as a field to be emptied rather than filled. In the paintings (Pl. 16), the limits of the canvas do not serve as a frame for the figure. The artist creates an indeterminate space within the frame by using discontinuous lines that suggest but do not define. His destruction of the frame results in "a true void," a quality of transparency described by Sartre as "layers of emptiness." The imprecise quality of the resultant emptiness contrasts sharply with the sense of space he found in Pompeian murals. Sartre objects violently to the artistic lie of perspective in wall paintings. Their function is to create grandiose dimensions of unambiguous space in the home.

> The painters were entrusted with the task of covering the walls with false perspectives; they painted columns, and behind these columns, receding lines, which gave the room palatial dimensions. I don't know whether those vainglorious Pompeians let themselves be fooled by these *trompe-l'œil* techniques, but I think that I would have loathed them.[7]

The creation of a false sense of precise space, through perspective in these enlarged horizons, denies the ambiguity of the world, which for Sartre is "the great universal Void." He damns the painters whose appetite for objects causes them to surcharge their pictures. "For five hundred years pictures have been filled to the

7. "Les peintres s'en chargeaient en couvrant les murs de fausse perspective: ils peignaient des colonnes et, derrière ces colonnes, des lignes fuyantes qui donnaient à la pièce des dimensions de palais. Je ne sais pas s'ils se laissaient prendre, ces vaniteux Pompéiens, à ces trompe-l'œil, mais il me semble que j'en aurais eu horreur." Quoted by Simone de Beauvoir in *Force de l'âge*, p. 270.

bursting point; the whole universe is crammed into them." [8]
Giacometti avoids false emptiness and excessive filling of the
canvas by avoiding a precise figure-ground relation.

This ambiguity is achieved not only by the indeterminate
interior frame suggested by the discontinuous lines but also by
the way in which Giacometti represents the figure itself. Sartre's
objection to the carving technique in sculpture has a counterpart
in painting. The use of line and pigment results in surface and
volume and creates the solidity characterized by definite contours
or limits to the body. The sharp distinction between the figure
and his environment results from lines and edges. In the painting
Sartre does not like, the subject is separated by these lines from
the space in which he is contained. Here we see a carry-over from
his attitude toward the imprisoning effect of stone or bronze:
"Line portrays arrested flight; it represents an equilibrium between the outside and the inside, it fastens itself around the form
the object takes under the pressure of exterior forces; it is a
symbol of inertia, of passivity." [9] Immobility and fixity result
from the use of stone or line unless they are used imaginatively
by Hare or Giacometti. Sartre finds in Giacometti's representation of the figure a comprehension of the dynamic qualities of
the subject and a corresponding stylistic solution through the use
of line to suggest centripetal force. There is a multiplicity of
movement through the layers of the void toward the focal point
of the figure. Line moves across the surface planes, breaking up
the edge and rendering the exact limits of the figure indeterminate—just as it has done with the frame. In this use of line
Giacometti avoids defining the contours of the body. In this way
the figure does not become a vessel of porcelain in anthropomorphic form. The flesh is not hardened and fixed as in the
Bouville portraits or the paintings of Ingres. This technique of
striation, which characterizes Giacometti's use of pigment, relates
the figure to the created ambiguity of space but offers as well
an answer to Sartre's criticism of artificial divisibility in the
representation of the human figure—particularly the face.

In the essay on David Hare, Sartre formulated his criticism of
this inherent divisibility in the art of classical sculpture. He saw

8. "Depuis cinq cents ans, les tableaux sont pleins à craquer: on y
fait entrer de force l'univers." *Situations*, 4: 353.
9. "La ligne figure une fuite arrêtée, elle représente un équilibre
entre l'extérieur et l'intérieur, elle se noue autour de la forme qu'adopte
l'objet sous la pression des forces du dehors; c'est un symbole de
l'inertie, de la passivité." *Ibid.*, p. 354.

the classical sculptor's technique of carving as a fragmentary assemblage of individual parts of the body. These details of the anatomy are joined according to a predictable ideal of scale and proportion. Head, arms, and other fragments of the body exist independent of the whole. Sartre carries this idea to his discussion of body imagery in painting. His dramatic illustration centers on the representation of the face through the accumulation of precise details that fail to achieve the wholeness of the experience of the human physiognomy. Here he suggests that painters historically have accumulated realistic details of the head in a way comparable to Giuseppe Arcimboldo's fruit and vegetable assemblages (Pl. 17). The technique of reproducing a cheek or an eye like an apple, or a grape, and juxtaposing them in the shape of the face, results in cadavers. What Sartre called the "présence indécomposable" in his discussion of sculpture becomes in painting "the indissoluble unity of a face." [10] Giacometti achieves this unity through his use of line to suggest the perception of the body or face—not as they *are* but as they are seen. "He wants his figures, at the heart of their original void, on his immobile canvas, to oscillate ceaselessly between continuity and discontinuity." [11] Sartre sees his own concept of existence in the paintings of Giacometti. Other painters have represented *being* in their portraits. The rigidity of *being* of the cadaver or Chinese pot is found in the reassurance implied in the traditional portrait. Ingres's *Odalisque* (Pl. 18) is not only an example of a ceramic body but is used here by Sartre as an example of composite detail which can be examined piece by piece in full awareness that the viewer can return to any detail. This example serves the same purpose in his writing on painting as Praxiteles or Donatello in his essays on sculpture. The indissoluble unity of the human figure is never achieved by the older painter in his representations of the human body. The viewer experiences the fixity of *being* but not the presence of *existence*. Unlike Ingres's technique, Giacometti's white lines of pigment contribute to an impression of unity because they do not delineate form but force the eye to follow without fixing on them. Sartre is drawn to these lines because they are opposed to the creation of an impression of passivity and inertia by volume and surface. Through them the eye is drawn across the surface of the painting without coming to

10. "L'indissoluble unité d'une figure." *Ibid.*, p. 358.
11. "Il veut que ses figures, au cœur de leur vide originel, sur sa toile immobile, passent et repassent sans cesse du continu au discontinu." *Ibid.*

rest on the detail of the figure. The movement toward the center suggested by these lines creates a dematerialized body. The desired wholeness or unity results from the impression of continuity in the viewer's experience of the painting.

Sartre praises Giacometti's portraits, which avoid weight, substance, volume, and materiality. Hallucinatory and phantomlike are among the words with which he describes one of Giacometti's portraits. The apparition that comes before the viewer is compared to a fleeting image seen in the flames of a fire. Only a glimpse is caught of the shape of the human body, suggested but not defined by the flicker. The texture of painting admired by Sartre is that of flames, which consume the stylistic rigidity of older portraiture. Like the Calder mobile, the canvas and pigment of Giacometti's painting are described as a trap in which the tenuous, fragile existence of man is caught momentarily. Giacometti's techniques produce magic qualities which create the illusion of a human presence in all its unity. The dexterity of the magician is invoked by Sartre in his comparison of Giacometti to a prestidigitator who tricks the viewer into belief. A shock of recognition is experienced as the painter-magician reveals the nature of human experience through illusion. Giacometti's flickering canvases "arouse in us feelings and attitudes ordinarily produced by encounters with real men." [12] The concept of space, the figure-ground relation, the use of line, and the texture of the painting are the stylistic problems for which Giacometti's solutions are welcomed by Sartre. Through these formal elements of the painting, Sartre finds a representation of man that parallels his own reflections on the existence of each man in his solitude. In the works of Tintoretto, Sartre will find an older artist who solved these same problems in a satisfactory way.

JACOPO ROBUSTI TINTORETTO

In general, Sartre disapproves of older art. In his early works he attacks the classical statue and portrait. Simone de Beauvoir certainly contributed to Sartre's reluctance to respond positively to painting and sculpture. His early enthusiastic response to paintings such as those of Guido Reni met with derision from his

12. "Suscitent en nous les sentiments et les attitudes que provoque à l'ordinaire la rencontre d'hommes réels." *Ibid.*, p. 354. Compare this description of Giacometti's portrait with Sartre's earlier discussions of faces seen in the fire. *L'Imaginaire*, pp. 52–55.

companion. In *La Force de l'âge* she subtly represents herself as superior to Sartre in her appreciation of the art of painting. Her account of their visit to the Prado with Fernando Gerassi (who served as the model for the painter Gomez)[13] reveals the contrast between their individual experience of painting, as she sees it.

> I had gone through the galleries of the Louvre several times with Sartre, and had discovered that, thanks to my cousin Jacques, I understood painting a little better than he did; for me a picture was first of all a surface covered with colors, while what Sartre reacted to was the subject and the expressions of the figures, to such an extent that he liked the works of Guido Reni. I attacked him severely for this, and he hastily withdrew.[14]

Her accounts of his reaction to painting on this occasion and during their travels permit her to illustrate what she had previously described as his "aesthetic of opposition."[15] As I have indicated, Sartre responded to paintings in which the human body in moments of pain and stress was represented in an expressionistic manner. Simone de Beauvoir wins a certain victory over Sartre in his first groping attempts to experience painting. She is delighted that her influence brought him to dislike paintings that repeat the "errors" she would have him avoid. "Sartre," according to her, "with vigilant loathing was tracking down all the painters in whom he thought he could see the errors of Guido Reni; I readily agreed to his pulverizing of Murillo, Ribera, and many others."[16] His stubborn resistance to her attempts to convert him to what she calls "pure art" centers on the work of Titian. Her praise of his canvases in no way convinces

13. I am indebted to Professor Meyer Schapiro of Columbia University for this information.

14. "Plusieurs fois, j'avais parcouru les galeries du Louvre avec Sartre et j'avais constaté que, grâce à mon cousin Jacques, je comprenais un peu mieux la peinture que lui: un tableau, pour moi, c'était d'abord une surface couvert de couleurs, tandis que Sartre réagissait au sujet et à l'expression des personnages, au point qu'il goûtait les œuvres de Guido Reni. Je l'avais vivement attaqué et il avait battu en retraite." P. 91.

15. "Esthétique d'opposition." *Force de l'âge,* p. 83.

16. "Sartre, poursuivant d'une haine vigilante tous les peintres en qui il lui semblait reconnaître les erreurs de Guido Reni, je consentis avec empressement qu'il réduisit en poudre Murillo, Ribera et bien d'autres." *Ibid.,* p. 92.

Sartre of their merit. In this matter he will not share her admiration for Titian's brilliant technique. She suggests that his refusal to accept her position is due to the lesson he has learned too well from her in the Guido Reni affair.

> Still, technical virtuosity fascinated me, and I willingly stood there gaping at the canvases of Titian. On this point Sartre immediately took a radical position: he turned away in disgust. I told him that he was exaggerating, that these canvases were extraordinarily well painted. "What then?" he answered, adding, "Titian is pure Opera." In reaction to Guido Reni, he would no longer permit a picture to make any concessions to gesture or expression.[17]

However, his rejection of Titian's paintings was undoubtedly based on his natural opposition to the Renaissance style of Titian and not simply on her reproach of his predilection for Guido Reni. In the thirties, Sartre's attraction to a particular representation of the human body in space is already apparent in the Avignon *Pietà* (Pl. 19), the Grünewald *Crucifixion* (Pl. 20), and the paintings of Guido Reni.

In these works there are clues to his predilections for the stylistic elements he praises in the painting of Tintoretto. In the Avignon *Pietà* the expressive representation of the human figure to which Sartre is attracted is set in space which is not based on consistent perspective. The figures exist in an ambiguous space and are related to one another in such a way that they are inextricable from the experience they share. The clarity of measurable space constructed according to the rules of single point perspective is not present. Matthias Grünewald shows a suffering Christ whose body is violently twisted in pain. The shared emotional experience of the witnessing figures is intensified by the contorted position in which they are portrayed. His treatment of space is characterized by a slightly greater traversability, but in the construction of the painting he is opposed to centrality and regularity— stylistic traits to which Sartre reacts negatively. Stable figures in symmetrical composition are alien to this German

17. "Cependant, la virtuosité technique m'éblouissait et je restais volontiers plantée devant les toiles du Titien. Sur ce point, Sartre fut tout de suite radical: il s'en détournait avec dégoût. Je lui dis qu'il exagérait, que c'était quand même fameusement bien peint. 'Et après?' me répondait-il; et il ajoutait: 'Titien, c'est de l'Opéra.' Par réaction contre Guido Reni, il n'admettait plus qu'un tableau sacrifiât au geste ni à l'expression." *Ibid.*

painter. "Grünewald's basic sensibility expressly rejected tectonic and regular structure as inadequate,"[18] as Heinrich Wölfflin has shown in his discussion of this *Crucifixion* admired by Sartre. On another occasion Wölfflin finds in the works of Guido Reni the same treatment of the frame and the space created that Sartre likes in Giacometti's paintings.

> The rectangularity of the picture-space as active, form-defining principle is already essentially negated. The main current runs diagonally, and even if the distribution of the masses does not far depart from renaissance bilateralism, the recollection of Titian would suffice to bring home to us the baroque character of this Magdalene.[19]

The same tension in the representation of the body to reveal a figure in torment is joined with a spatial concept which contrasts with the style of the classic Renaissance painter. Wölfflin explores the opposition between the Renaissance and the baroque style.[20] The baroque style with its painterliness, its recessional space, its open form, its unity, and its relative unclearness strikingly resembles the qualities Sartre selects for praise in the paintings of Giacometti. Sartre's interest in this style, often summarized as one of *becoming* by art historians, is indicative of his interest in " 'becoming' rather than 'being,' and thus preferring contortion to composure, complexity and involution to simplicity and clearness, oblique recession into space to frontality, the 'open-form,' viz., incompleteness and asymmetry, to the closed."[21] Sartre's own inclination towards a pictorial style in older art culminates in his discovery of a champion who struggled against the aesthetic of fixity and *being*.

Sartre's essay on Tintoretto[22] is based on the historical conflict between Titian and Tintoretto, who represent two poles of the depicting of man in space. Tintoretto is Sartre's inevitable choice. In the galleries of the Louvre and the Prado, he has already indicated his preference—in reaction to Simone de Beauvoir's taste for the works of Titian. In style and in content the enemy is Titian, a painter of official portraits and the epitome of the use of classical Renaissance style that tends to create *being*. Titian is

18. Wölfflin, *Sense of Form in Art,* p. 109.
19. Wölfflin, *Principles of Art History,* p. 138.
20. In his books, *Principles of Art History* and *Sense of Form in Art.*
21. Panofsky, *Early Netherlandish Painting,* 1: 345.
22. "Le Séquestré de Venise," reprinted in *Situations,* 4: 291–346.

revealed to us in Sartre's depicting of the fictional painters Renaudas and Bordurin. Bouville and Venice choose painters whose style is the very antithesis of those qualities Sartre singles out in the work of Giacometti. Titian as a court painter involved in the creation of the myth of power and right is certainly present in Sartre's mind when he writes of Roquentin's resistance to the portraits enshrined in the Bouville museum. Roquentin's experience is that of the spectator who refuses to accept the use of the human body as a carrier of abstract values. The portrait of Philip II that provided the initial experience through which Roquentin rejects court painting seems unquestionably related to the style of Titian. The work in the library at the Escorial by the Spanish painter Juan Pantoja de la Cruz [23] may well be replaced in Sartre's mind by one of Titian's several portraits of the Spanish monarch (Pl. 5)—particularly if we recall his violent reaction to Titian's works in the Prado. In any case Sartre's satirical representation of the style in which the Bouville portraits were painted was an attack on a style linked with Titian and the classical Renaissance aesthetic of the state portrait.

Tintoretto's rebellion took the form of rivalry with the court portraitist on his own ground rather than in the passive, ironic stance of Roquentin. Characteristically, Sartre in his attitude of "esthétique d'opposition" builds his own case for Tintoretto by attacking Titian's paintings for their content and for their style. The subject matter is the representation of kings, princes, battles, and religious subjects. Titian's role is to paint these individuals and events in a style that will reassure the ruling group. Painting in Titian's hands serves to create the myth of a stratified world, which the ruling class clearly dominates. Disrupting elements and fleshly conflicts are subjected to the ordering of Titian's brush. The human body in a moment of torment or anguish in a battle, a crucifixion, or an expulsion from the Garden of Eden is submitted to the harmonizing devices of perspective and color. The brilliant technique that Simone de Beauvoir attempted to force Sartre to admire is characterized by Sartre as an attempt to hide man's experience of injustice, suffering, and the pain of

23. Vivanco, *Escorial*, pp. 31–32. Pantoja was a student of Alonsa Sánchez Coello, one of three official court painters to Philip II. Titian and Mor completed the triumvirate. Coello's stylistic treatment of space is interesting in light of the Bouville portraits. "Space is indicated by various accessories, such as a red curtain, a velvet-draped table or a leather-backed chair," as George Kubler and Soria Martin have described it in their *Art and Architecture in Spain and Portugal*, p. 206.

existence. Sartre describes the role Titian accepted as that of an apologist for the establishment. Sartre complains that in his paintings, "discord is only an illusion, the worst enemies are secretly reconciled by the colors of their cloaks. Violence? A ballet danced by counterfeit tough guys with fleecy beards: there you are, war justified!" [24] What Sartre rejects in Titian's painting is the watering down of man's experience in the flesh. Human emotion so expressively represented in the Avignon *Pietà* and the Grünewald *Crucifixion* is in Titian's work but the pale reflection of man's suffering in his corporeal existence. Movement is not the fast pace of the violence of battle but the gentle rhythm of the dance. Beards and flesh in this vision of the world are reduced to the softness of princely fabrics. Titian, the brilliant colorist, reconciles the conflict between men in his painting and in so doing, "spends most of his time soothing princes, guaranteeing them, with his canvases, that everything is for the best in the best of all possible worlds." [25]

The elements of his style that create what Sartre considers to be a false vision of the world are criticized in an analysis of Titian's *Assumption of the Virgin* (Pl. 20). Sartre returns to the formal elements he treats in the paintings of Giacometti. The space of Titian's painting depends upon the requirements of the hierarchical relationship between man and the divinities. The ambiguous space of the void in Giacometti's works is absent. The organization of the painting relates to the worth of the individual portrayed. Perspective is used to place each figure precisely in his respective space at a clearly defined distance from God the Father. The privileged position is created through vertical distance and centrality. The light source reveals, not man's fleshly condition, but his position in the hierarchy: "This half-light corresponds to the obscurity of his position." [26] The vital experience of man called for by Sartre in painting takes on the character of empty ceremony. The body seen in action is avoided and Titian's technique strips it of its force: "Sacrificing movement to order and contrast to unity, he caresses the bodies with

24. "La discorde n'est qu'une apparence, les pires ennemis sont secrètement réconciliés par les couleurs de leurs manteaux. La Violence? Un ballet dansé sans trop de conviction par de faux durs aux barbes de laine: voilà des guerres justifiées." *Situations*, 4: 339.

25. "Passe le meilleur de son temps à tranquilliser les princes, à leur certifier par ses toiles que tout va pour le mieux dans le meilleur des mondes possibles." *Ibid.*, pp. 338–39.

26. "Cette pénombre correspond à l'obscurité de sa condition." *Ibid.*, p. 339.

his brush instead of modeling them." [27] Order and unity oppose the contrast and movement of the surface of the canvas that are critical to Sartre's aesthetic. The portrayal of the body in the *Assumption* may be seen as a multiple official portrait in the style of the Bouville paintings. Line and contour that define and limit with precision in order to create *being* are used by the artist to make power and merit unmistakably clear. Sartre criticizes Titian's tendency to give greater individuality to the figures portrayed in direct relation to their position in the hierarchy. The more important the concept embodied, the more distinct the body containing it becomes. Sartre rejects the orchestration of color, which endows the picture with the harmony the painter wishes to convey to the viewer. Most striking is the absence of the painter in his painting. Sartre's desire for the presence of man —whether subject or artist—is reiterated in his criticism of the "licked style." Titian, like Renaudas and Bordurin, removes all trace of his signature brushwork from the painting before offering it to the public. "He begins to 'lick' his canvas with his brush: scrapings and polishings, lacquers and varnishes. He will spare no effort to hide his labors; he ends up eliminating all trace of himself from the painting." [28] The individuality of the artist, which Sartre sees written across the canvases of Giacometti, is eradicated. The sweat of creation as it might have been revealed in the impasto is brushed away by Titian's slick canvas just as the Americans have deodorized the paintings in their air-conditioned, antiseptic Museum of Modern Art. If man is not present in the flesh—in sweat and blood—Sartre resists the brilliance of the style. But in the canvases of Tintoretto, Sartre believes he finds the painter's imprint. In Tintoretto's art Sartre discovers a man revealed in his paintings because this sixteenth-century rebel permits his struggle to appear boldly on the surface of the painting.

Tintoretto's revolt against the official stylistic representations of Titian is dramatized by Sartre in his essay. The creative endeavor is reconstructed through an analysis of the struggle of the man. Sartre examines the record of this life and unveils the complicity of a city and its art historians. The recurrent elements of the legend behind which the painter disappears hinge on two

27. "Sacrifiant le mouvement à l'ordre et le relief à l'unité, il caresse les corps plus qu'il ne les modèle." *Ibid.*

28. "Il se met à lécher sa toile: grattages et polissages, laques et vernis. Il n'épargnera rien pour cacher son travail; il finit par s'escamoter." *Ibid.*, p. 340.

anecdotes repeated again and again until they become a substitute for the absent facts of the painter's early life. Both revolve around Titian—the enemy. At the age of twelve Tintoretto is supposed to have been dismissed from Titian's *atelier* because of the master's jealousy and fear of the talent of the young genius. The second is an attempt to explain his style by espousing the myth that the painter inscribed on the walls of his studio as his motto, "The color of Titian and the draftsmanship of Michelangelo." In his essay Sartre carefully disproves the slanderous charges implied in these two "facts." Sartre draws on the absolute necessity of learning the craft of painting in a studio and points up the difficulties the young Jacopo would have encountered had Titian in fact closed the door of his workshop on the child of twelve. The elder painter is linked by Sartre to the establishment in his authoritarian hold over Venetian painting of the period. He was the king of painters with the right to choose his heir. Titian did this in designating Veronese to succeed him. For Sartre, the critical moment in the life of the young rebel occurred when he dared to break from current stylistic representation and reveal himself in the painting of *The Miracle of the Slave* in 1548 (Pl. 22). The reaction of Venice to the work was violently negative. Sartre suggests a cabal. The style scandalized and confounded official Venice. In this painting consistent with his own aesthetic inclinations, Sartre sees the real Tintoretto—his Tintoretto.

The rejection by the Rialtans of this portrayal of the human figure in space explains for Sartre why the subsequent paintings do not continue the early boldness. Drawing upon the social and economic conditions of the period, Sartre describes Tintoretto's position in the Venetian art market as untenable. The personal necessity to survive as a craftsman earning his living in a competitive market obliged Tintoretto to paint in the style of his contemporaries. Because he was forced to imitate their works, Tintoretto gave himself the task of outdoing each of these painters by excelling in their own style. For Sartre his painting in the style of Veronese with its vast, measurable architectural space was alien to Tintoretto's vision (and to Sartre's own preference for deep ambiguous space). The means the painter must use in order to express himself against the imposed taste and rules explain Sartre's subheading, "Les Fourberies de Jacopo" ("Jacopo's Capers"). The example of these double-dealings dramatized by Sartre is the competition for the ceiling panel at the Scuola San Rocco. Tintoretto submitted no sketch, but revealed a fully finished painting installed in the ceiling of the school at the moment of the judging and made the Brotherhood a gift of it. Through this trick he won the right to paint the vast empty walls of the school, and it is in these works painted for Scuola San Rocco that Sartre sees the real Tintoretto's style. The animosity he incurred from his fellow painters was but a part of the burden he had to bear.

The painters with whom Tintoretto competed were in the service of those wealthy Rialtans who dwelt on the right side of the canal. Painting as a manual occupation was scorned by the artists of the period, contrary to popular tradition. Sartre attempts to show that the Renaissance painters were frustrated in their role of craftsman and felt strongly the inferiority of their social position. In cataloging the literary pretensions of Raphael, Michelangelo, and Titian, Sartre contrasts Tintoretto's acceptance of the challenge of his trade. "What enchants him in the craft of painting is that in it professional know-how is pushed to the point of prestidigitation and the delicacy of the merchandise reduced to its quintessence." [29] In this Sartre returns to the characterization of the artist's creative act that he had previously used in describing the painting of Giacometti. Tintoretto is, in Sartre's eyes, a magician, a seller of visions, but above all a worker who did not choose to use his art to glorify the elite in order to bask in the reflected light of the privileged ruler. "This sacred personage transfers to the elect a share of his supernatural powers; the glory of his throne falls on them like a ray of sunlight, and they in turn reflect it on the people; the divine right of kings creates painters of divine right." [30] Their art participates in the creation of the myth of privilege and *being*. They depend on the monarchy, yet create it in embodying the abstract concept in their works. Sartre refuses their role and their style, which go hand in hand. He condemns the admirers of these painters of the classical Renaissance tradition: "Even today, nostalgic republicans worship in them, in the name of genius, the light of that dead star, Monarchy." [31]

Tintoretto's choice of clientele is welcomed by Sartre as an

29. "Ce qui l'enchante dans le métier de peindre c'est qu'on y pousse l'habilité professionnelle jusqu'à la prestidigitation et la délicatesse de la marchandise jusqu'à la quintessence." *Ibid.*, p. 319.

30. "Ce personnage sacré cède à ses élus une parcelle de ses pouvoirs surnaturels; la gloire du trône tombe sur eux comme un rayon du soleil, ils la réfléchissent sur le peuple; le droit divin des rois fait les peintres de droit divin." *Ibid.*, p. 318.

31. "Aujourd'hui encore, les républicains nostalgiques adorent en eux, sous le nom de génie, la lumière de cette étoile morte, la monarchie." *Ibid.*

occasion to relate the painter's art to his audience. Tintoretto did at times accept commissions from foreign princes, but Sartre asserts that he did not create his masterpieces for them. Sartre applies the vocabulary of the movie industry to these works that left his native Venice: they are "B" pictures. The real Tintoretto chose to be seen only at home in his native city. In this belief Sartre coincides with Taine, who praises the work of Tintoretto so highly and who insists, "There is a man of genius, Tintoretto, almost all of whose works are in Venice. One does not suspect his worth, until one is here." [32] But Sartre reduces the number of Tintoretto's major works even further by dividing the paintings commissioned by his Venetian clientele into two distinct groups. Tintoretto's paintings for officialdom—in general, the result of a group effort of the entire workshop—are eliminated from the work of the man, Jacopo Robusti, who created for his fellow Venetians. For Sartre, the real Tintoretto exists far from the Doge's Palace, in the Scuola San Rocco whose works are commissioned by the people of Venice: "Sometimes the faithful of the parish, sometimes the members of the Confraternity: bourgeois great and small; this is his real public, the only one he loves." [33] In this audience Sartre sees a class threatening the patriciate just as Tintoretto is threatening the position of Titian. In this way Sartre is able to identify Tintoretto with a social struggle that reinforces the artist's aesthetic rivalry with the old master. Tintoretto, the worker-painter, creates for the "workers," and unlike Titian, the frustrated son of a peasant, remains in his city with his own kind, demonstrating to them that he is one of "the little fellows who bear the burden of a heavily hierarchical society." [34] "He esteems their high regard for work, their moralism, their common sense; he likes their nostalgia and, above all, he shares their deepest aspiration: all of them, if only to produce, to buy and sell, need freedom." [35] This freedom to create and to express

32. "Au contraire, il y a un homme de génie, Tintoret, dont l'œuvre presque entière est à Venise. On ne soupçonne pas ce qu'il vaut, tant qu'on n'est point ici." *Voyage en Italie,* 2: 358.

33. "Tantôt les fidèles de la Paroisse, tantôt les membres de la Confrérie: des bourgeois, grands et petits; voilà son vrai public, le seul qu'il aime." *Situations,* 4: 321.

34. "Les petites gens qui supportent le poids d'une société lourdement hiérarchisée." *Ibid.,* p. 309.

35. "Il apprécie leur goût du travail, leur moralisme, leur sens pratique, il aime leur nostalgie et, surtout, il partage leur aspiration profonde: tous, ne fût-ce que pour produire, pour acheter et pour vendre, ils ont besoin de la liberté." *Ibid.,* pp. 323–24.

himself in stylistic opposition to Titian and the Renaissance heritage is visible only in a choice few of his works. For Sartre, it is first in *The Miracle of the Slave* of 1548 and most fully in those works of the Scuola San Rocco accomplished single-handedly by the painter that Tintoretto's freedom is expressed in a style of his own.

These works are placed by Sartre against the background of the state of art at the time they were painted. Art had long been in the service of the church and now passed from a sacred to a secular role. Sartre links this change to the development of Renaissance perspective, drawing on his memories of the Pompeian wall paintings. He derides a Florentine banker for having had "the ridiculous idea of decorating his house with frescoes." [36] In subject and in technique Sartre records the profanation of art. Perspective is forced upon the sacred subject at a time when painters are not yet ready for it. "In sixteenth-century Italy, faith still burns in the hearts of artists, wrestling with the atheism of their eyes and hands. In wanting to seize the Absolute, they perfected techniques that thrust in the middle of a relativism they detest." [37] The Renaissance artists find themselves in a situation in which the light of God that guarantees their art and the myth of divine right disappears. God cannot be represented with man's body according to laws of perspective used to define the finite. Sartre records this historical development, but gives it his own interpretation when he writes that "perspective is a violence which human weakness imposes on God's little world." [38] The crisis in painting,[39] as Sartre conceives of it, reveals the fragility of man's existence, but the darkness and emptiness revealed force Tintoretto to work furiously to conquer this nothingness. "Perspective cannot be transcended as long as the right to create other plastic spaces has not been won." [40] In *The*

36. "L'idée saugrenue d'embellir par des fresques sa maison." *Ibid.*, p. 328.

37. "Au XVI⁰ siècle, en Italie, la foi brûle encore le cœur des artistes, elle combat l'athéisme de l'œil et de la main. En voulant serrer de plus près l'Absolu, ils ont mis au point des techniques qui les jettent dans un relativisme qu'ils détestent." *Ibid.*, p. 330.

38. "La perspective est une violence que la faiblesse humaine fait subir au petit monde de Dieu." *Ibid.*, p. 329.

39. Compare this same idea in his essay "Doigts et non-doigts," "Art crumbles at the same time as its guaranty, divine Creation." "L'art tombe en poussière en même temps que sa garantie, la Création divine." *Ibid.*, p. 418.

40. "On ne dépasse pas la perspective tant qu'on ne s'est pas donné le droit de créer d'autres espaces plastiques." *Ibid.*, p. 332.

Miracle of the Slave, Sartre sees Tintoretto's attempt to express himself by revealing to his fellow citizens this experience of the Infinite: "The Infinite is the emptiness, the darkness, within the creature and without." [41] But the city turned on him for this revelation. Venice preferred the reassuring style of his rival, Titian.

In creating a portrait of Tintoretto, Sartre attempts to reveal the passionate struggle of the artist within his craft, his art, and his city. In his writing on Giacometti there is a closer analysis of the paintings themselves. The work of art forms the basis for the discussion of the artist's vision of the world. Why then does Sartre avoid a lengthy discussion of the style of Tintoretto in individual paintings? A partial answer is in his characteristic "esthétique d'opposition." He analyzes at some length the style of the enemy, Titian, in the *Assumption.* Sartre tells us what he sees the project of Tintoretto to have been and indicates those stylistic qualities which form a part of his enterprise by contrast with those of Titian. Sartre puts the man back in the work. Jacopo's life is written across the painting's surface; hence, we are forced by Sartre to return to those works in the Scuola San Rocco. If he does not take us through each painting to point out the signature elements of the Robusti style, it is partly because he has done it by implication. There is perhaps another reason. Sartre's admiration for Tintoretto's painting established at the time of his encounter with the San Rocco *Crucifixion* (Pl. 23) in the thirties is shared by Giacometti. In a letter to Pierre Matisse published in the catalogue of the 1948 exhibition for which Sartre wrote the introduction, Giacometti reveals that he spent his days in Venice looking at the paintings of Tintoretto, "not wanting one of them to escape [him]." [42] This continued interest in Tintoretto's art is demonstrated in the publication of a brilliant essay by Jules Vuillemin [43] the same year that Sartre wrote his essay on Giacometti's painting. Vuillemin's essay discusses the style that develops in Tintoretto's works and fully treats the aesthetic qualities that conform to Sartre's taste. In suggesting Sartre's predilection for stylistic treatment of the figure in space in the baroque tradition, I do not suggest that Sartre would accept it without certain necessary qualifications. This is appropriate as well in

41. "L'Infini, c'est le vide, c'est le noir, dans la créature et hors d'elle." *Ibid.,* p. 331.

42. "Ne voulant pas qu'il y en ait un seul qui [lui] échappe." Reproduced in Peter Selz's *Alberto Giacometti,* p. 15.

43. "La Personnalité esthétique du Tintoret."

dealing with the style of Tintoretto, as Vuillemin points out, because the Venetian does not easily fall into a single category. But in the works at San Rocco and the early *Miracle of the Slave,* Vuillemin's vocabulary echoes Sartre's own treatment of the paintings of Giacometti. However, Vuillemin's essay fails to portray *il furioso* with all the dash and vigor recaptured in Sartre's portrait. After publishing Vuillemin's study in *Les Temps modernes,* Sartre apparently does not feel obliged to repeat the long description and analysis of these paintings found in writers such as Taine and Ruskin.[44] But in writing his "Sequestré de Venise," Sartre could not resist another opportunity to champion the cause of a major opponent of Titian's style of painting, as he had done earlier in his satire of the Bouville official portraits. Against the background of the situation in which Tintoretto finds himself, Sartre shows us the choices the artist made in striving to express, with brush and pigment, a vision of the world with which the writer is sympathetic.

ROBERT LAPOUJADE

In 1961, on the occasion of an exhibition of the work of Lapoujade, when Sartre again turns his attention to the art of painting, he once more attacks those betrayers of human experience—Titian and his fellow privileged painters. The representation of the human figure in space has undergone an extraordinary change at the moment when Sartre arrives at a consideration of the abstract canvases of "Le Peintre sans privilèges." [45] Lapoujade's work falls logically within Sartre's own aesthetic inclination in subject matter and especially in the painter's portrayal of man's experience. The abstract painter has taken the final step from the limiting contours to which Sartre has long objected by achieving the dissolution of the figure. The measurable, traversable space of

44. Sartre's essay, "Le Séquestré de Venise," is a part of a longer study on Tintoretto's painting. The complete work may never be published, but a portion of it appeared in *L'Arc,* No. 30 (1966), pp. 33–52. This *"Saint-Georges et le Dragon"* is a detailed interpretation of a painting by Tintoretto in the National Gallery in London. The development of the essay applies Sartre's characteristic "esthétique d'opposition." He contrasts Carpaccio's *Saint George Bringing In the Dragon* with Tintoretto's painting of the same subject and demonstrates the superiority of the latter.
45. This is the title of the preface Sartre writes for the catalogue of the Lapoujade exhibition (March 10–April 15, 1961).

the Renaissance painters becomes the richly ambiguous whole of
the surface of the abstract canvas. Precision in the representation
of space through perspective, and in the representation of figure
through volume, mass, and contour disappears, but the subject
remains the shared distress before the tortured, broken bodies
already seen in the works of Grünewald and Tintoretto. The
exhibition's title, "Peintures sur le thème des Emeutes; Triptyque
sur la torture; Hiroshima," indicates its relation with the portrayal of human suffering to which Sartre is drawn in older art.

Before examining Lapoujade's paintings, Sartre again explains
how older art has failed in its treatment of these themes. Just as
he reconsiders older sculpture each time he begins to write on
Calder, Hare, or Giacometti, Sartre enumerates what he considers
to be errors of painting as exemplified by the canvases of Titian.
In accepting commissions for battle scenes, the painter's servitude
to the hierarchy requires the depicting of the beauty of the
human body so as to disguise the torment of the individual. The
brilliant style places the viewer in the position of forgetting the
content. The ceremonial aspect of the painting dominates and
thus obscures the meaning of the massacre. Again Sartre seems to
reply to Simone de Beauvoir standing before Titian's paintings in
the Prado when he insists that "he forced his brush to render
serene terrors, suffering empty of pain, the dead without death;
because of him Beauty betrays men and places itself on the side
of kings." [46] According to Sartre, the clarity of the painter's style
in depicting the mutilation to which the human body is subjected
results in one of two reactions on the part of the viewer. The first
is for the spectator to turn from a horror too real to be viewed
for long. The second is to be lost in admiration for the beauty of
the style as Simone de Beauvoir had been. In the history of art
Sartre sees only two exceptions to the problem he formulates:
Goya and Picasso (Pl. 24). The former does not attempt to
communicate the horrors of war, but rather assimilates them into
the visionary representation of "the naked horror of being
Goya." [47] Picasso's solution results from the auspicious moment
of the history of art in which he finds himself. Society, art, and
the painter are joined appropriately in an historical moment. An
act of violence (Guernica) occurs when the portrayal of the
human figure in art and in this artist's painting is ready to depart

46. "Il a forcé son pinceau à rendre des terreurs tranquilles, des
douleurs sans douleur et des morts sans mort: à cause de lui, la Beauté
trahit les hommes et se range du côté des rois." *Situations* 4: 367.

47. "L'horreur nue d'être Goya." *Ibid.*, p. 368.

from the traditional representation of the body. "This violence did not need to be hidden or transformed, it just identified itself with the disintegration of men by their own bombs." [48] So Picasso's style, unlike that of Titian, derives from art itself in the portrayal of such an event. Sartre is understandably more comfortable before a painting whose style has reached a stage in which the representation of the body is not that of the statue-like rigidity of a classical tradition. In Picasso's painting, the contortion of the body seen earlier in Tintoretto finally reaches an intensity sufficient to wrench the image of man from the fixity that contour and edge imply for Sartre.

The destruction of the simplicity and clearness of the Renaissance tradition of perspective and the ceramic-like qualities of the body as a container places new requirements of organization on the contemporary painter. Sartre has examined this reconstruction of a whole in his treatment of the fragmenting and reassembling of the image based on the body in David Hare's sculpture. In that work and in Giacometti's painting and sculpture as well, he insists on a quality he requires in a work of art which he calls presence. Sartre approaches this presence in terms of an indecomposable unity. His emphasis in this essay on nonfigurative (abstract) art is on the act of the painter and the act of the viewer that together bring this presence into being. This restating of his concept of the aesthetic experience expressed in *L'Imaginaire* [49] is particularly appropriate because it reveals Sartre's own preference for a style in painting. Sartre makes clear what he expects the painter to do stylistically in order to invite the participation of the viewer and in that way to avoid the reduction of the work of art to an ashy residue. A technique Sartre has long esteemed is the representation of movement in sculpture and painting. In general, the human body has been used to impart movement to the canvas. Through gesture, older painters have attempted to create this effect, but we know that for Sartre the action remains frozen. Giacometti's white striations to which Sartre is attracted are independent of the gesture of the figure represented. The lines themselves draw the eye across the surface of the canvas to create a centripetal movement. Tintoretto has a comparable device in his dramatic use of light, and it is not by chance that lightning is frequently used by Sartre to

48. "Cette violence n'a pas eu besoin de se cacher ou de se transformer, elle s'est identifiée telle quelle avec la désintégration des hommes par leurs propres bombes." *Ibid.*

49. Pp. 239–46.

describe the phenomenon that brings about this dynamic effect. Nor is the unity created by the movement of the viewer's eyes unrelated to the ambiguous treatment of space and the unfinished texture of the surface of the work in the handling of the impasto by both Tintoretto and Giacometti. In writing of Lapoujade, Sartre makes explicit his requirement for the establishment of this unity that creates presence.

> Then Presence, intuition denied, lends us its aid; it does not itself determine the itinerary the viewer's eyes will follow, but it guides the eyes' movement. To *construct,* visual relations are adequate, but in order to guarantee this construction, in order to save it from absurdity, transcendental unity is necessary. This unity ensures a movement that can never be stopped. It is this ceaseless movement which produces the permanence of an invisible unity; we continue moving our eyes across the surface of the picture because if we were to stop, the whole thing would explode.[50]

In his stylistic preference he insists on the creation of movement freed from the tyranny of the body's action in measured space.

However, though his own experience of figurative art, Sartre is aware of the inhibiting effect of reality in creating this presence. In his treatment of the concept of presence, it is amply clear that this movement of the eye brings the work to life and that the work depends on it. The meaning of the work results from this activity which creates the presence and which is inherent in the style of *becoming* to which I have referred. The artist must impart this presence to what he receives from the real world through his style. The painters Sartre rejects consistently avoid a stylistic transformation of the experience of the world. He chooses Guardi (Pl. 25) over Canaletto (Pl. 26) because the latter appears to reproduce accurately a measurable, knowable world, but fails totally in creating the desired presence. "When Canaletto paints Venice, the resemblance is perfect; half sign, half image. The Queen of the Seas is careful to avoid confusion:

50. "C'est à ce moment que la Présence, intuition refusée, nous prête son concours: elle ne détermine pas elle-même l'itinéraire, elle le surdétermine; pour 'construire' il suffira d'établir des rapports visibles; pour garantir cette construction, pour la sauver d'une absurdité totale, l'unité transcendante est nécessaire. Par elle, le mouvement du regard est assuré de ne s'arrêter jamais: c'est ce tourniquet des yeux qui produit la permanence de l'unité invisible; donc nous tournerons; si nous nous arrêtions, tout éclaterait." *Situations,* 4: 371.

there is no chance of mistaken identity. So the painting has no meaning. No more than an identification card." [51] Photographic reality in the service of the city-state reveals Sartre's prejudice against precise, accurate representation of the world. We can see that the experience he calls for in painting is one in which the world is wrenched into meaning through ambiguity in the treatment of light and space and the resultant movement of the eye across the surface of the work: "a unity of diversity through rigorous imprecision." [52] Confusion or this relative unclearness, incompleteness, and complexity—to use terms applied to the baroque—reveal the world as it is experienced; it is never seen in the precision of fixity. For Sartre the photographic world reproduced by Canaletto tends to obscure the presence he requires. "Paradoxically, the incarnation of presence more or less fails because of a brutal, mechanical bond that ties the portrait to the sitter." [53] Canaletto's Venice is like the wax guard of the Musée Grévin. Like the sculptor, the painter must use reality as given to him only by alluding to it. The object or sitter is changed by the brush in a kind of sleight of hand. Sartre's continual recourse to terms of magic or alchemy to relate what occurs in painting is emphasized by his description of the brush as a wand whose power lies in the artist's life. He also characterizes this power as a catalyst that avoids using the elements of the external world other than as a point of departure. The danger inherent in the use of the seen world is that it may become sign or symbol. The greed of the surrealist painter such as Dali, to whom Sartre refers indirectly, leads to a false trickery, as in the painter's visual puns that depend on language. In order to experience the painting's meaning, Sartre requires that the possibility of signs and symbols be brushed aside. In writing of Calder he introduces the idea of a trap set up by the artist. The springing of this trap is related to the sudden coagulation or the abrupt fixing of an image in the flames that Sartre uses in his essay on Giacometti. Sartre returns to these terms to explain the artist's use of the real world in order to create a work of art.

51. "Quand le Canaletto peint Venise, la ressemblance est parfaite: moitié signe, image à moitié, la Reine des mers a pris soin d'éviter les confusions: on ne peut pas s'y tromper. Donc le tableau n'a pas de sens. Pas plus qu'une carte d'identité." *Ibid.*, p. 372.

52. "Unité du multiple par le moyen d'une rigoureuse imprécision." *Ibid.*

53. "Paradoxalement, l'incarnation de la présence y est plus ou moins manquée par un lien brutal et mécanique assujettissant du dehors le portrait au modèle." *Ibid.*

Lapoujade has the advantage of no longer being obliged to reproduce this inhibiting reality of the seen world. Yet in this new freedom from direct reference to photographic reality, Sartre makes the same demands on nonfigurative art. He relentlessly pursues the presence he has always sought in his experience of painting. The organization of the canvas continues to depend on a multiplicity that creates a unity of the whole. In the work of Lapoujade (Pl. 27), the lightning of Tintoretto and the flicker of Giacometti become storms, turbulences, whirlwinds freed from body imagery. The words may differ, but Sartre's taste remains the same. "In order to maintain the rhythm of explosive space, to prolong the vibration of colors, to exploit in depth the strange and terrifying disintegration of being and its whirling movement, it is absolutely necessary for the brush to impose a meaning on the picture and on us." [54] The meaning, however, derives from the experience of the artist who expresses it in his style. Sartre's choice of the terms "explosive," "whirling," and "vibrating" is an attempt to suggest the action of the artist as he forcefully projects himself onto the canvas without the aid of signs or symbols. Sartre would undoubtedly agree with Meyer Schapiro, who maintains that "the object of art is, therefore, more passionately than ever before, the occasion of spontaneity or intense feelings. The painting symbolizes an individual who realizes freedom and deep engagement of the self within his works." [55] The unity of Lapoujade's painting is called lyrical by Sartre, who explains that lyrical painters "endeavor to give to the canvas the unity of emotion, élan, or a relaxed moment; in short, they choose to force those who attend their shows to experience their singular adventure." [56] In communicating his experience, the abstract painter directly expresses himself to his viewer by removing from the canvas barriers such as the use of the human figure to portray crowds seen from the outside. In the work of Lapoujade, "the presence that is incarnated is his own." [57] His humanity is revealed from within the crowd. Sartre contrasts

54. "Pour garder à l'espace explosif son rythme, pour prolonger la vibration des couleurs, pour exploiter à fond l'étrange et terrifiante désintégration de l'être et son mouvement tourbillonnaire, il est indispensable que le pinceau lui impose un sens et nous l'impose." *Ibid.*, p. 377.

55. "The Liberating Quality of Avant-Grade Art," p. 38.

56. "Prétendent donner à la toile l'unité de leur émotion, d'un élan ou d'une détente, bref ils choisissent le public des expositions pour lui faire éprouver leur aventure singulière." *Situations*, 4: 378.

57. "La présence qui s'incarne c'est la sienne." *Ibid.*

the direct revelation of the painter's own experience within the crowd with that of the older painter who is protected from the crowd by his position of privilege. Lapoujade is one of the populace just as Tintoretto is seen by Sartre to be one of the Rialtans. In the paintings of San Rocco he revealed himself. Titian does not. Although Sartre does not invoke the "style léché" in contrast to the personal statement of Lapoujade's own handwriting on the canvas, it is evident that the modern artist no longer is separated from the people by the self-effacement required by the mask of privilege. The crowd of which he is a part has been represented historically as viewed from the outside rather than from within its ranks. Lapoujade's titles for his paintings reveal his desire to express his identity with the tortured and the suffering. As an abstract painter, Lapoujade represents the culmination of traits first admired by Sartre in Guido Reni, Grünewald, and the Avignon *Pietà*. Lapoujade's choice of subject matter, his treatment of the surface of the canvas, his attitude toward the human figure, and most significantly his "unprivileged" relation to the viewer coincide with Sartre's own stylistic preferences.

ANDRÉ MASSON

In his involvement with those who demonstrate against the suffering of the individuals tortured during the revolt in Algeria, Lapoujade finds expression for his commitment through his painting. André Masson, a friend of Sartre's of long standing, was also a signer of *Le Manifeste des 121,* a protest against the tortures in Algeria. As a result of this activity, Sartre and Masson saw one another more frequently. In the course of their meetings in the company of Pierre Boulez, Masson recounted to them "stories of the heyday of surrealism." [58] These evenings appear to have given rise to the essay Sartre wrote as a preface for a series of Masson's lithographs entitled *Vingt-deux Dessins sur le thème du désir (Twenty-two Drawings on the Theme of Desire).* [59] Masson had earlier created the sets for *Morts sans sépulture (The Dead without Tombs)* when it was produced in 1946 at the Théâtre Antoine. Both Sartre and Simone de Beauvoir had been

58. "Des histoires sur les beaux temps du surréalisme." De Beauvoir, *Force des choses,* p. 604.
59. "André Masson." This essay was reprinted in *Situations,* vol. 4, pp. 387–407, in 1964.

drawn to the painter's work in the Surrealist exhibit of 1938 at the Galerie des Beaux-Arts, but it was probably the sets designed by the painter for *La Numancia* of Cervantes at the request of Jean-Louis Barrault that were responsible for his part in *Morts sans sépulture*.[60] The later series of lithographs, *Vingt-deux Dessins*, based on drawings done in a single day in 1947,[61] gives Sartre the opportunity to discover in the work of his friend those stylistic characteristics he prefers.

Sartre does not limit himself to a consideration of the drawings in this collection but examines aspects of the work of Masson from its beginning in order to present the steps that lead to the lithographs at hand. Sartre draws heavily from a book published in a series called "Les Grands Peintres par leurs amis." *André Masson et son univers,* a collection of prefaces and essays written by Michel Leiris and Georges Limbour, is illustrated with a generous selection of paintings, sculptures, and drawings representative of Masson's career. Sartre's analysis of the artist's work is based entirely on paintings and drawings reproduced in this volume and the twenty-two drawings for which Sartre writes his essay. From these numerous examples, Sartre characteristically chooses the works that permit him to see Masson in the context of his own ideas on painting. As in the case of Tintoretto, he places Masson in opposition to those painters who depict *being* through a representation of the human figure. The works to which Sartre refers are almost exclusively anthropomorphic in character. He avoids the examples that do not fall into the evolution of the representation of the human figure as the basis for movement. Those qualities he has praised in Giacometti, Tintoretto, and Lapoujade are discussed largely in terms of the use of contour by the artist rather than in terms of space and perspective; here, however, the ambivalence of these artists' treatment of space is echoed in Sartre's fascination with the ambiguities which Masson's "mythological" subject matters offers to the viewer.

Sartre is careful to separate this mythology from the literary use of classical allusions. Masson's mythology is justifiable because Sartre conceives of it as arising from the very act of drawing or painting. It is not symbolic or metaphorical but derives from the artist's relation with the process of the creation

60. Simone de Beauvoir recounts Sartre's enthusiasm for Masson's sets for *La Numancia* in a letter which he wrote to her in 1937. *Force de l'âge,* p. 304.

61. Juin *André Masson,* p. 124.

of the work of art. The growth of the drawing or painting creates its own meaning, and this act is interpreted by Sartre as the means by which Masson frees himself from any fixed mythology. From the unfinished, ambiguous form, the artist is forced to find a response to the image in process. Sartre contends that the decision made in the accomplishment of the drawing causes Masson to invent "an interpretation based on the figure and the figure based on the interpretation." [62] The creatures that take their form on paper or canvas are "a provisional answer to the question put to the painter by his painting." [63] In interpreting the mythology of Masson in terms of his technique, Sartre is able to place the artist's mythology on a level "on which the project of painting cannot be distinguished from the project of being a man." [64]

Sartre believes this project is translated by artists and poets into their work in one of two opposing attitudes. Titian in opposition to Tintoretto has already been considered in Sartre's writings on painting. He now expands this opposition between what I have referred to as a style of *being* and a style of *becoming* to include the different kinds of inspiration that relate to these styles. "Expansive" and "retractile" are used to characterize these two types of inspiration. Rimbaud and Mallarmé as poets head the list of the two categories in which Masson and the Impressionists are separated from painters such as Rouault. The painting of Rouault is criticized by Sartre because of the painter's technique of compartmentalizing the anatomy through the use of heavy black lines derived from stained-glass windows. These lines are damned because "they express nothing visible but rather a sacred terror, a hatred of change and plurality, a profound love of order which, beyond the convulsions of time and space, aim at restoring to objects their calm perennity." [65] Another aspect of "expansive" painting is related to the painter's involvement in his art. Sartre accepts the idea that an experimenter is unable to withdraw from the experiment he is conducting in order to

62. "L'interprétation à partir de la figure et soumet la figure à l'interprétation." *Situations,* 4: 388.

63. "Une réponse provisoire à la question que pose au peintre sa peinture." *Ibid.,* p. 389.

64. "Où le projet de peindre ne se distingue pas du projet d'être homme." *Ibid.*

65. "Ils n'expriment rien de visible mais plutôt une terreur sacrée, la haine du changement et de la pluralité, un amour profond de l'ordre qui, par-delà les déchirements du temps et de l'espace, vise à restituer aux objets leur calme pérennité." *Ibid.,* p. 390.

contemplate it from without. For Sartre the scientist is always a part of the experiment. The artist, too, cannot be outside of his work because, like the scientist, he participates in the process as a variable. Here Masson joins Lapoujade, whom Sartre has seen as refusing to paint men from the outside. Sartre continues this idea of the world—an involved rather than a detached point of view —when he praises Masson for his awareness that "the experimenter is an integral part of the experimental system, that he is a real factor in the physical event, and that he modifies what he sees—not in his mind, as the idealists wish to believe, but here in the world—by the simple fact of observing it." [66] Although Sartre does not allude to the Venetian artist in this essay, Titian's position of detachment in his portrayal of the hierarchy in its stability is an important element in Sartre's rejection of the "retractile" category. By contrast with the latter group of painters, Masson's mythology is related to the "expansive" painters such as Giacometti, Tintoretto, and Lapoujade who undertake the representation of movement. In this explosive, dynamic quality here described in terms of André Breton's "explosante-fixe," Sartre returns to the opposition between true and false movement expressed previously in the David Hare essay: "He [Masson] does not attempt to depict real movement on an immobile canvas but rather to reveal the virtual movement of immobility." [67] In Masson's desire to give new meaning to the limiting quality of line by transforming it into a force of movement—a trajectory or a vector—Sartre believes he finds "the original myth of Masson, his myth as man and as painter." [68]

Sartre discovers in Masson's drawing the revitalizing of line through the artist's recourse to the human figure. Sartre has continually rejected the representation of the body in a linear style that defines and limits. His friend's work suggests the possibility of the use of line to create the frenetic pace of the original centripetal force of Giacometti's men or the lightning flashes that illuminate the paintings of the Scuola San Rocco. In writing of the problem that faces Masson, Sartre states his own

66. "L'expérimentateur fait partie intégrante du système expérimental, qu'il est un facteur réel de l'événement physique et qu'il modifie ce qu'il voit—non pas en son esprit, comme veulent les idéalistes, mais là-bas, dans le monde—par le seul fait de le voir." *Ibid.*, p. 392.

67. "Il [Masson] ne cherche point tant à figurer un mouvement réel sur une toile immobile qu'à révéler le mouvement virtuel de l'immobilité." *Ibid.*

68. "Le mythe originel de Masson, son mythe d'homme et de peintre." *Ibid.*

attitude toward the undertaking: "If the contour of pictured objects is only line, the whole thing sinks into the eternity of inertia; but if the painter is able to cause these contours to become vectors, then the viewer's eyes confer on them the lively unity of a melodic sequence." [69] The active movement of the eye across the surface of the canvas that Sartre requires in painting finds yet another expression in the work of Masson through the painter's use of the figure. Things animal, mineral, and vegetal are seen through men: "Man is the refractive medium through which Masson sees things and through which he wishes to force us to see them, a distorting mirror in which faces are reflected." [70] Unlike the women of Titian who are painted as desirable, those of Masson are desired. The latter are praised by Sartre because of the artist's technique through which "the contours of a breast are drawn by a hand that caresses it; the whole body becomes a bolt of lightning, the flash of a rape, it carries its own devastation." [71] Sartre traces the energetic dynamism he discovers through a series of Masson's works in the same way he has done in writing on the sculpture of David Hare.

It is not by chance that he follows the same method in these two artists' works because surrealism—a term Sartre carefully avoids in discussing the work of Masson—permeates the early works of Hare and Masson. The literary temptation of Hare in his sculpture as revealed in the girl whose sex is a keyhole-rattrap has its parallel in Masson's *Piège à soleil* (*Sun Trap*). Sartre suggests here, as he had before in the Hare essay, that after a brief flirtation Masson leaves behind the symbolism to which he had been drawn. The works Sartre discusses illustrate Masson's progression toward *Vingt-deux Dessins sur le thème du désir*. These works are seen by Sartre to be a final liberating step from the detested use of line and contour.

One of these is a landscape of 1941, *Paysage de la Martinique* (Pl. 28), in which elements of nature are depicted with refer-

69. "Si le contour des objets peints n'est qu'une ligne, tout s'enfonce dans l'éternité qui est une intemporelle inertie; mais si le peintre peut faire que les contours deviennent des vecteurs, alors les yeux du spectateur leur conféreraient l'unité vive d'une succession mélodique." *Ibid.*, p. 394.

70. "L'homme est le milieu réfringent à travers lequel Masson voit les choses et veut nous les faire voir, la glace déformante qui lui réfléchit les visages." *Ibid.*, p. 396.

71. "Les contours d'un sein sont tracés par une main qui le caresse, le corps entier devient une foudre, l'éclair d'un viol, il porte sur lui son propre saccage." *Ibid.*

ence to the human body. The human presence is clearly visible in the artist's use of the male and female figures as elements of the scene. The explosive force of movement is imparted to the line serving as contour by the underlying musculature, and the individual details of the body depicted permeate the whole with the vitality of the human gesture. The hated passivity that characterized the *Odalisque* of Ingres or the women of Titian should be contrasted with Sartre's admiration for the figures of Masson whose "legs and calves assume the function of those arrows drawn on battle maps used for tactical operations: they transform those contour lines, contours of nipples, into vectors." [72] In answering the accusation that Masson uses a mythology of eroticism, Sartre describes Masson's use of the female sex as an example of the human body whose representation transforms the static line into a vector. A clearer example is that of two nude figures of 1922, which illustrate Masson's portrayal of the female sex organ as two vectors that result in "the rupture of flesh crackled as a result of this tension." [73] The tension comes to represent in Masson's work an element of a personal mythology in which the female sex is seen as a wound. For Sartre this depiction occurs in response to the technical requirements of Masson's use of the human figure as a means to represent true movement in the work of art rather than action captured or frozen in photographic fashion. In this interpretation of conflict and movement in the artist's work, Sartre draws upon the writings of Georges Limbour, but only because Sartre's own predilections find an echo in Limbour's experience of Masson's works.

The recurring movement and conflict are frequently extensions of the violence of the male-female battle. The sex-wound motif and the use of themes of struggle, violence, and rape avoid a symbolism Sartre would reject because they are seen to be a means of avoiding the effect of a fixed image, which the contour might otherwise create. The dynamic quality of erotic acts depicted with contour-vectors creates "not finitude but explosion, not inertia heaped on a being that is what it is and nothing else, but a certain manner of being all that it isn't and never being

72. "Jambes et mollets assument la fonction de ces flèches que l'on trace sur une carte de bataille, d'opération stratégique: elles transforment les lignes de crête, les contours des mamelons en vecteurs." *Ibid.,* p. 399.
73. "L'éclatement de la chair fendillée sous l'effet de cette tension." *Ibid.*

exactly what it is." [74] The ambiguity Sartre discovers here is not initially in the imprecise representation of the space in which the figure exists, as in Giacometti's work, but in Masson's treatment of the human body as an element of the landscape. Rather than being *in* nature, the figure is *of* nature, as in his *Paysage de la Martinique*. The ambiguity is evident in a second drawing, *Deux Arbres* (*Two Trees*), in which the tree-couple represent an indeterminate state of metamorphosis—that of becoming—somewhere between plant and human. This is a dramatic reversal of the "thingification" of man that Sartre rejects in classical art. The look of Medusa that has attracted and repulsed Sartre is no longer at work. Masson reverses the process of making men of stone by representing elements of nature with the attributes of men and women. The anthropomorphic tentatively lends to mountains, rocks, and trees the vitality of human existence, Sartre's "astonishing adventure of the flesh." [75] The body becomes the means by which the elements of nature are made ambivalent.

In one of the drawings (Pl. 29) of this series, *Hommes ailés pris dans des rocs de glace et ne se dégageant de cet Himalaya de polyèdres qu'au prix de l'abandon de leur peau* (*Winged Men Caught in Icy Rocks Freeing Themselves from This Himalaya of Polyhedrons Only at the Cost of Their Skins*), the appeal of the subject matter is clearly related to that in Dürer's *Melencolia I*. The winged figure confronting the weight and density of stone is here multiplied. Not one but several figures are portrayed in their opposition to the volume of the depicted polyhedrons. Sartre admires this representation of the body, which suggests an escape from the pull of gravity governing it as an object. He considers the wings that cap the movement of the body to be an important stylistic element, but the representation of the forceful musculature, man's own active participation in overcoming his earthly condition, receives Sartre's highest admiration. The opposition between man and stone centers on the overcoming of inertia by human effort. The elements used by Masson suggest a direct encounter between the passivity of matter and the actions of men. Movement of the body here joins the dynamic shifting

74. "Non pas la finitude mais l'explosion, non pas l'inertie tassée de l'être qui est ce qu'il est et rien d'autre, mais une certaine manière d'être tout ce que l'on n'est pas et de n'être jamais tout à fait ce qu'on est." *Ibid.*, p. 400.

75. "L'étonnante aventure de la chair." *Situations,* 3: 308.

of the viewer's eyes across the drawing in order to create the unity Sartre so earnestly desires. In discussing other drawings of the series for which he is writing the preface, Sartre again stresses the rapid movement of the eye across the surface of the drawing that this uncertainty imposes on the viewer. The appeal of the search for meaning in the labyrinth of the painting's surface returns us to the Sartrian requirement for the viewer to bring the work of art to life. Forced by this created ambiguity,

> it is our eyes that bring about the transubstantiation, haunting flesh with the memory of marble, marble with the specter of animal warmth. Everywhere expectations are frustrated, disappointed, a deliberate transmutation of sensations: that sex organ explodes, that head breaks out in flowers, that female body frays into fog, the fog bleeds.[76]

In the experience of these drawings, the viewer's inability to discover a place in the picture at which he can rest his eyes brings to mind the phenomenon of the flickering that creates a unity of multiplicity. Like the image in the flames, the suggested metamorphosis created through the use of the human figure implies the phantom-like suspension of the Giacometti paintings.

In the works that do not depend upon Masson's mythology of metamorphosis in the suggested ambivalence of the mineral or vegetal substance as human figure, Sartre discovers the artist's tenacity in his search for a means to overcome the limitations of contour. What has been rejected by Sartre in the work of all of the painters on whom he has written is weight, substantiality, and volume. The dematerializing of the individual by Giacometti is also evident in *André Masson par lui-même* (*Torrential Self-Portrait*) (Pl. 30). Sartre sees in this drawing a solution to the problem of volume created through line and contour. The spatial ambiguity, the frenetic movement, and the explosive quality are reflected in Masson's self-portrait.

> Sometimes he works the interior of the body with broad strokes; at the same time he reduces to a minimum the line that forms the outer edge: the accent is placed on the substance; furrows, striae, fissures appear as internal move-

76. "C'est notre œil qui opère la transsubstantiation, c'est lui qui fait hanter la chair par le souvenir du marbre, le marbre par un fantôme de chaleur animale. Partout des attentes contrariées, déçues, une transmutation délibérée des sensations: ce sexe explose, cette tête éclate en fleurs, ce corps féminin s'effiloche en brouillard et ce brouillard saigne." *Situations,* 4: 403.

ments of the flesh while the tracing that delimits, dead, inert, loose, seems a provisional limitation of its expansion. [77]

The hard ceramic quality created by "retractile" painters to contain merits and rights is destroyed here by the artist, who represents the fleshly limits of the human physiognomy as a "thin, impotent membrane." [78] In the work of Lapoujade the flesh of the individual bursts from the limits of contour to be spread across the surface of the canvas. Sartre conveniently discovers the same phenomenon in the work of Masson: "After 1948, contour gives way, living substance breaks its shell and is strewn across the picture; nothing any longer stands in the way of Masson's revealing to us his Dionysiac myth in all its purity." [79] Sartre gives no examples of the works in which he finds that this occurs. Nor does he relate this final step to the impact that the light of the American cities had on Masson, who wrote in 1953: "From the object, which has now stopped oppressing me, there comes a tension that grows gradually more luminous and continues in all directions up to the edges of the pictorial surface." [80]

But according to Sartre the development of Masson's style reaches a point at which he may take leave of his preoccupations with a mythology, however personal it may be. Sartre has prepared us for this rejection he sees by insisting that each work that depends on such content leads Masson to the works under discussion, which the painter creates "in order to take his leave of all mythology." [81] For the metamorphosis of tree into man, Sartre describes Masson as substituting the very process of transformation: "Here is what he wants to paint now: neither flight, nor pheasant, nor the flight of a pheasant: a flight that is becoming pheasant; he crosses a field, a flare explodes in the brush, explo-

77. 'Tantôt il laboure l'intérieur des corps à gros traits, en même temps qu'il amenuise à l'extrême la ligne extérieure qui dessine leur forme: l'accent est mis alors sur la substance, les sillons, les stries, les clivages apparaissent comme des mouvements internes de la chair, tandis que la tracé qui la délimite, mort, inerte, délié, semble un arrêt tout provisoire de son expansion." *Ibid.,* pp. 404–05.

78. "Mince membrane impuissante." *Ibid.,* p. 405.

79. "A partir de 1948, le contour cède, la substance vivante brise ses coquilles et se répand à travers le tableau; rien ne s'oppose plus à ce que Masson nous révèle dans sa pureté son mythe dionysiaque." *Ibid.,* pp. 405–06.

80. Quoted by Werner Haftmann in his *Painting in the Twentieth Century,* 1: 276.

81. "Pour prendre congé de toute mythologie." *Situations,* 4: 389.

sion-pheasant: there is his picture." [82] Sartre encourages in painting the same ambiguity found in Hare's statue, described as "a
horror which 'gorillas,'" [83] and in the canvases of Masson he
delights in suggesting that this ambivalence prepares yet another
step in future works. The indetermination and the whirlwind
effect burst the limits of contour as Sartre once again selects
elements of an artist's painting that may be characterized as a
style of *becoming*.

WOLS

The most recent of Sartre's writings on painting, "Doigts et
non-doigts" ("Fingers and Non-fingers"), was published in
Wols's *En personne*.[84] Otto Wolfgang Schülze, better known as
Wols, represents painting in its encounter with existentialism.
Even before the publication of Sartre's essay, his work had been
referred to as "une peinture existentielle." [85] In Wols's contact
with the ideas of Sartre, Pierre Restany asserts that the painter
finds "an additional justification of his refusal of contingency, a
lucid analysis of the reign of Being-in-itself, the existential
projection of being in the cosmos." [86] As an artist in exile from
the oppressive atmosphere of Nazi Germany, Wols's existence
before his death was one of wandering and flight. In poverty and
alcoholism during his last years in Paris, he found a friend in
Sartre, who helped him to the point of renting a room for him in
the Hôtel des Saints-Pères.[87] So it seems natural that Sartre and
another of the artist's friends, Henri-Pierre Roché, wrote brief
essays to join the more complete and more traditional study of
the work done by Werner Haftmann for this volume of Wols's
aphorisms, drawings, and watercolors.

The idea of the self-destruction of the artist in the accomplishment of his art touched upon by Sartre in writing of Gauguin in

82. "Voilà ce que Masson veut peindre à présent: ni l'envol, ni le
faisan, ni l'envol du faisan: un envol qui devient faisan; il passe dans
le champ, une fusée éclate dans les buissons, éclate-faisan: voilà son
tableau." *Ibid.*, p. 406.
83. 'Une horreur qui gorille." "Sculptures à 'n' dimensions," p. 2.
84. Reprinted in *Situations*, 4: 408–34.
85. Restany, "Peinture existentielle: Wols," p. 55.
86. "Une justification supplémentaire de son refus de la contin-
gence, une analyse lucide du règne de l'en-soi, la projection existentielle de l'être dans le cosmos." *Ibid.*
87. De Beauvoir, *Force des choses*, p. 256.

L'Age de raison reappears in this work. The gradual transformation of the artist's body, as revealed in the Gauguin self-portraits,
suggesting the sacrifice of the artist's flesh for his art, is echoed in
Sartre's conception of the life and death of Wols. The artist's
death by accidental food poisoning plays little part in Sartre's
interpretation of his gradual self-destruction in alcoholism. Like
the Gauguin of the early self-portrait, the handsome young Wols
is seen as consciously undertaking the same project of transforming his fleshly existence into "a lush, overripe tropical fruit with
pockets full of water." [88] This contrast between the two Gauguin
self-portraits comes to mind when Sartre writes: "He had been
handsome, he no longer was; at thirty-three you would have
taken him for fifty except for the youthful sadness of his eyes." [89]
The theme of the bottle in Wols's work is to Sartre evidence of
his undertaking: "I now believe that he had thrown himself into
a short-term adventure, just one: to kill himself, convinced that
one cannot express anything without destroying oneself." [90] Two
of Wols's early self-portraits, *La Pagode* (*Pagoda*) and *Le Pan-
tin* (*The Puppet*), underline Sartre's feeling of experiencing
Rimbaud's famous "Je est un autre" ("I is an other"). The
torment of an individual who willingly submits himself to the
machinations of the universe in order to record his experience of
them in his art is related to the activities of the lowly termites.
Wols himself provides Sartre with the basis for this interpretation in his fascination with Maeterlinck's description of the
termites' existence. The artist's own "Aphorismes," which accom-
pany him wherever he goes, reveal his interest in their endless
burrowing and the resultant structures: "The butterfly contents
himself with being beautiful for a day. / The style of termitaries
is pure and gigantic." [91] The image of the ugliness of the flesh
of the late self-portrait of Gauguin is echoed in the art of Wols,
whose self-immolation leaves the residue that forms the very
material of the painting.

88. "Un fruit gras et mou des tropiques avec des poches pleines
d'eau." *L'Age de raison*, p. 78.

89. "Il avait été beau, il ne l'était plus: à trente-trois ans on lui en
eût donné cinquante sans la jeune tristesse de son regard." *Situations*,
4: 408.

90. "Je crois à présent qu'il s'était lancé dans une entreprise à court
terme, une seule: se tuer, convaincu que l'on n'exprime rien sans se
détruire." *Ibid.*

91. "Le papillon se contente d'être beau pour un jour. Le style des
termitières est pur et gigantesque." *En personne*, p. 51.

Others in any case—that's their lot—will substitute substance for the "otherness" of the finite mode. Wols, a superb termite, constructed palaces with his own excretions, as a matter of course. The creature dreamed of his own decomposition with his product, in such a way that nothing would remain except the original purity of their elements. His gouaches bear witness to it; they are beautiful. But it is impossible to decide whether beauty is a promise or the most frightful dream of the termitary.[92]

The idea of the presence of the artist's *being* in the painting derives from Sartre's growing interest in the experimenter-experiment relation. This idea first appears in his writings on art in "Sculptures à 'n' dimensions" of 1947, when he applies the scientist's idea of participation in the observation of the phenomenon: "Scholars today say that the experimenter is a part of the experimental system. Hare could say that the sculptor is a part of the sculptural whole." [93] Once again in the work of Lapoujade and Masson, this relation between the artist and the work is incarnated on the canvas. Now in writing of Wols Sartre categorically expresses the idea hesitantly proposed in reference to Hare's sculpture: "He [Wols] understood that the experimenter is of necessity a part of the experiment and the painter of his picture." [94] Sartre's long-standing insistence on the artist's *being* as it is revealed in the style of the work—most dramatically illustrated in the attack on "Maudrian" and the Americans who refuse any trace of the artist's *existence* become *being*—is obvious in his opposition to the "style léché." In the works of Tintoretto the brush stroke reveals the artist's involvement in his creation and hence his presence in the work of art. Sartre's predilection for placing artists and styles in opposition to order to clarify his own point of view, as he had done with Tintoretto and Titian,

92. "Autres de toute façon—c'est leur lot—ils substitueront à l'être-autre du mode fini celui de la substance. Wols, termite superbe, construisait avec sa fiente des palais, par ordre. La bête rêvait de se décomposer, avec son produit, et qu'il ne restât plus rien d'eux sinon la pureté originelle de leurs éléments. Ses gouaches en témoignent: elles font peur, elles sont belles. Mais l'on ne peut décider si la beauté est une promesse ou le rêve le plus affreux de la termitière." *Situations,* 4: 412–13.

93. "Les savants disent aujourd'hui que l'expérimentateur fait partie du système expérimental. Hare pourrait dire, lui, que le sculpteur fait partie du tout ensemble sculptural." P. 2.

94. "Il [Wols] a compris que l'expérimentateur fait nécessairement partie de l'expérience et le peintre du tableau." *Situations,* 4: 415.

and Tintoretto and Carpaccio, occurs again in the comparison he makes between Wols and Klee. In Sartre's discussion of the relationship between the artist, the world, and the act of painting, Klee confirms the experimenter-experiment concept that Sartre has put forward more and more vigorously. Sartre draws upon Klee's theoretical writings, *Das bildnerische Denken* (*The Thinking Eye*), as a basis for the development of the artist-art object discussion in his essay on Wols. Three articles of Klee [95] contained in this volume provide the basis for describing the art object as uniting the self (the artist) and the other (the object), and revealing their relation to one another and to the cosmos. From these articles Sartre arrives at his own statement on the artist and the world as it is seen in the work of art:

> The painter and his sitter together belong to a totality which rules their relationships and, moreover, is wholly incarnated in each of them. The object is revealed in its functional relation with the world and, at the same time, reveals the artist in his physiological relation with the invisible whole. The seer is the thing seen, clairvoyance is rooted in visibility. Inversely, the artist gives what he does not have, his being; this fretwork of shadows, once projected, is returned to him by the lattice of the plastic object. [96]

But if both Wols and Klee are examples of the artist whose painting gives an image of the world and of the painter, they are separated by the very lives they lived. Like Titian and Tintoretto they stand at opposite poles, because their attitudes toward the world and their experience in the world show Klee to be linked with the divine and the angelic, Wols with the terrestial: "Klee is an angel, Wols a 'poor devil.' One creates, or re-creates, the wonders of this world, the other puts to the test its wondrous

95. "Die Dinge in der Natur, auf ihr Inneres untersucht: Wesen und Erscheinung," "Wege des Naturstudiums," "Exakte versuche im Bereiche der Kunst," in *Das bildnerische Denken*, pp. 59–62, 63–67, and 69–71.

96. "Le peintre et son modèle appartiennent également à la totalité qui règle leurs rapports véritables et, d'autre part, s'incarne tout en chacun d'eux. L'objet se dévoile dans son rapport fonctionnel avec le monde, et du même coup, dévoile l'artiste dans sa relation physiologique avec l'invisible ensemble. Le Voyant est chose vue, la Voyance s'enracine dans la visibilité. Inversement, l'artiste donne ce qu'il n'a pas, son être; cette dentelle des ténèbres, sitôt projetée, lui est retournée par les nervures de l'objet plastique." *Situations*, 4: 414.

horror." [97] Rouault, Gris, Cézanne, and Klee relate their artistic activity to a world made in the image of divine creation. Like Titian they depend on the divinity to guarantee their vision. In this stance Wols finds himself separated from the group whose inspiration Sartre refers to as "retractile." [98] "The whole difference is there; freed from any catechism, Klee nonetheless retains a Christian, Faustian view of the world: 'In the beginning was the Word.' " [99] Wols and Tintoretto before him do not depend upon the infinite but reject the ambiguity of the unifying hierarchy depicted in *The Assumption of the Virgin* (Pl. 25). Sartre sees Wols as experiencing the world in another fashion. His project is not to create an ordered world supported by the guarantee of the divine. Sartre's painters are in the world, within the crowd, among the Rialtans: "For Klee the world is inexhaustibly to be created; for Wols it is created with Wols in it." [100] Wols is yet another of Sartre's unprivileged painters who paints his experience of "the universal horror of being-in-the-world." [101]

Klee's tenuous link with the world is seen by Sartre to be a desire to free himself from the weight which is imposed upon him by the earth. The human condition from which the American, Ritchie, would hide himself in art permits Sartre to call him pejoratively a cherubim or seraphim. Klee's own desire to free himself from mud and earth, "the aspiration of freeing ourselves from the terrestrial ties in order to attain, beyond swimming and flight, total mobility," [102] is quoted by Sartre to illustrate his relation with the angelic or celestial. The weight of the earth and the roots that Sartre emphasizes in the works of Wols show the artist's use of the nonphotographic as the young painter has learned it from his "maître angélique." Klee has shown Wols the way to avoid the realistic, but the pupil refuses to escape from the things of this world. These things possessing a fascina-

97. "Klee, c'est un ange et Wols un pauvre diable. L'un crée ou recrée les merveilles de ce monde, l'autre en éprouve la merveilleuse horreur." *Ibid.*, p. 413.

98. "Expansive" and "retractile" referred to in the essay on Masson were first applied by Sartre to modern poetry in his *Saint Genet*, pp. 429–30.

99. "Toute la différence est là; dégagé de tous les catéchismes, Klee n'en conserve pas moins une vision chrétienne et faustienne de l'univers: 'Im Anfang war der Tat.' " *Situations*, 4: 418.

100. "Pour Klee, le monde est à faire intarissablement; pour Wols, il est fait avec Wols dedans." *Ibid.*, p. 421.

101. "L'horreur universelle d'être-au-monde." *Ibid.*, p. 422.

102. "L'aspiration à s'affranchir des liens terrestres pour atteindre, par-delà la nage et le vol, à la libre mobilité." *Ibid.*, p. 416.

tion for the painter are revealed in the drawings and gouaches. Like Roquentin, Wols is seen by Sartre as discovering himself in these objects: "They are himself, outside him: to see them is to dream of himself, they hypnotize him." [103] From them Wols learns what Roquentin had learned in Bouville: "the impossible refusal to exist." [104] For Sartre, Wols's work falls into two major periods separated by the early forties. In his experience of objects, Wols is gradually able to release himself from them through the process of transforming them. The evolution that has been seen in Sartre's consideration of the work of Masson follows the initial pattern. Sartre's admiration for an art that becomes more and more ambiguous is repeated as he recounts the process by which men and objects of the everyday world become gradually less and less precise. An excellent example of this first style is to be found in one of the four illustrations Wols did for Sartre's *Visages*. This engraving (Pl. 31) takes as its point of departure parts of the anatomy. From the familiar aristocratic nose of the official portrait of François I, which Sartre discusses in the essay, Wols creates an amorphous biological creature that might well inhabit an aquarium. The official portrait is the basis for the man in the flesh in this dry point. No ceramic quality is imparted to this portrait. The body is stripped bare of accessories of right and merit; the biological existence of the man remains in all of its ambiguity. But in considering the whole of the artist's work, Sartre characterizes this stage of his stylistic development as unsatisfactory because the experience of the work remains on the level of magic. In discussing his other essays on painting, I have noted Sartre's preoccupation with prestidigitation. The term "sorcery" was first used in connection with the Bouville portraits and the statue of Impétraz. Subsequently, Sartre applied the vocabulary of magic in a positive way to the art of Giacometti, Guardi, or Lapoujade, but the sleight of hand of Wols, as the artist uses it to depict the human figure, reveals itself to be as undesirable as the mythologies of Masson. Like Masson's, Wols's technique is seen to arise from the artist's vision of the universe; however, his view of the world as revealed in his work of the late forties takes on an entirely new dimension:

> Before this, he used objects of everyday life to construct traps, to suggest the elusive, and beyond them, as it were,

103. "Ils sont lui-même hors de lui: les voir, c'est se rêver, ils l'hypnotisent." *Ibid.*, p. 421.
104. "L'impossible refus d'exister." *Ibid.*, p. 422.

their inherent contradictions; after 1942 conjured by different means, being appears immediately and suggests these
objects allusively. The procedure reverses itself: being now
is alluded to—the flip side of man; now it is man who is the
flip side of being.[105]

Sartre compares the artistic production of Wols's first stylistic
period with that of Dubuffet in that the two artists treat the
human body as an enigmatic, organic substance and thereby
reveal the diseased nature of existence in the flesh—in this instance a finger. From this portrayal of the body eaten by "the
cancerous presence of All Things," [106] Sartre takes his title for the
essay. He develops the idea in order to contrast the early style
with Wols's later style. Haftmann uses the term "psychic
improvisation" [107] to describe the process of the abstract works of
this period. Sartre prefers to call it automatism. This automatism,
as Sartre explains, "consists in revealing the 'otherness' of the
finger through deliberately painting non-fingers. Non-fingers,
precisely, whose 'otherness' will be fingers, unseen, unnamed,
always present." [108] From a fascination with his vision of the
world of objects, Wols steps to the fantastic revelation of his
own psyche—just as Sartre suggests that Goya moves from
the representation of the atrocities of war to the depicting of "the
naked horror of being Goya." Sartre's early predilection for
the work of Bosch [109] finds another form in his admiration for the
work of a contemporary artist.

Sartre's lyrical praise of Wols's style centers on a gouache that
fills him with uneasiness (Pl. 32). This gouache, *La Grande*

105. "Avant, les objets quotidiens lui servaient à construire ses pièges,
suggérer l'insaisissable, comme au-delà de leurs contradictions; après
1942, convoqué par des moyens différents, l'être paraît d'abord et les
suggère allusivement. Tout se retourne: l'homme, à présent, qui est
l'envers de l'être." *Situations*, 4: 424.

106. "La présence cancéreuse de Tout." *Ibid.,* p. 109.

107. *Painting in the Twentieth Century*, 1: 346.

108. "Consiste à révéler l'être-autre du doigt en peignant délibéré-
ment des non-doigts. Non-doigts dont, précisément, l'être-autre sera le
doigt, jamais vu, jamais nommé, toujours present." *Situations*, 4: 425.

109. "We never tired of losing ourselves in his tormented creatures,
his monsters; he stirred our imaginations to such a degree that we were
unable to worry about the precise quality of his painting." "Nous n'en
avions jamais fini de nous perdre parmi ses suppliciés, ses monstres; il
remuait trop nos imaginations pour que nous nous inquiétions de
l'exacte qualité de sa peinture." *Force de l'âge*, p. 91.

Barrière qui brûle (*The Great Burning Barrier*), summarizes the distance Sartre has come from his experience of the paintings of the Bouville museum to his experience of the nonfigurative painting of Wols's final period. In this gouache the human figure is eliminated. With it goes the ceramic quality imparted to the flesh, the *trompe-l'œil* representation of materials and textures of symbolic objects, and the varnished surface of the canvas. The Renaissance perspective used to establish precise relations within a hierarchy is replaced by indetermination in the disposition of the non-objects in planes. The prestidigitation is of the highest level because it deals with the very nature of the enigmatic substance of things rather than the sorcery of divine right. The elements of the gouache place the viewer in an attitude of total uncertainty as the work reveals itself to be truly in the process of *becoming*. Sartre describes the work as being in the process of both composition and decomposition, in which the totality of the animal, vegetable, and mineral world is revealed to him as "transsubstantiation permanente." Sartre has moved from an image in the flames to the fixed unity of an image of *becoming* which is the work of art itself. His experience is that of a presence of unity in its multiplicity: "This unity escapes me if I seek to discover it, but the detail forces me to return to it unceasingly; through its fixed, incessant metamorphosis, it reveals itself as an 'integral part' of the totality, omnipresent in its presence, which is the Thing itself." [110]

In *La Grande Barrière qui brûle,* Sartre sees a perfect example of the work of art as something which does not *exist* but *is*. Confronted with this work, Sartre experiences himself and not the fixity and stability of the other as in the case of the official portrait. The work is read as a projection into the future because it embodies the qualities of the whirlwind and the explosive that are permanently suspended in the art object. Wols has made the final break with the human figure and with the temptation of the translation of the pictorial into language. Sartre not only emphasizes that the artist usually refuses to give his works titles but also that the component elements of his world refuse to be fixed by a verbal mask: "The superiority of Wols is that Things, in his

110. "Cette unité m'échappe si je la cherche, mais le détail m'y renvoie sans cesse; par sa métamorphose figée, incessante, il se révèle comme 'partie intégrante' d'une totalité, omniprésente dans son absence, qui est la Chose elle-même." *Situations,* 4: 431.

gouaches, are unnamable. This means that they are not within the realm of language and that the art of painting has been liberated from that of literature." [111] Nothing remains but the formal elements of the work of art itself, but for Sartre this organization of the picture represents alienation and anguish in plastic form. In this work he sees an example of "anguish become thing" which he has consistently sought and which he had found earlier in the work of Tintoretto. Wols has rid himself of the storytelling criticized in *La Nausée* and has succeeded in creating an object of beauty, but this beauty is linked to the suffering and anguish of the works of Grünewald (Pl. 23) and of the Avignon *Pietà* (Pl. 22). There is no betrayal of anguish and suffering in this work because there is no distraction of the beauty of the body condemned by Sartre in the battle scenes of classical painting. *La Grande Barrière qui brûle*—and by extension all those works of Wols's later style—uses beauty to create "the verisimilitude of horror." The painter succeeds in creating an object in which "the rigorous integration of forms and the marvelous tenderness of colors have the function of disclosing our damnation." [112]

In each of these essays on painting, Sartre creates his own version of the artist and his project and moves toward a concept of painting that suits his own attitudes toward the human condition. His rejection of the measurable elements of line and contour as they are used to create a hierarchical version of the world guaranteed by the reassuring glance of a creator results in painting which itself contains a myth. But this myth is one of *becoming* and not of *being*. In Sartre's own stylistic preferences, uncertainty, ambivalence, and imprecision depict the continuous process of the individual as he seeks to define himself. For Sartre, painting that defines man limits man. In his essay on Masson he quotes from Spinoza in relation to the artist's project: "'All determination,' said Spinoza, 'is negation.' It is this negation that Masson attempts to repudiate." [113] The same might be applied to Sartre, who seeks painting that defines by negating the definition.

111. "La supériorité de Wols, c'est que les Choses, dans ses gouaches, sont innommables: cela veut dire qu'elles ne sont pas de la compétence du langage et que l'art de peindre s'est entièrement dégagé de la littérature." *Ibid.,* p. 433.

112. "L'intégration rigoureuse des formes et leurs merveilleuses couleurs tendres ont pour office de manifester notre damnation." *Ibid.,* p. 434.

113. "'Toute détermination,' disait Spinoza, 'est négation.' C'est cette négation que Masson tente de nier." *Ibid.,* p. 404.

For him those painters on whom he has written succeed in varying degrees in creating an image of man whose existence is characterized by a bursting vitality in his projection towards the future, but an image in which Sartre repeatedly discovers the anguish of his *becoming*.

7

Poetry and Poets

SARTRE'S best known expressions of his attitudes concerning poetry are in *Qu'est-ce que la littérature?* (*What Is Literature?*). His definition of poetry in opposition to prose is discussed in the first chapter of this study. The distinction he makes between the poet's use of language and that of the prose writer serves his desire to commit literature. However, this important manifesto is not the only source that should be considered for his ideas on poetry and poets. His interest in the creative activity of Ponge, Senghor, Baudelaire, Genet, and Mallarmé is an extension of his own youthful attempts at poetry, which he describes in *Les Mots* (*Words*),[1] and to which Simone de Beauvoir refers in *La Force de l'âge*.[2] These studies are related to the characters he has created in his short stories and novels. Lucien Fleurier in "L'Enfance d'un chef" ("Childhood of a Leader") and Philippe Grésigne in *Les Chemins de la liberté* are represented as young men whose poetic projects are ways by which they attempt to give form and meaning to their *existence*. The attempts of these characters to apply the myths of Baudelaire, Rimbaud, or Mallarmé to their own lives are portrayed by Sartre as fictional examples of the quest for *being*. The work of art, as has been seen, represents the possibility of eternal hardness for the man of flesh. The ironic comment of the self-taught man in *La Nausée* who imagines that Roquentin is endeavoring to eliminate the alexandrines from his prose[3] is intimately connected with the project of justification of the protagonist—particularly when the failure of this aesthetic enterprise becomes clear to the reader. Sartre's interpretations of the works of Ponge, Baudelaire, Genet,

1. P. 116.
2. P. 49.
3. P. 45.

and Mallarmé continue the exploration of the inevitable failure which he believes characterizes the writing of poetry. He repeatedly emphasizes in their poetic endeavors the same preoccupation with the transformation of gratuitous flesh into the hardness of sculpture. These studies reveal not only a negative attitude towards this project of *being* but a clear preference for a style of poetry that parallels the representations of man he has praised in his writings on sculpture and painting.

FRANCIS PONGE

The petrification to which Sartre returns in his consideration of the work of Francis Ponge is initially subordinated to his praise for the style of the poems of *Le Parti pris des choses.* "L'Homme et les choses" ("Man and Things"),[4] Sartre's first essay written on a volume of poetry, reveals the extent to which he relates the created poem to painting. Parallels are drawn between Ponge and painters such as Juan Gris, Georges Braque, Salvador Dali, and Fra Angelico that foreshadow in a remarkable way the treatment of painting and sculpture in his subsequent essays. Drawn to those artists who use the materials with which they work in order to free themselves from *trompe-l'œil* reality, Sartre discovers in Ponge a poet who uses language to render the qualities of ambiguity and discontinuity. The flickering, dynamic movement of his preferred painters is found in the poetic technique of Ponge, but the poet is criticized for permitting this tendency to be dominated by the solidification that Sartre abhors.

For Sartre, description of the external world is not the province of the artist. In this essay on Ponge he deems absurd the advice supposedly given by Flaubert to Maupassant; to sit before a tree and describe it results in the circumscription of the object without revealing the complexities of its nature. This is the same point Sartre makes by the contrast which he draws between Canaletto and Guardi. Ponge belongs to that group who struggle against the use of the mind to define an object in the world by reproducing it photographically or by mapping its exterior. The negation that characterizes definition is for Sartre the result of the application of language as a social phenomenon.

4. This essay, first published as "A propos du *Parti pris des choses*" in *Poésie,* no. 20 (Jul.–Oct. 1944): 58–77, and no. 21 (Nov.–Dec. 1944): 74–92, was reprinted as *L'Homme et les choses* and in *Situations,* 1: 245–97. Quotations will be from the latter.

Unlike Flaubert, Ponge uses words in order to look at things "with the same eye that Rimbaud cast on 'idiotic paintings,' to seize them at the very moment when man's creations warp and buckle, escaping from men by the secret chemistry of their meanings." [5] The word as thing in all of its materiality is the basis for the construction of the poem-object. The unity on which Sartre insists results from the elimination of the rational links of everyday language. The breakdown of the artificial wholeness of the intellectual image is applied to an anthropomorphic example in the work of Ponge. The head of a gymnast becomes "an interrogative movement at the tip end of an annelid." [6] Through the poetic metaphor, the intellectual wholeness of the body is stripped of its fixed image. The application of the wriggling movement of a worm to the representation of the gymnast's head results in a feeling of unity which the process of accumulation of an Arcimboldo or Ingres cannot create. Comparing Ponge to Virginia Woolf and Colette, who, like Canaletto, excel in external appearances, Sartre finds Ponge to be more appealing because "he speaks of a cigarette without saying a word about the white paper in which it is rolled, of the butterfly almost without mentioning the pattern which mottles its wings: he does not concern himself with *attributes* but with the thing." [7] His poetic process is the rejection of mere description. The building up of the poem by the process of almost imperceptible agglutination stands opposed to the naming of the individual parts of the body. Sartre might well be referring to a Giacometti figure when he speaks of Ponge's refusal simply to reproduce individual elements to represent the component parts of the body: "And the poem, precisely because of the profound unity of the words in it, because of its synthetical structure and the agglutination of all of its parts, will not be a simple copy of the thing but thing itself." [8] Ponge makes

5. "Avec les yeux que Rimbaud tournait vers les 'peintures idiotes,' les saisir au moment même où les créations de l'homme se gauchissent, se gondolent, échappent à l'homme par les secrètes chimies de leurs significations." *Situations*, 1: 252.

6. "Un mouvement interrogateur au sommet d'un annélide." *Ibid.*, p. 255.

7. "Il parle de la cigarette sans dire un mot du papier blanc qui l'entoure, du papillon sans presque mentionner les dessins qui jaspent ses ailes: il ne soucie pas des *qualités* mais de l'être." *Ibid.*, p. 263.

8. "Et le poème, précisément à cause de l'unité profonde des mots en lui, à cause de sa structure synthétique et de l'agglutinement de toutes ses parties, ne sera pas simple copie de la chose mais chose lui-même." *Ibid.*, p. 265.

an object. He does not imitate nature. Sartre relates this activity
to what he calls "this trend shared by literature and painting in
the twentieth century which wants a painting, for example,
instead of being a translation of nature, however free, to have a
nature of its own." [9]

These objects created by Ponge are seen to be worthy of praise
because they are multifaceted. The term "layers of emptiness" is
here applied for the first time by Sartre to describe the shifting
movement of the eye of the viewer over the art object as a whole
without fragmenting it. Concerning the construction of a poem,
he explains that "you don't go from one facet to another, instead
you must inscribe in the whole construction a rotatory movement
that brings the new facet before our eyes." [10] The organic unity
of the poem is described as phantom-like because of the effect of
a frenetic discontinuity forcing the eye, and not the mind, to
create the whole. Sartre's admiration for this stylistic effect,
expressed in this essay on poems and throughout his writings on
art, undoubtedly has its source in his experience of the paintings
of the Cubists, whose style is related to the flickering images seen
in the fire he discusses in L'Imaginaire. He relates this marvelous
spasmodic effect to the painting of the first quarter of this
century:

> It constitutes perhaps the most immediate charm, and the
> most difficult to explain, of the works of Ponge. His sen-
> tences appear to me, in their relation to one another, to be
> like those solids seen in the paintings of Braque and Juan
> Gris, between which the eye must establish a hundred
> different unities, a thousand relationships and correspond-
> ences, in order to finally compose with them *one* painting.
> These solids are surrounded by lines so thick and somber, so
> profoundly centered on themselves, that the eye is perpet-
> ually shifting from continuity to discontinuity in an attempt
> to fuse the various patches of the same violet, but each time
> stumbling against the impenetrability of the mandolin and
> the water jug. [11]

9. "Cette tendance commune à la littérature et à la peinture du XX°
siècle et qui veut qu'un tableau, par exemple, plutôt qu'une traduction,
même libre, de la nature, soit une nature à lui tout seul." *Ibid.*, p. 266.
10. "On ne passe pas d'une facette à l'autre, mais, plutôt, il faut
imprimer à la construction entière un mouvement de rotation qui
amène une facette nouvelle sous notre regard." *Ibid.*, p. 270.
11. "Il constitue peut-être le charme le plus immédiat et le plus
difficilement explicable des œuvres de Ponge. Il me semble que ses

This dynamic effect achieved in the poem as object, for Sartre "a bewitched statue," causes him to remark that in these poems, "we are dealing with marble haunted with life." [12] As in the works of David Hare, what is revealed in Ponge's poems is "the inner substance of the object at the precise point at which it determines itself." [13] Sartre's praise for Ponge is centered on the poet's proclaiming the continuous decomposition and recomposition of things through recourse to the transmutations of animal, mineral, and vegetable elements. The anthropomorphic transforms the very qualities of objects, and man is in turn transformed by vegetable and animal attributes as in the example of the gymnast. This process, for Sartre the veritable domain of the poet and the painter, is reinforced by his explanation that it was precisely this metamorphosis that Proust created as the stylistic accomplishment of his fictional painter, Elstir.

For Sartre, Ponge's tendencies in his poetic imagination towards those metamorphoses in which earth becomes water are subordinated to his need for expressions of density. Despite the qualities of Ponge's style in which Sartre takes such delight, "this perpetual flickering from interiority to exteriority which constitutes the originality and power of the poems of Ponge," [14] Sartre reluctantly reveals the dominance of solids in the poet's sensitivity. The poetic act of Ponge ends in the same petrification that Sartre discovers in the work of all artists and poets: "Everything that comes from his hands is *thing,* including and above all his poems." [15] Sartre's conception of the creative act is that of the creation of *being.* Almost as if to reinforce this opinion he finds the mineralization of the metamorphic style of Ponge in his

---

phrases sont entre elles à l'image de ces solides qu'on voit dans les tableaux de Braque et de Juan Gris, entre lesquels l'œil doit établir cent unités différentes, mille relations et correspondances, pour composer enfin avec eux *un seul* tableau, mais qui sont cernés de lignes si épaisses et si sombres, si profondément centrés sur eux-mêmes que l'œil est perpétuellement renvoyé du continu au discontinu, tentant de réaliser la fusion de différentes taches du même violet et butant à chaque coup sur l'impénétrabilité de la mandoline et du pot à eau." *Ibid.,* p. 274.

12. "Nous avons affaire à des marbres hantés par la vie." *Ibid.,* p. 275.

13. "La substance interne de l'objet, au point précis où elle se détermine elle-même." *Ibid.,* p. 276.

14. "C'est ce papillottement perpétuel de l'intériorité à l'exteriorité qui fait l'originalité et la puissance des poèmes de Ponge." *Ibid.,* p. 286.

15. "Tout ce qui sort de ses mains est *chose,* y compris et surtout ses poèmes." *Ibid.,* p. 287.

creation of a poetic residue.[16] By the writing of the poem, Ponge is seen already to feel the look of Medusa: "He is transformed into statue; everything is finished; he is of the nature of pebble and rock, the stupefaction of stone paralyzes his arms and legs." [17] Attracted and repelled by the project of the poet as it is revealed in the work before him, Sartre, like Roquentin, is forced to see the inevitable failure of the artistic enterprise: "Ponge's endeavor is doomed to failure like all others of its kind." [18]

BAUDELAIRE

The paradox he finds in the work of Ponge is discovered to a lesser degree in the poetic style of Baudelaire. In the preface he writes for Baudelaire's *Ecrits intimes*,[19] Sartre examines this desire for fixity in the poet's life and works. This essay has provoked a good deal of critical commentary and cries of betrayal of Baudelaire from many quarters.[20] It is of interest in the context of Sartre's own obsession with the concept of the artist's attempt to substitute the finality of a statue carved in stone for his *existence*. The mythification of the poet as the result of his own efforts to be seen by others in his chosen stance is derived by Sartre not only from the private revelations of Baudelaire but from a sensitive reading of his poetry. If the result of this existential psychoanalysis is criticized for its negative judgment of the poet,

16. In his article on Ponge in his *Onze Etudes sur la poésie moderne*, pp. 161–81, Jean-Pierre Richard praises Sartre for his study of Ponge because of his appreciation of the formal discontinuity discussed above. B. Margaret Douthat, in her *"Le Parti pris des choses?"* finds Ponge to be a "poète existentialiste," and suggests that "sa conception du monde, son esthétique, sa morale le rapprochent nettement de Sartre— beaucoup plus, à [son] avis que Sartre ne le croit." "His conception of the world, his aesthetic, his ethics clearly place him beside Sartre—to a much greater extent, in her opinion, than Sartre believes." P. 51.

17. "Il se transforme en statue; tout est fini, il est de la nature du roc et du galet, la stupéfaction de la pierre paralyse ses bras et ses jambes." *Situations,* 1: 287.

18. "La tentative de Ponge est vouée à l'échec comme toutes les autres de même espèce." *Ibid.,* p. 289.

19. Sartre's preface for this work was reprinted as *Baudelaire* by Gallimard in 1947. Quotations will refer to the 1947 version.

20. Anglès, "Sartre versus Baudelaire"; Bataille, "Baudelaire 'mis à nu': l'analyse de Sartre et l'essence de la poésie"; Blin, "Jean-Paul Sartre et Baudelaire"; Chacal, "Baudelaire y el *Baudelaire* de Sartre"; Jourdain, "Sartre devant Baudelaire"; Lupo, "Un Affronto a Baudelaire"; Salel, "A propos de *Baudelaire* de Jean-Paul Sartre."

it is because of Sartre's own rejection of this dream of stone as I have discussed it in interpreting *La Nausée, Huis clos,* and *Les Chemins de la liberté.* Like Ponge, Baudelaire represents the failure of the artist to justify his own *existence* through his creative endeavors, except, as Roquentin discovered, "in the past, only in the past." It is in the context of Sartre's own ideas on art and the artist that this attack on Baudelaire is most revealing.

His reading of the poetry of Baudelaire traces those elements of the poet's work that affirm the attraction of *being.* The statue in stone that first appears in Roquentin's search for justification enlightens us as to Sartre's explanation of the artist's attempt at self-portraiture. For Sartre, Baudelaire's attempt to reconcile *being* and *existence* is seen as his desire to be his own sculpture: "His dearest wish is to *be* like a stone, a statue, in the peaceful repose of immutability." [21] This desire attributed to Baudelaire is clearly explained in terms of the *being* of a work of art in contrast with the *being* of an object. Sartre carefully distinguishes between the two in the poet's yearning for the permanence of a sculptural object.

> This man tried all his life, through pride and rancor, to *turn himself into a thing* in the eyes of other people and in his own. He wanted to stand aloof from the great social fête like a statue, like something definitive, opaque, inassimilable. In a word, we can say that he wanted to *be*—and by that we mean the obstinate, rigorously defined mode of being of an object. But for Baudelaire this being, which he wanted to force others to observe and to enjoy himself, would have been intolerable if it had had the passiveness and unconsciousness of a utensil. He certainly wants to be an object, but not an object created by pure chance.[22]

This distinction, with its emphasis on the role to be played by the poet-artist, seizes upon the elements in Baudelaire's life and

21. "Son souhait le plus cher est d'être, comme la pierre, la statue, dans le repos tranquille de l'immuabilité." *Baudelaire,* p. 196.

22. "Cet homme a toute sa vie, par orgueil et rancune, tenté de se *faire chose* aux yeux des autres et aux siens propres. Il a souhaité se dresser à l'écart de la grande fête sociale, à la manière d'une statue, définitif, opaque, inassimilable. En un mot, nous dirons qu'il a voulu *être*—et nous entendrons par là le mode de présence têtu et rigoureusement défini d'un objet. Mais cet être qu'il voulait faire constater aux autres et dont il voulait jouir lui-même, Baudelaire n'eût pas toléré qu'il eût la passivité et l'inconscience d'un ustensile. Il veut bien être un objet mais non pas un pur donné de hasard." *Ibid.,* p. 90.

poetry that show him to be consciously painting his own portrait or sculpting his own image in stone. Sartre believes that this project of *being* is one in which Baudelaire continually modifies his created self. "He wants to take himself up, to correct himself as one corrects a painting or a poem. He wants to be his own poem for himself; that is the game he plays." [23] Like Anny in *La Nausée,* Sartre's Baudelaire tries to create, for others, an object of himself that would be at the same time an object he might see.

Sartre bases his interpretation of the poet's life on Baudelaire's choice of perpetual oscillation between *being* and *existence.* This choice, compared repeatedly by Sartre to creating a self-portrait in pigment or in marble, is the necessary foundation on which Sartre rests his consideration of the major themes of Baudelaire's poetry. The poet's attitude towards nature is the first aspect on which Sartre erects his argument for the dominance of petrification in Baudelaire's poetic imagination. The profound antipathy towards trees, plants, insects, and all the creatures of nature that haunts the poet is contrasted with his urge to replace or transform natural elements into sharply defined objects. One amorphous aspect of the landscape, water, is despised by Baudelaire except when it accepts the rigid, geometrical form of the containing walls of the quays of the Seine. This city dweller prefers the handiwork of man. Paving stones and building blocks of marble and granite are used to construct barricades against the formlessness of woods and forests through which streams meander. Water contained in stone basins and the poet protected by his precisely laid out city are used by Sartre to illustrate Baudelaire's preference for art in its struggle with nature. As I have indicated previously, Sartre is delighted to discover his own ideas concerning an artist in the critical essays of others. In this particular case he weights his interpretation of Baudelaire's hatred of the fecundity of nature and his predilection for a mineral world with references to the critical writings of Georges Blin.[24] Baudelaire's attraction towards the stability of the mineral world of the city in which the hard edge of geometric forms opposes the amorphous elements in nature obviously fascinates Sartre, but he rejects it.

This opposition between art and nature is considered to be a source for the poet's cult of the artificial. Cosmetics and clothing, attacked earlier in "Portraits officials," are seen to hide the

23. "Il veut se reprendre, se corriger, comme on corrige un tableau ou un poème; il veut être à lui-même son propre poème et c'est là sa comédie." *Ibid.,* p. 182.

24. *Baudelaire* (Paris: Gallimard, 1939).

nakedness of the body and to provide the edge and contour the flesh lacks. Sartre takes Baudelaire to task for his preference for the clothed or partially clothed over the revealing frankness of the naked. This inability to confront the body as flesh is coupled with the frigidity that Sartre discovers as a dominant attitude in the poetry: gems, metal, jewelry, mirrors, and the moon are inextricably woven into this interpretation. Artificial objects serve the poet in his desire to *be,* because they are seen to lend an image of sterile hardness to the poet who would be his poem. Sartre relates the desire to be an object to the mirror-moon imagery and to the poet's relations with women, in particular his relationship with Madame Sabatier. Baudelaire, in choosing an apparently unattainable partner, places the woman on a pedestal, turned to stone. "In this way he is able to enjoy his idol as he wishes, love it in secret, and be overwhelmed by its disdainful indifference. No sooner does she give herself than he departs. She no longer interests him. He can't play his game any longer. The statue has come to life, the cold woman grows warm." [25] Baudelaire, for Sartre, is a reverse Pygmalion who prefers his look to be that of Medusa.

This gorgonizing eye is required in his narcissism as well. In the icy sterility of the mirror Baudelaire seeks a reconciliation between *existence* and *being.* His dandyism is considered to be the means by which he attempts to catch some degree of permanency by seizing his own reflection, "to be his own object, to deck himself in all his finery, to paint himself like a reliquary in order to be able to possess the object, to be absorbed in contemplation of it, and, finally, to melt into it." [26] In *Les Chemins de la liberté* both Ivich and Daniel suffer from this same disease. Sartre also forces Baudelaire the dandy into the mold of the outsider who is required to use his image to find a place in the hierarchy of nineteenth-century society, but repeatedly the poet is unable to find a niche in a society of the living. In his pose as Narcissus, Baudelaire stares into the mirror of the dead and attempts to integrate himself into the portrait gallery of poets and artists of

25. "Ainsi peut-il jouir tout à son aise de son idole, l'aimer en secret, être comblé par son indifférence dédaigneuse. A peine s'est-elle donnée à lui qu'il s'en va: elle ne l'intéresse plus et il ne peut plus continuer sa comédie. La statue s'est animée, la femme froide se réchauffe." *Baudelaire,* pp. 140–41, n. 1.

26. "Être à soi-même objet, se parer, se peindre comme une châsse, pour pouvoir s'emparer de l'objet, le contempler longuement et s'y fondre." *Ibid.,* p. 156.

the past. Edgar Allan Poe becomes Baudelaire's image reflected in the mirror portrait of death and the past. Sartre's fictional account of young Philippe Grésigne gazing into the eyes of the portrait of a dead child is echoed in his description of Baudelaire's search for consecration and justification by seeing himself as a dead Poe. "Once dead, on the other hand, his portrait is complete in all its distinctness and clarity, and it is quite natural to name him poet and martyr; his existence is a destiny, his misfortunes seem to have been predestined. Then the resemblances acquire their full value; they make Poe into an image of Baudelaire in the past, something like a John the Baptist of this accursed Christ." [27] Death and dandyism standing face to face permit Sartre to borrow an idea from another scholar, Jacques Crépet; the belief that suicide was the supreme sacrament of dandyism is extended by Sartre when he postulates that dandyism was a club whose members sought a permanent suicide.[28] In this, Sartre prepares us for his interpretation of the poetry of Mallarmé whose poems are characterized as miniature suicides.

In Baudelaire's poetry Sartre discovers the paradox of man's duality that haunts the poet.

> I am the wound and the knife, . . .
> The victim and the torturer.[29]

To stand on both sides of the canvas, to be both alive and dead, to be poet and poem, these are the irreconcilable opposites that characterize the impossible undertaking of Baudelaire: "Because he wanted at the same time to be and to exist, because he persistently flees from existence to being and from being to existence, he is nothing but the great gaping mouth of a fresh wound." [30] I have previously referred to the self-inflicted wound

27. "Mort, au contraire, sa figure s'achève et se précise, les noms de poète et de martyr s'appliquent à lui tout naturellement, son existence est un destin, ses malheurs semblent l'effet d'une prédestination. C'est alors que les ressemblances prennent toute leur valeur: elles font de Poë comme une image au passé de Baudelaire, quelque chose comme le Jean-Baptiste de ce Christ maudit." *Ibid.*, p. 165.

28. In Eugène Crépet's *Baudelaire* (Paris: Messein, 1907).

29. "Je suis la plaie et le couteau

. . . .

Et la victime et le bourreau."

From Baudelaire's "L'Héautontimorouménos," *Œuvres complètes*, ed. le Dantec, p. 150.

30. "Parce qu'il a voulu à la fois être et exister, parce qu'il fuit sans relâche l'existence dans l'être et l'être dans l'existence, il n'est qu'une plaie vive aux lèvres largement écartées." *Baudelaire*, p. 91.

in Sartre's work and have demonstrated the relation between Gauguin's brush or palette knife and the razor in Daniel's stance before the mirror contemplating suicide. Self-destruction through the creation of an art object dominates Sartre's consideration of the aesthetic enterprise, a project of *being* in Sartre's own terminology. He again confirms this in his study of Baudelaire by stating categorically that "he is his own witness and his own executioner, the knife that turns in the wound and the chisel that carves the marble." [31] Baudelaire's painful probing of the wound that he is occurs in his poetic endeavors. The knife-pen-chisel participates in the suicidal stance of the poet. Each of the actions and attitudes taken by the poet in his life appears to Sartre as a symbolic equivalent of suicide. These tiny moments of *being* created by his ritual postures are above all in his poems: "Poetic creation, which he preferred to any form of action, is linked for him with the suicide he continually ruminates on." [32] The use of the pen to create his own myth becomes the process through which the poet attempts to achieve in life a rigid form of being for which he would be entirely responsible. "He shapes his feelings as he had shaped his body and its attitudes," [33] but this project of edge and contour resulting in petrification is doomed to failure. Only in death can a man *be*. There is no synthesis of being and existence. The poet cannot carve his being from his own flesh without destroying himself. There is your tomb figure, a dead poet.

Sartre's condemnation of the frantic search for *being* runs throughout his work as novelist, dramatist, and essayist. In his interpretation of Baudelaire's poetry, Sartre expounds upon his concept of the choice that leads to the writing of poetry, and he studies the major themes of the poetry in relation to this fundamental decision.[34] This essay demonstrates to us once again

31. "Il est son témoin et son bourreau, le couteau qui fouille la plaie et le ciseau qui sculpte le marbre." *Ibid.,* p. 216.

32. "Et la création poétique, qu'il a préférée à toutes les espèces de l'action, se rapproche, chez lui, du suicide qu'il ne cesse de ruminer." *Ibid.,* p. 220.

33. "Il met en forme ses sentiments comme il a mis en forme son corps ou ses attitudes." *Ibid.,* p. 221.

34. Perhaps the most sympathetic evaluation of Sartre's interpretation of the life and poetry of Baudelaire is Martin Turnell's foreword to his translation of Sartre's *Baudelaire*. Turnell praises him not only for the work as a whole but also for his treatment of individual themes: "His emphasis on Baudelaire's preoccupation with sterility gives us a fresh appreciation of the function of metal and stone in his poetry." P. 10.

Sartre's unending fascination with and revulsion towards the artist's temptation to overcome temporality and gratuitousness through the creative act. Unlike Ponge, Baudelaire offers to Sartre no example of those qualities of dynamic movement or metamorphosis which oppose the permanence of *being* with the flux and ambiguity of *existence* in the flesh. His evaluation of Baudelaire's life and work is ferociously negative because he finds in *Les Fleurs du mal* a basis for his interpretation of the poet's quest for permanency in a myth of bronze and marble.

French African Poets

In contrast to Baudelaire's work, which provided an image of the artist-poet in search of *being,* the poetry of French Africa, collected in an anthology by Léopold Sédar-Senghor, is held up by Sartre, in his preface,[35] as an example of the orphic vision of the turbulence of *existence.* Baudelaire's poetry belongs to a tradition Sartre describes as a progressive tendency toward the representation of man in terms of the solidity of the mineral world. These African poets derive their power from the use of organic images: "This profound unity of vegetal and sexual symbols is certainly the greatest originality of black poetry, especially in a period in which, as Michel Carrouges has shown, most of the images of white poets tend towards a mineralization of the human." [36] These poems are seen to reverse the direction of a stylistic representation of man in stone by substituting animal or vegetal metamorphosis for mineral. The position of the black African as poet is related to the problem of language—a language learned from French colonials. Prose is inadequate in the African's revolt because the language itself is discovered to contain the values of a culture that exploits the black race. The civilizing of the African is interpreted by Sartre as a substitution of urban fixity for the amorphous vegetal growth of the jungle. The Medusa look of the city dweller gives rise to the poetic attitude of refusal to use language. For Sartre, it is only through the poetic act that

35. "Orphée noir," *Anthologie de la nouvelle poésie,* pp. ix–xliv. Reprinted in *Situations,* 3: 229–86. Quotations will refer to the latter.

36. "Cette unité profonde des symboles végétaux et des symboles sexuels est certainement la plus grande originalité de la poésie noire, surtout à une époque où, comme l'a montré Michel Carrouges, la plupart des images des poètes blancs tendent à la minéralisation de l'humain." *Situations,* 3: 269. Sartre is undoubtedly referring to Carrouges's study *Eluard et Claudel* but, as in the case of the poets, Sartre uses Carrouges to strengthen his own case against mineralization.

the exploited African is able not only to refuse the exploiter's language but to turn his language against him. This truly revolutionary undertaking of the black poet is focused on the concept of negritude. Negative blackness becomes in their poetry a positive representation of their condition in that it frees them from the imposed fixity of the language of the colonial hierarchy. The creation of this negritude is deemed by Sartre to be appropriate for a poet because through this act poetic ambiguity denies prose values. In sculpture, poetry, and painting, subjectivity is praised by Sartre for its lack of definition in prose language. Negritude is not described or copied from an experience in the visible world, but it is created poetically. Indicative of his animosity towards the photographic eye is Sartre's insistence that "Césaire's words do not describe negritude, they do not designate it, they do not copy it from outside as a painter does a model: they make it; they compose it under our eyes; from then on it is a thing which one can observe and from which one can learn." [37] Like the painters and sculptors he prefers, these poets do not imitate or copy but create an object that represents suffering in its total ambiguity.

The Orphic descent into the self results in the creation of the poem-object that fulfills Sartre's aesthetic requirement of the representation of man's *becoming*. The familiar vocabulary used in writing of the art of Ponge, Calder, and Giacometti is applied to the unbearable tension of a vacillating world of movement. Sartre gingerly relates these adjectives of flickering and turbulence to that of Nietzsche's "Dionysian." The Nietzschean antithesis between the "Dionysian" and the "Apollonian" is well suited to Sartre's "esthétique d'opposition" and his categories of *being* and *existence*. Nietzsche himself defines the Apollonian as

> that state of rapt repose in the presence of a visionary world, in the presence of the world of "beautiful appearance" designed as a deliverance from "becoming"; the word "Dionysos," on the other hand, stands for strenuous becoming, grown self-conscious, in the form of the rampant voluptuousness of the creator, who is already perfectly conscious of the violent anger of the destroyer.[38]

37. "Les mots de Césaire ne décrivent pas la négritude, ne la désignent pas, ne la copient pas du dehors comme un peintre fait d'un modèle: ils la font; ils la composent sous nos yeux: désormais c'est une chose qu'on peut observer, apprendre." *Situations,* 3: 260.

38. In his notes concerning *The Birth of Tragedy* published by Elizabeth Förster-Nietzsche as part of her introduction to the philosopher's study of tragedy. Nietzsche, *Complete Works,* ed. Levy, 1: xxv–xxvi.

The static surface of the urban world of the white poet conveys the eternity that dominates the Apollonian. The frenetic movement, sought by Sartre as a means of suggesting the blinding light of the phantom-like African continent as it is consumed in fire, is seen in Nietzschean terms: "It is the rhythm, in fact, that cements together these multiple aspects of the black soul; it is just that which imparts its Nietzschean lightness to their weighty Dionysian insights; it is the rhythms of the tom-tom, of jazz, of the throbbing of these poems that express the temporality of black existence." [39] Negritude is perceived in the rhythmic sequences of their poetry and in the poems' exploding forces of "fixed flickering of being and non-being." [40]

In this essay Sartre lays the groundwork for the two major categories of modern poetic imagination on which he will expound at length in writing of the poetry of Jean Genet. Although he invokes Nietzsche's classifications, he will absorb them in the "retractile" and the "expansive" imaginations as he enlarges his considerations on poetry to include not only the poetic but the artistic imagination in general. The Dionysian of Nietzsche is here related for the first time to André Breton's description of the work of art as "explosante-fixe." However, in this African poetry, the destruction of language through the systematic coupling of opposites in a poetic context is seen to be superior to the same technique that in the hands of the surrealists results in impassivity and impersonality: "Unlike them, a poem of Césaire bursts and becomes a fuse itself, which is like those bursting suns that explode into new suns in an unending chain reaction." [41] Sartre never tires of describing the work of art that fulfills the requirements of fire and light to which he continually returns as a means of expressing his animosity toward the passivity of stone. This African poetry is enthusiastically received by Sartre as the embodiment of poetry, as it represents man in the process of *becoming* and, above all, avoids the mineral world of Baudelaire's poetic act. There is, as well, the implication that the

39. "C'est le rythme, en effet, qui cimente ces multiples aspects de l'âme noire, c'est lui qui communique sa légèreté nietzschéenne à ces lourdes intuitions dionysiaques, c'est le rythme—tam-tam, jazz, bondissement de ces poèmes—qui figure la temporalité de l'existence nègre." *Situations,* 3: 272.
40. "Papillotement figé d'être et de non-être." *Ibid.,* p. 250.
41. "Un poème de Césaire, au contraire, éclate et tourne sur lui-même comme une fusée, des soleils en sortent qui tournent et explosent en nouveaux soleils, c'est un perpétuel dépassement." *Ibid.,* p. 257.

poetic act of these men is not a project of *being* but the means by which they may free their existence from the contamination of definition and *being*.

JEAN GENET

In the second of his studies referred to as existential psychoanalyses, Sartre treats the work of Jean Genet. *Saint Genet, comédien et martyr* is a penetrating examination of the work of this novelist, playwright, and poet, which offers an explanation of the life of the man who produced the novels, plays, and poems. From this encyclopedic treatment of Genet, a relatively small portion deals with Genet as poet, but this material permits Sartre to deal once again with a project of *being* and to root his earlier observations on poetry in these poems. Through his examination of these works he is able to clarify and develop his ideas on the opposing categories of imagination of modern poetry.

The opposition between prose and poetry expressed in *Qu'est-ce que la littérature?* is reiterated in conjunction with Sartre's insistence on Genet's overriding intention to communicate. By examining Genet's long poem, *Le Condamné à mort* (*The Condemned Man*),[42] Sartre renews his theory that poetry arises from a nonverbal rhythmic sequence that has its source in the poet's past. He relates Genet's first line, "The wind which rolls a heart on the stones of the courtyards,"[43] to Valéry's experience, which has been discussed in the first chapter. The poem is born from a haunting refrain that has long obsessed the poet: "Undoubtedly Genet heard it months, perhaps years before, deep within his throat; now he brings it forth from his memory in order to set it in his poem."[44] These obsessive patterns, however, are betrayed by their integration into a whole more prosaic than poetic in conception. In this early poem (1945), Genet's product is described by Sartre as that of an apprentice learning a trade of poetic mystification through recourse to techniques of broken syntax. His crime is substituting a prose meaning for the poetic "sens" felt to be present in the few authentic lines to which Sartre is drawn. The source of this opposition between "sens" and

---

42. Genet, *Œuvres complètes*, 2: 179–86.
43. "Le vent qui roule un cœur sur le pavé des cours." *Ibid.*, p. 179.
44. "Très certainement Genet l'a entendu dans sa gorge des mois auparavant, des années peut-être; il le tire de sa mémoire pour l'enchâsser dans son poème." *Saint Genet*, p. 402.

"signification" is here revealed. It was Breton who objected to
the substitution of the prose meaning—"carafe"—for a poetic
expression—"mamelle de cristal (breast of crystal)"—of Saint-
Pol Roux. Genet's bent for communication in his poem is compared unfavorably with the verses of Cocteau's "Plain Chant":
"The superiority of Cocteau's lines is that they create an object to
be seen. The art of Genet will never have as its aim the creation
of an object to be seen; as we have discovered, his aim is to
annihilate the real, to disintegrate perception." [45] The intuition
discovered in the poem of Cocteau or in the works of other poets
whose verses are compared to those of Genet is refused. Genet
borrows only technique from their works. When Sartre speaks of
the visual aspect of the poem in a positive sense he is again
relating the creation of an object by the painter to his concept of
the poem as thing. This poem-object resulting from the poetic
vision retains the ambivalent qualities of the work of art by the
very fact that communication is not its *raison d'être.* In order to
prove that Genet's poem fails to create this ambiguity and that
the poet intends to communicate, Sartre translates the poem into
prose. When he cannot do this, as in the first verse of *Le
Condamné à mort,* the verse is considered successful by Sartre's
criteria for poetry.

The poetic imagination of the mature Genet is a triumph over
prose but, as in the case of Baudelaire, one to which Sartre is
antagonistic. Enlarging on the categories to which he has linked
the Nietzschean Apollonian and Dionysian, Sartre distinctly separates the unifying factors of modern poetic imagination into
"expansive" and "retractile." The work of Rimbaud represents
for Sartre all the characteristics of the "expansive" imagination
that have been singled out for praise in the writings on painting
and sculpture. The explosive unity that breaks the limiting bonds
of contour in painting or shatters the massive volume of stone in
sculpture is now applied to poetry. The centrifugal force of
Breton's "explosante-fixe," long admired by Sartre, becomes a
key element in his description of this style:

> Plurality, far from being denied, is discovered everywhere;
> it is exaggerated in order to present it as a moment of
> progression, an abstract moment that is congealed into an

45. "La supériorité des vers de Cocteau, c'est qu'ils 'donnent à voir.'
L'art de Genet ne vise pas, ne visera jamais à donner à voir: nous
l'avons vu, ses tentatives magnifiantes ont pour but avoué d'anéantir le
réel, de désintégrer la vision." *Ibid.,* p. 408.

"explosante-fixe" beauty. From impenetrability, that inert resistance of space, and the weighty collapse of the body, a conquering force and a glorious burst of continuity is created; beings become a bursting spray whose dynamic unity is deflagration.[46]

This Dionysian imagery, which Sartre hesitantly terms leftist, "aims at depicting the unity that human labor imposes upon the disparate." [47] The familiar conflict between the hierarchical world of Titian and the dynamic turbulence of Tintoretto is echoed in this establishment of the opposing styles that result from the expansive and retractile imaginations: "If unity is not dynamic, if it manifests itself in the form of limiting contours, it reflects their chains; revolutionaries break the shells of being and the yolk flows everywhere." [48]

Genet, on the other hand, is accused of essentialism in his perversion of the centrifugal movement into a centripetal force. His work becomes a continuation of the stability of the closed form of the classical artist: "Everywhere, his patient insistence on unification performs its constricting influence, lays out its boundaries, and contains everything. His aim is not to show exteriority as an expansive force, but to make of it a nothingness, a shadow, the pure perceptible guise of secret unities." [49] The hierarchical world of Bouville made manifest by its official painters and architects and the frozen Paris of Baudelaire are earlier instances of the work of the artist who transforms the biological existence of man and the amorphous forms of nature into the rigidity of *being*. Now Sartre treats Genet's representation of nature—in

46. "Loin de nier la pluralité, on la découvre partout, on l'exagère mais c'est pour la présenter comme le moment d'une progression: c'est l'instant abstrait qui la fige en une beauté 'explosante-fixe.' De l'impénétrabilité, résistance inerte de l'espace, effondrement cadavérique, on fait une force conquérante, de la divisibilité infinie un éclatement glorieux de l'étendue, les êtres sont des gerbes jaillissantes dont l'unité dynamique est la déflagration." *Ibid.,* p. 430.
47. "Vise à représenter l'unité que le travail humain impose de force au disparate." *Ibid.*
48. "L'unité, si elle n'est pas dynamique, si elle se manifeste sous la forme de contours limitatifs, leur envoie l'image de leurs chaînes; les révolutionnaires brisent les coquilles de l'être, le jaune d'œuf coule partout." *Ibid.*
49. "Partout, sa patiente volonté d'unifier opère des resserrements, des rassemblements, trace des limites, enferme. Le but n'est pas de présenter l'extériorité comme une puissance expansive, mais d'en faire un néant, une ombre, la pure apparence sensible d'unités secrètes." *Ibid.*

this case a flowering branch—as yet another example of the poet's tendency to fix the natural explosive force in a rigid, dead form:

> A flowering branch normally suggests the image of blossoming, of expansion, in brief, centrifugal explosion; poetic movement weds natural movement and proceeds from the tree to the bud, from the bud to the flower. But Genet's image, instead of causing the flowers to burst forth from the branch, draws them back toward it, and glues them against the wood. The direction of the image is from the outside to the inside, from the wings to the center.[50]

This static, closed tendency of the poetic imagery of Genet is related by Sartre to that of the geometrical figure. Genet is at the head of a long and distinguished list of poets and writers who are, according to Sartre, practitioners of essentialism and Platonic idealism. Mallarmé, Valéry, Baudelaire, and Proust in their feminine imaginations are assaulted by the masculine imaginations of Rimbaud, Breton, and Nietzsche—and surely Sartre in his own eyes. It is clear that Sartre is expressing stylistic preferences of long standing, and these opinions culminate in this striking codification of the aesthetic imagination. He is, however, careful to qualify his categorical opposites: "It goes without saying that between Mallarmé and Rimbaud, who represent the epitome of opposing types of imagination, there exists a series of 'mixed,' transitional types." [51] In each case, Sartre illustrates his placing of the poet or writer in a particular camp with an analysis of an image or a passage of prose, but characteristically he chooses an adversary for Genet. For Titian he chose Tintoretto. Genet is pitted against André Breton, but Sartre does not dwell on the work of the Surrealist poet. Instead he attacks Genet through Mallarmé. Sartre's fascination with Mallarmé is evident in the recurrent use of the latter's poetry as parallel examples of the poems of Genet. Sartre repeatedly holds the Mallarméan aes-

50. "Un rameau fleuri suggère normalement l'image d'une éclosion, d'un épanouissement, bref d'un éclatement centrifuge; le mouvement poétique épouse le mouvement naturel et va de l'arbre au bourgeon, du bourgeon à la fleur. Or l'image de Genet, au lieu de 'faire sortir' les fleurs de la branche, les ramène contre elle, les colle au bois; le mouvement de l'image va de l'extérieur à l'intérieur, des ailes à l'axe." *Ibid.*, p. 431.

51. "Il va de soi qu'il existe entre Mallarmé et Rimbaud, les deux types purs et opposés d'imagination, une série de types 'mixtes' qui font la transition." *Ibid.*, p. 434.

thetic up as an example of the Genet he opposes. This entrancement with the rejected style of the retractile dominates Sartre's writings on poetry.

MALLARMÉ

As in the case of Flaubert, Sartre is both attracted and repelled by the life and work of Mallarmé. Simone de Beauvoir recounts in *La Force des choses* (*Force of Circumstance*) that during the period of the writing of *La Mort dans l'âme,* Sartre began a work on Mallarmé. She reveals in a brief footnote that "he wrote hundreds of pages of it that he later lost." [52] The relation between the poetry of Mallarmé and Daniel in *La Mort dans l'âme* was discussed in dealing with Sartre's unfinished *Les Chemins de la liberté,* and unless the lost manuscript is one day recovered, Sartre's Mallarmé is to be found only in the trilogy, in the frequent references to the poet in *Saint Genet,* and in the brief but important four-page article he contributed to *Les Ecrivains célèbres,* edited by Raymond Queneau.[53]

Sartre traces the career of the poet as yet another project of *being* and condemns his poetry as the product of a retractile imagination. Mallarmé's abhorrence of the material world, of society, of family, and of himself, as it is described by Sartre, suggests itself as a source for Sartre's Roquentin as well as his Daniel Sereno. The face in the mirror and the touch of things are seen to be the origin of "a revolt that does not find the point at which it should be applied." [54] The feeling of nausea which objects caused Mallarmé to experience [55] is not focused on by Sartre, but the task of destroying the world ends in failure

52. "Il en écrivit des centaines de pages que plus tard il perdit." P. 179, n. 1.
53. "Mallarmé." This little known essay was recently reprinted as the preface to a 1966 edition of Mallarmé's *Poésies.* Quotations will refer to the Queneau collection.
54. "Une révolte qui ne trouve pas son point d'application." "Mallarmé," p. 148.
55. In his *L'Univers imaginaire de Mallarmé,* Jean-Pierre Richard writes of the poet's attitude towards the material world: "Dès sa jeunesse son 'odeur de cuisine' provoquait en lui une nausée: plus tard il atténue sa répugnance, lui donne des formes plus souriantes et plus allusives, mais toujours, et très fidèlement, elle survit en lui." "From his youth its 'odeur de cuisine' made him nauseous; later he subdued this loathing and gave it more allusive and more appealing forms, but it remained always, and quite faithfully, with him." P. 376.

because this revolt would require physical contact with the bomb as object. Sartre interprets Mallarmé's initial response as a withdrawal into a rigid code of etiquette dominated by distance: "He chooses the terrorism of politeness; with things, with men, with himself, he always maintains an imperceptible distance. It is this distance that he first wishes to express in his verse." [56] Writing the poem becomes the means to create the fissure Mallarmé would establish between himself and the world. This act is used to create the necessary reassurance "that one is indeed where one should be." [57] To hold the world at arm's length becomes the goal of his poetry: "It will serve as an alibi; he disguises the resentment and hatred which incite him to absent himself from being by pretending to withdraw in order to join the ideal." [58]

Art requires a hierarchy dominated and made secure by a deity. In Sartre's novels and critical essays, painting and poetry crumble without the guaranty of God.[59] Mallarmé's dilemma is his discovery that his inspiration is terrestrial if God is dead. Sartre's frequent description of poetic creation as an indistinct stirring or rhythmic structure from the past is interpreted here as "an ancient verse that wants to be resurrected." [60] According to Sartre, the problem of inspiration as memory gives rise to Mallarmé's impotence, because the poet refuses to accept the material world as the basis for his poetics: "In epochs without futures, obstructed by the voluminous stature of a king or by the indisputable triumph of a class, invention seems pure reminiscence; everything has been said, one arrives too late." [61] With the death of God and the ordered world, man is confronted with the need to replace the unifying principle in the universe: "Man is a volatile illusion that hovers above the movements of matter. His impotence is 'theological'; the death of God created for the poet

56. "Il choisit le terrorisme de la politesse: avec les choses, avec les hommes, avec lui-même, il conserve toujours une imperceptible distance. C'est cette distance qu'il veut exprimer d'abord dans ses vers." "Mallarmé," p. 148.

57. "Qu'on est bien là où l'on doit être." *Ibid.*

58. "Elle servira d'alibi: on dissimulera le ressentiment et la haine qui incitent à s'absenter de l'être en prétendant qu'on s'éloigne pour rejoindre l'idéal." *Ibid.*

59. *Situations*, 4: 328–29, 418.

60. "Un vers ancien qui veut ressusciter." "Mallarmé," p. 148.

61. "Aux époques sans avenirs, barrées par la volumineuse stature d'un roi ou par l'incontestable triomphe d'une classe, l'invention semble une pure réminiscence: tout est dit, l'on vient trop tard." *Ibid.,* p. 149.

the necessity of replacing him, but he fails." [62] Sartre describes this frustrating failure to unify the infinite multiplicity as the basis for Mallarmé's preoccupation with suicide.

For Sartre's Mallarmé, the impotence of the poet comes to symbolize the impossibility of being man. Self-destruction would be a denial of his *being* as created by God: "By disappearing, one can restore being to its purity." [63] Mallarmé would deny the materiality of his fleshly *being* by an act that would render *being* only *being* and create a permanent distance between himself and things. Yet in doing this, he would perform an act of unification impossible in a world disintegrating because of the absence of the eye of God:

> Suicide is an act because it effectively destroys a being and causes the world to be haunted by an absence. If being is dispersion, man wins perfect unity by losing his being; even better, his absence has an astringent effect on the being of the universe; like Aristotelian forms, absence draws things tighter and penetrates them with its secret unity.[64]

Sartre finds Mallarmé's solution to his poetic dilemma in his contemplated suicide. The poem will repeat the drama of the act of suicide, but it is clear that the destructive endeavor is contrary to the style of Sartre's expansive category of poetic imagination: "It is a question of squeezing multiplicity so tightly that elements interpenetrate in order to make an invisible totality." [65] Mallarmé's horror of the diversity of the world and of its materiality gives rise to poetic negation. Sartre's analysis of the negation in the poet's style leads to the conclusion that the technique of Mallarmé's poetry is essentialist in nature.[66] Mallarmé denies the

62. "L'homme: l'illusion volatile qui voltige au-dessus des mouvements de la matière. Son impuissance est 'théologique': la mort de Dieu créait au poète le devoir de le remplacer: il échoue." *Ibid.*

63. "Disparaître: on rendrait à l'être sa pureté." *Ibid.*

64. "Le suicide est un acte parce qu'il détruit effectivement un être et parce qu'il fait hanter le monde par une absence. Si l'être est dispersion, l'homme en perdant son être gagne une incorruptible unité; mieux son absence exerce une action astringente sur l'être de l'univers; pareille aux formes aristotéliciennes, l'absence resserre les choses, les pénètre de son unité secrète." *Ibid.*, p. 150.

65. "Il s'agit donc de resserrer la multiplicité jusqu'à ce que les éléments s'interpénètrent pour faire une totalité invisible." *Saint Genet,* p. 433, n. 1.

66. Sartre cites a number of examples from Mallarmé's poetry in *Saint Genet,* p. 434, n. 2.

explosive force that Sartre seeks in poetry. The circularity of the
internal movement of his sonnet, "The Virgin, hardy, and beautiful today," [67] its false explosion, and its dissolution of contour
only prove to Sartre that "lack of being is a manner of being." [68]
Mallarmé's platonic essentialism and his retractile imagination
are rejected by Sartre.

Sartre considers the failure of the poet to be consciously
desired, and therefore he relates the project of *being* to Mallarmé's unfinished book. Sartre views this task of which Mallarmé speaks throughout his later years as the central element in
the poet's own process of mythification. His unfinished work
becomes a significant failure in a way the short poems could
never be.[69] These works play an important rôle in the dramatic
process of the creation of the myth of the poet:

> In the complicated rules of this game, his poems had to fail
> in order to be perfect. To abolish language and world was
> not enough for these poems, not even if they canceled each
> other out; they also had to be vain sketches in comparison
> with the unprecedented, impossible work that the accident
> of death prevented him from beginning.[70]

Of all the poets, Mallarmé's defeat is the most remarkable
because the myth of the unrealizable Book represents the poet's
perfect *being* in his own failure to be: "Such as into Himself
eternity at last changes him." [71] The poet has applied his creative

67. "Le Vierge, le vivace et le bel aujourd'hui," *Œuvres complètes,*
p. 67.
68. "Le défaut d'être est une manière d'être." "Mallarmé," p. 150.
69. Jean-Pierre Richard in his *L'Univers imaginaire de Mallarmé,*
p. 463, does not accept Sartre's interpretation of the unfinished book:
"Tout le dossier publié par Jacques Scherer nous prouve d'ailleurs que
celui-ci fut loin d'être un mythe comme le croyait Sartre." "The whole
dossier published by Jacques Scherer proves to us moreover that it was
far from being the myth Sartre believed it to be." This, however, does
not minimize the role of the unfinished book as part of Mallarmé's
myth.
70. "Dans le système complexe de cette comédie, ses poésies devaient
être des échecs pour être parfaites. Il ne suffisait pas qu'elles abolissent
langage et monde, ni même qu'elles s'annulassent; il fallait encore
qu'elles fussent de vaines ébauches au regard d'une Œuvre inouïe et
impossible que le hasard d'une mort l'empêcha de commencer." "Mallarmé," p. 151.
71. "Tel qu'en Lui-même enfin l'éternité le change." *Œuvres complètes,* p. 70.

capacity to his own existence in order to prepare the phantom *being* he will become in death.

Sartre's consideration of the work of these poets reveals specific examples to support his view of the creative act as an attempted creation of *being*. That Sartre considers this enterprise to be condemned to failure—with one exception—becomes clearer with each poet discussed. The expansive style alone redeems the undertaking of writing poetry. It is Baudelaire who is most severely judged because of the degree of petrification discovered in the style of his myth of *being,* but Genet and Mallarmé are condemned by Sartre for their use of negation to create their ideal *being.* Francis Ponge belongs to that group of artists whose representations of man clearly overcome the nature of their enterprise, by his use of ambiguity, metamorphosis, and discontinuity as elements of his style. Sartre's disappointment with the poetry of Ponge occurs because of a progressive discovery of mineral elements in his work. Only the French African poets overcome the temptation of the myth of *being.* Through their dynamic use of organic elements of growth and the frenetic shifting of images of fire and light, they seek in the poetic act a means by which they may live. *Existence*—not *being*—is seen to be the end result of their rhythmic verse, and this revolutionary poetic act is warmly praised by Sartre.

Appendix

Music and Musicians

ALTHOUGH SARTRE INCLUDES music when he discusses his ideas on art, he has not found a contemporary musician whose works have inspired him to explore music in the same way as he has done with sculpture and painting. The jazz theme and the works of Chopin in *La Nausée* are echoed in certain instances in the plays and in *Les Chemins de la liberté:* the melody of the flute in *Les Mouches* and in *Les Jeux sont faits* (*The Chips Are Down*); the haunting melodies sung by Lola Montero in *L'Age de raison;* the polonaise that accompanies Daniel Sereno's reflection on his existence in *Le Sursis.* However, there are no studies comparable to the Giacometti, Calder, Masson, or Lapoujade essays. It is in the preface he writes for a book written by a friend, a contemporary musician, that he addresses himself to some of the problems of music.[1] In this book, *L'Artiste et sa conscience: Esquisse d'une dialectique de la conscience artistique,* René Leibowitz attempts to deal with the problem of "musique engagée." As a musician he is disturbed by Sartre's elimination of music from the commitment offered to the prose writer. In response to the *Prague Manifesto* published on the occasion of the Second International Congress of Composers and Music Critics, Leibowitz undertook an exposition of the means by which the musician may commit himself. Because of their friendship—and certainly because of Sartre's own position with respect to music as stated in *Qu'est-ce que la littérature?*—Leibowitz requested a preface of Sartre.

His observations on music are consistent with the ideas he has expressed towards painting and sculpture. He reiterates his criticism of art in an official role. In this instance the Communist musician is condemned for his tendency to perpetuate values

1. "L'Artiste et sa conscience," in Leibowitz, *L'Artiste et sa conscience.* Reprinted in *Situations*, 4: 17–37.

given to him by the elite of the society: "They would like the artist to submit to a society-object and to sing the praises of the Soviet world as Haydn sang those of divine creation." [2] The official musician is rejected together with the official portrait painter. They are guilty of presenting man as fixed in relation to the social order. When Sartre writes, "They ask him to copy what *is,* to imitate without transcending, to serve as a model, for his public, of submission to an established order," [3] he is applying his objections first expressed in "Portraits officiels" to the art of music. The content of such art is the message which Sartre would deny to music, painting, and sculpture. His criticism of Greuze's desire to speak in his works is applied to the work of Beethoven and Chopin. Sartre insists once again on the distinction he makes between "sens" and "signification" in relation to the work of art by drawing a parallel between his experience of the Mona Lisa and a concerto of Bach:

> When I listen to a *Brandenburg Concerto,* I never *think* of the eighteenth century, of the austerity of Leipzig, of the puritanical ponderosity of the German princes, of that strange moment in the history of the intellect in which reason, in full possession of its techniques, nevertheless is kept in check by faith, and in which logic of concept is transformed into logic of judgment; but it is all there, in the sounds, just as the Renaissance smiles on the lips of the *Mona Lisa.*[4]

The meaning of the work cannot be translated into a prose meaning and communicated independently of the music. Haydn and Rigaud are considered to be verbal propagandists. Sartre condemns words in music used in order to convey specific messages. The insistence of the writers of the *Prague Manifesto* on those musical compositions such as oratorios, operas, and cantatas

2. "Ils voudraient que l'artiste se soumît à une société-objet et qu'il chantât les louanges du monde soviétique comme Haydn chantait celles de la Création divine." *Situations,* 4: 20.

3. "Ils lui demandent de copier ce qui 'est,' d'imiter sans dépasser et d'offrir à son public l'exemple de la soumission à un ordre établi." *Ibid.*

4. "Lorsque j'entends un *Concerto Brandebourgeois,* je ne 'pense' jamais au XVIIIe siècle, à l'austérité de Leipzig, à la lourdeur puritaine des princes allemands, à cet étrange moment de l'esprit où la raison, en pleine possession de ses techniques, demeure pourtant soumise à la foi et où la logique du concept se transforme en logique du jugement: mais tout est là, donné dans les sons, comme la Renaissance sourit sur les lèvres de *la Joconde.*" *Ibid.,* p. 31.

to the detriment of symphonies or quartets is viewed by Sartre as the use of the verbal to betray the music. In such musical compositions, he contends that the words carry the content: "Change the words; a hymn to the Russian dead at Stalingrad will become a funeral oration for the Germans who fell before that very same city. What do the sounds convey? A great blast of sonorous heroism. It is the words which will make it explicit." [5]

In contrast to the official artist discussed above, the modern artist is tempted to demonstrate his commitment in his life rather than in his work. Sartre is concerned that the modern artist who accepts the concept of the work of art as an appeal to human freedom may find his personal actions to be a sufficient demonstration of his commitment to man's liberty: "A musician's life may be exemplary: his chosen poverty, his rejection of easy success, his continual dissatisfaction, and the permanent revolution he carries on against others and against himself. But I fear that the austere morality of his person remains a commentary external to his work." [6] The important image of the human condition lies not in the artist's life but in his works. In his essay on Tintoretto, Sartre characterized the Venetian as a painter who expressed himself despite the limitations imposed upon him by his society. Bach is offered to the contemporary musician as an example in music. In his private life and actions, Bach, like Tintoretto, demonstrated an acceptance of the monarchy and religious absolutism, but in his music man's liberty is revealed: "Bach furnished an image of freedom which, although seeming to be contained within a traditional framework, transcended tradition toward new creation." [7] In music, the musician must create for the listener a demonstration of human worth. The restraining conditions of modern society must be transcended by the artist just as Bach did within the context of his contemporary

5. "Changez les mots: un hymne aux morts russes de Stalingrad deviendra une oraison funèbre pour les Allemands tombés devant cette même ville. Que peuvent donner les sons? Une grosse bouffée d'héroïsme sonore; c'est le verbe qui spécifiera." *Ibid.,* p. 27.

6. "La vie du musicien peut être exemplaire: exemplaire sa pauvreté consentie, son refus du succès facile, sa constante insatisfaction, et la révolution permanente qu'il opère contre les autres et contre lui-même. Mais je crains que l'austère moralité de sa personne ne demeure un commentaire extérieur à son œuvre." *Ibid.,* p. 28.

7. "Bach offrait l'image d'une liberté qui, tout en paraissant se contenir dans des cadres traditionnels, dépassait la tradition vers des créations neuves." *Ibid.,* pp. 33–34.

religious and political traditions. Bach went beyond the limitations imposed upon him to illustrate the world in terms of the individual, by judging his experience of it and showing this judgment in his music:

> Against the closed tradition of little despotic courts, he raised in opposition an open tradition; he learned how to discover originality in an accepted discipline, indeed, how to live: he manifested the play of moral freedom in the very heart of a monarchical and religious absolutism; he depicted the proud dignity of the subject who obeys his king, of the devout person who prays to his God.[8]

In *The Well-Tempered Clavier,* Sartre discovers that Bach's style suggests the infinite possibilities of his combinations to musicians of future generations: "The infinite variations he performs, the postulates he forces himself to respect, place those who follow him at the brink of changing the postulates themselves." [9]

To be committed, the composer today must do as Bach did in the eighteenth century; but to demonstrate this freedom not only to generations to follow, he must speak with a future voice in the present. The problem for the artist is to be so conscious of his existence in the twentieth century that he will show his contemporary audience their freedom in his work. Sartre admires Leibowitz for his desire to demonstrate to man that "he is not created, that he will never be created, that he will retain everywhere and at all times the freedom to create and to create himself beyond all that which is already created." [10] Today's listeners understand the work of previous centuries, but Sartre asks whether it is possible for them to understand what the artist is creating now. In the growing complexity of music, Sartre sees that fewer and fewer listeners are capable of understanding Leibowitz and his fellow musicians in their attempt to incorpo-

8. "A la tradition fermée des petites cours despotiques, il opposait une tradition ouverte; il apprenait à trouver l'originalité dans une discipline consentie, à vivre enfin: il montrait le jeu de la liberté morale à l'intérieur de l'absolutisme religieux et monarchique, il dé peignait la dignité fière du sujet qui obéit à son roi, du fidèle qui prie son Dieu." *Ibid.,* p. 34.

9. "Et les variations infinies qu'il exécute, les postulats qu'il s'oblige à respecter, mettent ses continuateurs à deux doigts de changer les postulats eux-mêmes." *Ibid.*

10. "Il n'est pas fait, qu'il ne sera jamais et qu'il conserve toujours et partout la liberté de faire et de se faire par-delà tout ce qui est déjà fait." *Ibid.,* pp. 20–21.

rate man's liberty in their music: "Indeed, to whom does it speak of liberation, of freedom, of will, of the creation of man by man?" [11] Sartre prescribes what the composer must do, but he wants the artist to discover for himself how to reach all men now —not in the next generation or in the next century. He asks the musician to reflect on his art in order to find a means of revealing the liberty of the human condition within his compositions— even to the untutored. The dilemma Sartre sees for the composer is how to reveal this stylistically. By his plea for "musique engagée," Leibowitz gives Sartre another occasion to express the difficulty of being understood by a contemporary audience. The problem is not solved, yet it reveals Sartre's own distance from the proletarian reader he so earnestly desires to reach, and it explains the myth he creates of Tintoretto as a painter who created for his own contemporaries in the works of the Scuola San Rocco.

11. "Mais à qui donc parle-t-elle de libération, de liberté, de volonté, de la création de l'homme par l'homme?" *Ibid.,* p. 21.

Selected Bibliography

Works of Jean-Paul Sartre

L'Age de raison (*Les Chemins de la liberté*, Vol. 1). Paris: Gallimard, 1945.

"André Masson." In *Vingt-deux Dessins sur le thème du désir.* Nice: Editions La Diane française, 1961. Also in *Situations* 4: 387–407.

"A Propros du *Parti pris des choses.*" *Poésie* no. 20 (Jul.–Oct. 1944): 58–77, and no. 21 (Nov.–Dec. 1944): 74–92. Reprinted as *L'Homme et les choses* and in *Situations* 1: 245–97.

"L'Artiste et sa conscience." In *L'Artiste et sa conscience* by René Leibowitz. Paris: L'Arche, 1950, pp. 9–40. Also in *Situations* 4: 17–37.

Bariona. Paris: Imprimerie Anjou, n.d.

Baudelaire. Paris: Gallimard, 1947. Portions of this essay appeared in *Confluences,* no. 1 (Jan.–Feb. 1945): 9–18 and *Les Temps modernes* no. 8 (May 1946): 1345–77.

Baudelaire, trans. with a foreword by Martin Turnell. Norfolk: New Directions, 1950.

"Calder's Mobiles." In *Alexander Calder.* Bucholz Gallery. New York: Curt Valentin, 1947.

Les Chemins de la liberté. 3 vols. Paris: Gallimard, 1945–49.

Le Diable et le bon Dieu. Paris: Gallimard, 1951.

"Doigts et non-doigts." In *En personne* by Wols. Paris: Delpire, 1963, pp. 32–43. Also in *Situations* 4: 408–34.

"Drôle d'amitié." *Les Temps modernes* no. 49 (Nov. 1949): 769–806; no. 50 (Dec. 1949): 1009–1039.

Esquisse d'une théorie des émotions. Paris: Hermann, 1939.

"Existentialist on Mobilist: Calder's Newest Works Judged by France's Newest Philosopher." *Art News* 46 (Dec. 1947): 22–23, 55–56.

L'Etre et le néant. Paris: Gallimard, 1943.

L'Homme et les choses. Paris: Seghers, 1947.

"Une Idée fondamentale de la 'Phénoménologie' de Husserl: L'Intentionnalité." *Nouvelle Revue française* 52 (1939): 129–31.

L'Imaginaire: Psychologie phénoménologique de l'imagination.
Paris: Gallimard, 1940.

L'Imagination. Paris: Alcan, 1936.

"Mallarmé." In *Les Ecrivains célèbres,* ed. R. Queneau. 3 vols.
Paris: Editions d'Art Lucien Mazenod, 1953, 3: 148–51. Reprinted as preface to Mallarmé's *Poésies.* Paris: Gallimard,
1966.

"Les Mobiles de Calder." In *Alexander Calder: Mobiles, Stabiles, Constellations.* Paris: Galerie Louis Carré 1946, pp. 9–
19. Also in *Situations* 3: 307–11 and *Style en France* no. 5
(April 15, 1947): 7–11.

La Mort dans l'âme (Les Chemins de la liberté, vol. 3). Paris:
Gallimard, 1949.

Les Mots. Paris: Gallimard, 1964.

Le Mur. Paris: Gallimard, 1939.

La Nausée. Paris: Gallimard, 1938.

"Orphée noir." In *Anthologie de la nouvelle poésie nègre et
malgache de langue française,* ed. Léopold Sédar-Senghor.
Paris: Presses Universitaires de France, 1948, pp. ix–xliv. Also
in *Situations* 3: 229–86 and in *Les Temps modernes* no. 37
(Oct. 1948): 577–606.

"Le Peintre sans privilèges." In *Lapoujade: Peintures sur le
thème des émeutes, triptyques sur la torture, Hiroshima.*
Paris: Galerie Pierre Domec, 1961. Also in *Médiations* no. 2
(1961): 29–44, and in *Situations* 4: 364–86.

"Les Peintures de Giacometti." *Derrière le miroir* no. 65 (1954).
Also in *Les Temps modernes* no. 103 (June 1954): 2221–
32, and in *Situations* 4: 347–63.

"Poème." *Art présent* no. 3 (1947): 45.

"Portraits officials." *Verve* nos 5–6 (July–Oct. 1939): 9–12.
Also in *Visages.*

"Présentation de *Temps modernes.*" *Les Temps modernes* no. 1
(Oct. 1945): 1–21. Also in *Situations* 2: 9–30.

"A propos du *Parti pris des choses.*" *Poésie* no. 20 (July–Oct.
1944): 58–77; no. 21 (Nov.–Dec. 1944): 74–92. Also in
Situations 1: 245–97. Published separately as *L'Homme et les
choses.*

Qu'est-ce que la littérature?. *Les Temps modernes* no. 17 (Feb.
1947): 769–805; no. 18 (Mar. 1947): 961–88; no. 19

(Apr. 1947): 1194–1218; no. 20 (May 1947): 1410–29; no. 21 (June 1947): 1007–1041; no. 22 (July 1947): 77–114.

"La Recherche de l'absolu." *Les Temps modernes* no. 28 (Jan. 1948): 1153–63. English translation in *Alberto Giacometti: Exhibition of Sculpture, Painting, Drawing*. New York: Pierre Matisse Gallery, 1948. Also in *Situations* 3: 289–305.

Saint Genet, comédien et martyr. Paris: Gallimard, 1952.

"*Saint-Georges et le dragon*." *L'Arc* no. 30 (1966): 33–52.

"Sculptures à 'n' dimensions." *Derrière le miroir* no. 5 (1947): 1–4. A portion of this essay appeared in *Arts*, no. 144 (Dec. 1947): 1.

"Le Séquestré de Venise." *Les Temps modernes* no. 141 (Nov. 1957): 761–800. Also in *Situations* 4: 291–346.

Situations vol. 1. Paris: Gallimard, 1947.

Situations vol. 2. Paris: Gallimard, 1948.

Situations vol. 3. Paris: Gallimard, 1949.

Situations vol. 4. Paris: Gallimard, 1964.

"La Structure intentionnelle de l'image." *Revue de métaphysique et de morale* 45 (1938): 543–609.

Le Sursis (*Les Chemins de la liberté* vol. 2). Paris: Gallimard, 1945.

Théâtre. Paris: Gallimard, 1947.

Théâtre. Paris: Gallimard, 1962.

"La Transcendance de l'égo: Esquisse d'une description phénoménologique." *Recherches philosophiques* 6 (1936–37): 85–123.

"Visages." *Verve* nos. 5–6 (July–Oct. 1939): 43–44.

Visages, précédé de Portraits officiels. Paris: Seghers, 1948.

OTHER SOURCES

Adam, Henri-Georges. "*Les Mouches*." *Cahiers Charles Dullin* no. 2 (Mar. 1966): 6–7.

Albérès, René-Marill. *Jean-Paul Sartre*. Paris: Editions universitaires, 1953.

Ames, Van Meter. "Existentialism and the Arts." *Journal of Aesthetics and Art Criticism* 9 (1951): 252–56.

Anglès, Auguste. "Sartre versus Baudelaire." *Yale French Studies* no. 2 (1948): 119–24.

Arnold, A. James. *"La Nausée* Revisited." *French Review* 39 (1965): 199–213.

Barnes, Hazel. *The Literature of Possibility: A Study in Humanistic Existentialism.* Lincoln: Univ. of Nebraska Press, 1959.

Bataille, Georges. "Baudelaire 'mis à nu': l'analyse de Sartre et l'essence de la poésie." *Critique* nos. 8–9 (Jan.–Feb. 1947): 3–27.

Baudelaire, Charles. *Ecrits intimes.* Paris: Editions du Point du Jour, 1946.

———. *Œuvres complètes,* ed. Yves le Dantec. Editions de la Pléiade. Paris: Gallimard, 1961.

Beauvoir, Simone de. *La Force de l'âge.* Paris: Gallimard, 1960.

———. *La Force des choses.* Paris: Gallimard, 1963.

Blin, Georges. "Jean-Paul Sartre et Baudelaire." *Fontaine* no. 59 (Apr. 1947): 3–17, and no. 60 (May 1947): 200–216.

Boudaille, Georges. "Henri-Georges Adam." *Cimaise* 56 (Nov.–Dec. 1961): 41–53.

Brée, Germaine, and Guiton, Margaret. *The French Novel from Gide to Camus.* New York: Harcourt, Brace and World, 1962.

Brombert, Victor. *The Intellectual Hero: Studies in the French Novel, 1880–1955.* Chicago: Univ. of Chicago Press, 1964.

Brown, Calvin S. "James Thomson and d'Annunzio on Dürer's *Melencolia." Journal of Aesthetics and Art Criticism* 19 (1960): 31–35.

Bucarelli, Palma. *Giacometti.* Rome: Editalia, 1962.

Butor, Michel, *Répertoire* vol. 2. Paris: Editions de Minuit, 1964.

Calder, Alexander. *Calder: An Autobiography with Pictures.* New York: Pantheon, 1966.

———. "Mobiles." In *The Painter's Object,* ed. Myfanwy Evans. London: Gerald Howe, 1937.

Campbell, Robert. *Jean-Paul Sartre ou une littérature philosophique.* Paris: Pierre Ardent, 1947.

Carrouges, Michel. *Eluard et Claudel.* Paris: Editions du Seuil, 1945.

Chacal, Rosa. "Baudelaire y el *Baudelaire* de Sartre." *Sur* no. 171 (Jan. 1949): 17–34.

Champigny, Robert. "Le Mot 'être' dans *L'Etre et le néant*." *Revue de métaphysique et de morale* 61 (1956): 155–65.

——. *Stages on Sartre's Way*. Indiana Univ. Publications, Humanities Series No. 42. Bloomington: Indiana Univ. Press, 1959.

Cohn, Robert G. "Sartre's First Novel: *La Nausée*." *Yale French Studies* no. 1 (1948): 62–65.

Cruickshank, John, ed. *The Novelist as Philosopher*. London: Oxford Univ. Press, 1962.

Cumming, Robert, "The Literature of Extreme Situations." In *Aesthetics Today*, ed. Morris Philipson. New York: Meridian, 1961.

Dali, Salvador. *Les Cocus du vieil art moderne*. Paris: Fasquelle, 1956.

Douglas, Kenneth. *A Critical Bibliography of Existentialism*. Yale French Studies, Monograph no. 1. New Haven: Yale Univ. Press, 1950.

——. "Sartre and the Self-Inflicted Wound." *Yale French Studies* no. 9 (1952): 123–31.

Douthat, B. Margaret. *"Le Parti pris des choses?" French Studies* 13 (1959): 39–51.

Dupin, Jacques. *Alberto Giacometti*. Paris: Maeght, 1962.

Elsen, Albert. *Rodin*. New York: Museum of Modern Art, 1963.

——. *Rodin's Gates of Hell*. Minneapolis: Univ. of Minnesota Press, 1960.

Evans, Myfanwy, ed. *The Painter's Object*. London: Gerald Howe, 1937.

Gautier, Théophile. *Œuvres complètes*. 2 vols. Paris: Charpentier, 1884.

Genet, Jean. *L'Atelier d'Alberto Giacometti*. Lyon: L'Arbalète, 1963.

——. *Œuvres complètes*. 3 vols. Paris: Gallimard, 1951–53.

Goosen, E. C., Goldwater, Robert, and Sandler, Irving. *Trois Sculpteurs américains: Herbert Ferber, David Hare, Ibram Lassaw*. Le Musée de poche. Paris: Georges Fall, 1959.

Grubbs, Henry A. "Sartre's Recapturing of Lost Time." *Modern Language Notes* 73 (1958): 515–22.

Haftmann, Werner. *Painting in the Twentieth Century*. 2 vols. London: Lund Humphries, 1960.

Hare, David. "The Spaces of the Mind." *Magazine of Art* 43 (Feb. 1950): 48–53.

Houston, Mona Tobin. "The Sartre of Madame de Beauvoir." *Yale French Studies* no. 30 (1963): 23–29.

Isère, Jean. "Ambiguïté de l'esthétique de Sartre." *French Review* 21 (1948): 357–60.

Jameson, Frederic. "The Laughter of *Nausea.*" *Yale French Studies* no. 23 (1959): 26–32.

———. *Sartre: The Origins of a Style.* Yale Romanic Studies. New Haven: Yale Univ. Press, 1961.

"Jean-Paul Sartre répond à la critique dramatique et offre un guide au spectateur pour suivre *Le Diable et le bon Dieu.*" *Figaro littéraire* June 30, 1951: 4.

Jourdain, Louis. "Sartre devant Baudelaire." *Tel Quel* no. 19 (Fall 1964): 70–85, and no. 21 (Spring 1965): 79–95.

Juin, Hubert. *André Masson.* Le Musée de poche. Paris: Georges Fall, 1963.

Kaelin, Eugene F. *An Existential Aesthetic: The Theories of Sartre and Merleau-Ponty.* Madison, Wisc.: Univ. of Wisconsin Press, 1962.

Klee, Paul. *Das bildnerische Denken.* Basel: Benno Schwabe, 1956.

Knight, W. F. Jackson. *Roman Vergil.* London: Faber and Faber, 1944.

Koefoed, Oleg. "L'Œuvre littéraire de Jean-Paul Sartre." *Orbis Litterarum* 6 (1948): 209–72; 7 (1949): 61–141.

Kohut, Karl. *"Was ist Literatur?:* Die Theorie der 'littérature engagée' bei Jean-Paul Sartre." Diss., Marburg Univ., 1965.

Kramer, Hilton. "Giacometti." *Arts Magazine* Nov. 1963: 52–59.

Kubler, George, and Martin, Soria. *Art and Architecture in Spain and Portugal and Their American Dominions: 1500– 1800.* Baltimore: Penguin, 1959.

Leibowitz, René. *L'Artiste et sa conscience: Esquisse d'une dialectique de la conscience artistique.* Paris: L'Arche, 1950.

Leiris, Michel, and Limbour, Georges. *André Masson et son univers.* Paris: Editions des Trois Collines, 1947.

Lupo, Valeria. "Un Affronto a Baudelaire." *Humanitas* 4 (1949): 404–19.

Magny, Claude-Edmonde. *Les Sandales d'Empédocle*. Paris: Baconnière, 1945.

Mallarmé, Stéphane. *Œuvres complètes,* eds. Henri Mondor and G. Jean-Aubry. Editions de la Pléiade. Paris: Gallimard, 1945.

———. *Poésies.* Paris: Gallimard, 1966.

Masson, André. *Vingt-deux Dessins sur le thème du désir.* Nice: Editions La Diane française, 1961.

Michelet, Jules. *Œuvres complètes.* 40 vols. Paris: Flammarion, n.d.

Mondrian, Piet. *Plastic Art and Pure Plastic Art 1937 and Other Essays 1941–43.* New York: Wittenborn, 1945.

Morpurgo-Tagliabue, Guido. *L'Esthétique contemporaine: Une Enquête.* Milan: Marzorati, 1960.

Murdoch, Iris. *Sartre: Romantic Rationalist.* New Haven: Yale Univ. Press, 1959.

Nerval, Gérard de. *Œuvres,* ed. Henri Lemaître. 2 vols. Paris: Garnier, 1958.

Nietzsche, Friedrich Wilhelm. *Complete Works,* ed. Oscar Levy. 18 vols. New York, 1909–1911; reissued by Russell and Russell, 1964.

Panofsky, Erwin. *Albrecht Dürer.* 2 vols. Princeton: Princeton Univ. Press, 1948.

———. *Early Netherlandish Painting.* 2 vols. Cambridge: Harvard Univ. Press, 1953.

Peyre, Henri. *The Contemporary French Novel.* New York: Oxford Univ. Press, 1955.

Ponge, Francis. *Le Parti pris des choses.* Paris: Gallimard, 1942.

———. "Reflections sur les statuettes, figures et peintures d'Alberto Giacometti." *Cahiers d'art* 26 (1951): 75–89.

Rau, Catherine. "The Aesthetic Views of Jean-Paul Sartre." *Journal of Aesthetics and Art Criticism* 9 (1950): 139–47.

Restany, Pierre. "Une Peinture existentielle: Wols." *Vingtième Siècle* no. 19 (June 1962): 53–56.

Richard, Jean-Pierre. *Onze Etudes sur la poésie moderne.* Paris: Editions du Seuil, 1964.

———. *L'Univers imaginaire de Mallarmé.* Paris: Editions du Seuil, 1961.

Robb, David. *The Harper History of Painting.* New York: Harper, 1951.

Rousset, Jean. *La Littérature de l'âge baroque en France.* Paris: Corti, 1953.

Salel, Jean-Claude. "A propos de *Baudelaire* de Jean-Paul Sartre." *La Table ronde* no. 3 (Mar. 1948): 470–75.

"Sartre Bibliography." *Yale French Studies* no. 30 (1963): 108–19.

"Sartre parle." *Clarté* 55 (Mar.–Apr. 1964): 41–47.

Schapiro, Meyer. "The Liberating Quality of Avant-Garde Art." *Art News* 56 (Summer 1957): 36–42.

Scully, Vincent. *The Earth, the Temple and the Gods: Greek Sacred Architecture.* New Haven: Yale Univ. Press, 1962.

Sédar-Senghor, Léopold, ed. *Anthologie de la nouvelle poésie nègre et malgache de langue française.* Paris: PUF, 1948.

Selz, Peter. *Alberto Giacometti.* New York: Museum of Modern Art, 1965.

Shattuck, Roger. "Making Time: A Study of Stravinsky, Proust and Sartre." *Kenyon Review* 25 (1963): 248–63.

Sweeney, James Johnson. *Alexander Calder.* New York: Museum of Modern Art, 1951.

Taine, Hippolyte. *Voyage en Italie.* 2 vols. Paris: Hachette, 1905.

Tardieu, Jean. "Giacometti et la solitude." *Vingtième Siècle* no. 18 (Feb. 1962): 13–19.

Thody, Philip. *Jean-Paul Sartre: A Literary and Political Study.* London: Hamilton, 1960.

Valéry, Paul. *Variété* vol. 3. Paris: Gallimard, 1936.

Vendôme, André. "Jean-Paul Sartre et la littérature." *Etudes* 259 (1948): 39–54.

Virgil. *Works,* trans. H. Rushton Fairclough. 2 vols. The Loeb Classical Library. London: Heinemann, 1947.

Vivanco, Luis Felipe. *The Escorial.* Barcelona: Noguer, 1956.

Vuillemin, Jules. "La Personnalité esthétique du Tintoret." *Les Temps modernes* no. 102 (May 1954): 1965–2006.

Weightman, John. "Jean-Paul Sartre." In *The Novelist as Philosopher,* ed. John Cruickshank. London: Oxford Univ. Press, 1962.

Wölfflin, Heinrich. *Principles of Art History.* New York: Dover, 1929.

———. *The Sense of Form in Art.* New York: Chelsea, 1958.

Wols. *En personne.* Paris: Delpire, 1963.

Index